For Sasha and Chantie

Acknowledgments:

There is simply not enough space to mention all the people that justly deserve acknowledgment fot their efforts in getting one man around the world, so I will restrict myself to those whose contribution made it possible.

Marain Tipler for her encouragement, tolerance and belief in me, David Arnold, Editor of Motoring And Leisue Magazine for launching me into journalism, and Brruno Tagliafrri at Triumph Motorcycles for helping me fly the British flag.

Derrick Lello of J. E. Bernard for his meticulous research, Mary Jennings for sending money under difficult circumstances and Simon Jones for his friendship and the first glass of champagne.

My thanks to Sundaraj Teitz for keeping me safe, Sue Rhodes (formally Al-Sobky) for keeping me sane and Khizar Edroos for keeping me solvent. A journey is not complete until the story has been told, so my thanks to TravellersEye and especially Joss Guttery for being an understanding editor.

Triumph Around The World

Robbie Marshall

Edited by Joss Guttery
Published by TravellersEye

Triumph Around The World
1st Edition
Published by TravellersEye Ltd 2001

Head Office:
Colemore Farm
Colemore Green
Bridgnorth
Shropshire
WV16 4ST
United Kingdom
tel: (0044) 1746 766447   fax: (0044) 1746 766665
email: books@travellerseye.com   website: www.travellerseye.com

Set in Times
ISBN: 1903070082
Copyright 2001 Robbie Marshall

Contents

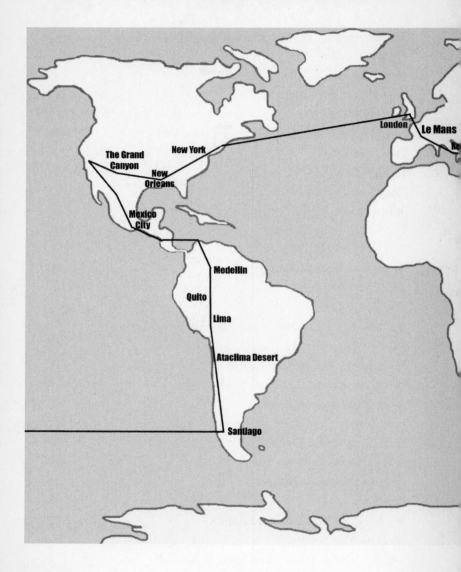

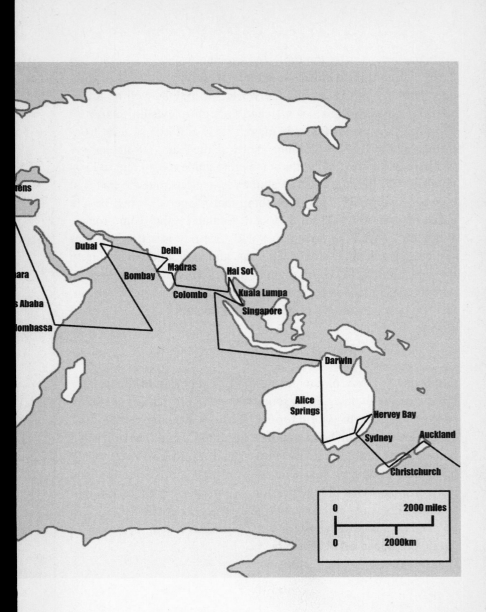

Dear Charles,

Someone has to share the trials and tribulations of an ignorant old hippy attempting to fulfil an adolescent dream riding a wholly unsuitable motorbike around the world. It may as well be a ten-year-old boy, who has not watched enough television to form a distorted view of our fantastic planet. This is it kid, straight from the hip, a blow by blow account. The fun, the fear, the pain and joy of 51 weeks on the road without a map to guide me, or tent to keep me dry. The journey was not about destinations, but the travel in between. Arriving is just something that happens. When people asked me where I was going, I said 'England – the scenic route'. When they asked me how, I just said 'one day at a time'. It was difficult, demanding, often dangerous, and very lonely listening to the wind alone with your thoughts – hour after hour. The adventure was not a statement of masculinity, moral fibre or even achievement, just the best education on offer, and the most rewarding event of my life.

Every day is a school day on the road. Every day the senses are bombarded with new sights, sounds, smells, just like being a new-born child seeing the world for the first time. Nothing was familiar except the throbbing heart of a British legend. I could have taken a horse. Some said I should have taken a horse. At least there would have been something to eat in times of hardship. Where the idea came from, or what fed the passion, is a mystery, but it turned into a manic obsession, and now it is over. The only challenge left is to do it again. I hope these words will illuminate, entertain, make you laugh, but above all else inspire.

1.The Beginning, the Old Bill and the Gods of Sundaraj

It was about eight in the evening, and the fat guy's uniform was fighting back the blubber attempting to escape between stretched buttonholes. He was probably tired and I was not doing too well with explanations as to why I had no return ticket.

This was to be my first lesson in tolerance of officialdom. Every country exists on its own rules that seem to exist for no reason, but they are *its* rules and being middle-class British is not a licence to avoid scrutiny. People queuing patiently behind the white line started twitching as the officer's plump fingers rested on a USA visa, complete with photograph. My unrehearsed monologue was thankfully overheard by fatty's colleague in the next booth. "No shit! A Triumph huh? I got a Harley. Let the guy through."

Someone once said 'A sure sign of the male menopause is when a man leaves his wife and buys a motorbike', and who was I to break the mould? The combination of bike and travel was too much to resist and, if I did not grab the opportunity, I would have become too old and feeble to even try. We all find valid justification for not fulfilling dreams, but the time had come to stop making excuses and gird the loins for action. My time of reckoning had arrived, and it was terrifying!

The only thing more ridiculous than an old man in love, is an ageing, nine stone hippy trying to ride a wholly unsuitable quarter-ton motorcycle around the world. I was both those things, and when I stepped out into that watery June dawn it was too late to bottle out. "Go west, you degenerate old fool," my girlfriend Marian whispered lovingly into my ear with a final kiss. I took her advice and headed for New York.

The plan was to depart this green and pleasant land riding a 1200cc Triumph, to explore some of the wildest and most remote parts of our fascinating planet, and capture on film a diverse patchwork of cultures and traditions. I had never been a motorcycle fetishist, although I had enjoyed them through my youth, before becoming an art student, husband and father all in a few weeks. Bikes had had to take a bow while my wife and I got better acquainted resulting in a second daughter whilst I was still a student.

Two decades passed before the trappings of wealth allowed me to indulge in another passion – aviation. After a particularly bad hang gliding accident in southern France I decided I needed an engine so qualified to fly microlights. This meant I was able to take off from one of my fields behind the house, provided my wife's racehorses and children's ponies would move out of the way. I spent Sunday afternoons flying the Sussex downs until a bad take-off had me flying through the roof of a neighbour's barn. Striking a concrete wall at 55mph can be very painful, but I was fortunate enough to escape uninjured. The investigating officer was there in minutes riding a booming Moto Guzzi motorcycle. "So, where's the fatality?" he enquired to a man in flying suit and helmet. "That would be me," I said feeling a little confused. "Nice bike, can I have a go?" The officer declined my request, which was probably a good thing as I had already escaped death once that day, but said his machine was to be auctioned the following week. I bought it as a mate for the Bultaco, which I kept for thrashing round the fields. My suppressed passion for road bikes had been rekindled, and as for the hole in my neighbour's barn, it turned out to be the best conversation piece ever.

I had just turned 40 and after 21 years of marriage my wife and I separated. Marian took a chance and moved into a little Brighton home with a man 16 years her senior in search of adventure. Now the silly old bugger wanted to circumnavigate the planet on a motorcycle.

The romantic fantasy was so much easier to handle than the reality. I was giving up my business and hard-earned career for this shit-or-bust endeavour. My trusty business partner Steve and I had sweated blood to make a success of our advertising agency, but in spite of aggressive competition, it was all working remarkably well. My biggest and most enjoyable client was Honda Motorcycles. Not only did I get to design their literature, but I also had the chance to ride some fabulous machines for photo shoots. Bruno Tagliaferri had run the marketing effort, but was snatched up by Triumph with the rebirth of the historic marque. We had stayed in touch and after deciding to fly the British flag around the world, I approached him for some help. "….but Robbie, I get a dozen requests like this every day. If I gave everyone a bike there would be none left to sell."

He had a very good point and if Triumph were to get involved, they would have to do it properly. Bruno did not have a sponsorship budget and frankly, without any proven track record, I was a bad risk. He must have seriously doubted my chances of success and could do without the blood of an Englishman on his hands. After some frantic negotiation, I did buy the bike at a slightly advantageous price, provided I promised to disappear into the great blue yonder, and leave him alone.

Preparation was practically non-existent as a business had to be wound up, farewells had to be said and, except for the odd visa, I was at a loss to know what to do.

An immaculate Triumph Trophy squatted in my front garden looking sleek and sexy. I only took it out on sunny afternoons to show it off.

Voluminous panniers were lined with foam rubber to protect a lap-top computer complete with printer, two hi-8 video cameras and stills cameras. The rucksack was half-filled with support equipment like the mother of all transformers to recharge batteries, spare video tape, film, paper – there was so much of it. Tools, spare parts, a ball of string (essential piece of travel equipment), and a bag of fake Swiss Army knives (useful bribes), left just enough room for a couple of pairs of spare knickers, and one or two T-shirts.

Being a hideous coward when it comes to the cold, I was disappointed that a flimsy sweatshirt was the only warm item I could find space for in my bulging rucksack. I also adopted a 'no map no tent' philosophy only because space was at an absolute premium. Besides, getting lost occasionally could be fun and, even if I couldn't find the popular destinations, surly the compensation would be finding locations off the tourist route. A compass was all I needed as an approximate direction finder and Marian's 1978 school atlas would tell me more or less which country to expect next. She was only thirteen when awarded it by The King's School, Peterborough, but I presumed the world had not changed too dramatically since publication.

It did cross my mind that getting wet at night, sleeping under the stars next to the bike, would be a lot less fun, but I planned to avoid cold, wet countries. Leave the northern hemisphere in mid-summer and a few months later be at the bottom of the southern to catch their's. Foolproof. It most certainly was not a macho statement. In good weather a tent creates more problems than it solves. Erecting and dismantling takes time and a rapid departure may be called for occasionally.

With all this weight on the back, I made several experimental rides to establish balance and stability. On one such ride, I followed a young police officer who was probably in nappies when I passed my test but was riding with far more confidence. On impulse, I wrote to the chief constable in the hope that a little extra training might increase my life expectancy.

The result was PC Bill Clemence giving up his own time to put me right on a number of riding skills. There was something very reassuring about following a dayglo yellow BMW through Sussex lanes. Periodically we would stop for a fag break and an assessment of my progress. He would laugh, then wrinkle his brow over many points in my riding style. Just because you have been doing something for a long time, it does not mean to say you are good at it. Bill's efforts were very worthwhile, increasing my confidence in the bike and ability to control such a massive machine. He gave me a bright yellow reflective overjacket as a parting gesture, hoping this would prevent me being knocked off on unlit roads at night.

An important but time-consuming part of the preparation was saying goodbye to friends. This included a brief trip to Hamburg to see my sister and her family. Some years previously she had adopted two remarkably beautiful Tamil boys, one of whom, Sundaraj, had returned to India to search for his parents. During his quest a Hindu priest blessed a small medallion to keep him safe while travelling. It became his most prized possession and had never left his neck until that blustery day in a Hamburg flat. It was not much to look at. A slim copper-coloured coin an inch across with a Hindu God etched on either side. He made no ceremony of handing over his charm to protect me in hostile places. His dark eyes did not reveal the wrench it must have been to place this token into my hand. I was a little concerned that he thought I needed such a valuable charm to keep me safe, but good luck and protection are not commodities to be rejected at any time.

The one sensible decision I did make was to have a finite start and finish point, or there would be too much of a temptation to keep going until the money ran out. For a decade I had been visiting the Le Mans 24 hour race and I did not see why a little thing like a round-world motorcycle trip should make me miss a favourite event, so it became a logical choice. Friends would be there to wave me goodbye, and be there again to pour beer down the dusty throat of a travel-weary old biker on his return. This was the theory, and I would have a whole year on the road before discovering the reality. From Le Mans, I planned to ship both myself and the bike to the United States, which was potentially very expensive and logistically tricky. Luckily, another old client came to the rescue. Derrick Lellow of J.E. Bernard Global Freight became an invaluable friend. He is the kind of guy who, despite always being frantically busy, invites people to take advantage of his fantastic knowledge, and in his methodical way he came up with a list of all their worldwide sister companies, even faxing some to warn them I may need help. This cumbersome document was going to be a pain in the arse to carry around, but any kind of introduction, especially where I did not speak the language, was potentially useful. He also arranged transport for the Triumph team to get to New York, but for reasons of cost and convenience we had to depart from Heathrow, which would mean returning to the UK after the Le Mans race. This proved to be a blessing in disguise as, travelling through central France, the Triumph's clutch started slipping badly.

There I was attempting to ride this thing across half a dozen continents, and it would not even get me halfway across France. For my sins, I had a very heated telephone conversation with an unsuspecting Mary at Redhill Motors in Brighton. Her boss, Tony Brown, was responsible for preparing the Triumph for its ordeal and I wanted blood.

The mother of all hangovers did not help the tense ride back after the race, as an overloaded bike struggled to climb any gradient towards Le Havre and a ferry home. Predictably, after profuse apologies for my irrational bad temper, Tony found the fault – and it was all mine. While replacing a damaged clutch lever, I had dropped a little brass bush, preventing the clutch functioning properly when hot, and Mary was added to my growing post card list in compensation. Thankfully, I did make amends, as Tony Brown was to have his patience severely challenged some nine months later in the face of severe adversity.

2. The Fat Lands

Sitting in Heathrow Airport waiting for my flight, I stared at the virgin notebook which was to become such a big part of my everyday activity, and a trembling pen etched its first words indelibly onto bleached paper. 'This is most definitely the first day of the rest of my life.' The words were harsh – threatening, not reassuring with a promise of fulfillment. 'This is the start of what will probably be the most outrageous adventure I am ever likely to undertake. Must phone Marian to say goodbye – I love you – and please ...' So much to say, but it had already been said before with a touch, a kiss, a look. No promises were ever exchanged. Had there been any doubts about our future together I would have been riding back to Brighton, not sitting with a trembling heart, waiting for British Airways to swallow me up, then spit me out into the unknown. She was singularly the most important thing in my life, yet after only four of years together, I had left her in the home we had made together for a different adventure. We planned to meet up in Bangkok for Christmas – if our relationship was strong enough to stand six months separation. The Gods of Sundaraj would protect my body but not my soul. A last cigarette before boarding. A cursory glance at a gleaming steel Zippo lighter given as a farewell gift by my business partner and most trusted friend, Steve. The straightforward inscription was to the point and so typical of Steve. 'Robbie – Trip of a lifetime.' The feeling of trepidation was crushing as dusty bike boots shed their last grains of British soil for an alien world.

New York greeted me with a thunderstorm worthy of a Dracula movie where sheet lightning conveniently illuminates the screen just long enough to catch a glimpse of a vampire's face. In this case it was a sullen black taxi driver's face I was staring at through a curtain of rain. "The nearest cheap hotel please" was not, I thought, an unreasonable request to a cab driver. "Any one in particular?" came the reply. "No, I'm a stranger in town, and if I knew of one, there would be no hesitation in asking for it." Being driven around a strange town always seems to take an eternity and I could not wait to lose myself in the bright lights of The Big Apple, a name that is still a mystery to me for a filthy, dangerous mass of high-rise buildings. We pulled up outside a neon sign claiming to be The Jade East Hotel, Jamaica, a part of town only exceeded by the Bronx in its undesirability, or so I was told. The fare came to eight dollars, so I handed over a twenty and asked for ten change. "Ain't you got any smaller? I don't carry that much dough at night." I ran into the hotel for some change, then asked the driver if he could give me a hand with some of my luggage. In an attempt to reduce the size of the bike crate and save some money, all my luggage had to fly with me and not the bike. Two 36 litre panniers, heavy rucksack and a bulging shoulder bag. "No, Sir. I never get out of my cab on this side of town." He nevertheless thought it was okay for me to struggle back and forth with just about everything I did not need.

It may have been the cheapest hotel around, but it was still $67 a night. The Russian owner showed surprise when I said I may need a room for a couple of days. Later I discovered rooms were generally rented by the hour. It must have been near midnight by the time a lone white stranger with his head in a different time zone hit the dark unwelcoming streets, but I was keen to have a look around and the rain had reduced to a persistent drizzle. The menacing looking Russian with almost black piggy eyes told me of a bar still open a couple of blocks away. He started to finger the handgun stuck in his trousers when he realised a guest was about to walk the streets. He offered to call me a cab, but I reassured him the British enjoy walking, especially in the rain. I caught a glimpse through the rain-streaked glass door of the rather sinister figure making the sign of the cross. He had already checked to see my room had been paid for in advance.

In reality the seedy little bar was only about three hundred yards away. The place was pretty spartan, with a few vacant wooden tables and a dozen or so drinkers sitting on tall bar stools served by bare-breasted women. The floor had been elevated on their side so skimpily-clad crotches were at eye height and they had to lean over to hear your order above nondescript music. Local etiquette lesson one. Watch what the others do before plunging in and making a prat of yourself. Most men were ordering, then stuffing a note in the waitress' G-string, which I took to be an invitation for her to keep the change. Some took advantage by fondling the swinging breasts before their eyes, as the waitress bent over to pass a bottle of Bud. Above the noise, I'm sure the gyrating triangle of sequined fabric framed by pubic hair said 'tits are optional', but it may have been 'tips'. With unceasing eye contact, my note was thrust firmly into a waiting hand. It is not my place to pass judgment and there are probably similar bars in Soho and Paris, but I hoped that that vile place, servicing the demands of inadequate people, was not typical. We can unwittingly dismiss or become enraptured with anything because of one experience and I needed to see more.

By morning, the hotel and just about everything else in New York was flooded, so there was no hot water and limited electrical power. This was brought to the attention of my host, but there was no apology and a refund was obviously not forthcoming, so I phoned JFK customs to check if the Triumph had arrived. It had not. "....but I was assured it would be landed on Saturday morning," I protested. "Sure," came the answer, "but today is Friday." This was confusing, and I assumed Americans had two Fridays each week.

Another day before Triumph and rider could be united gave me an opportunity to explore this vibrant Jekyll and Hyde city. I hastily scribbled an avalanche of postcards in a 5th Avenue bar over a pint of Guinness poured by a guy from Galway. Central Park was rivetting, with its endless procession of roller skaters, joggers and cyclists. Everyone, from toddlers to old wrinklies, dressed for the part so there was no confusion which activity they were participating in. The North Americans do not do anything by halves and designer uniforms are obligatory for all recreational pursuits.

After a long day playing tourist I boarded the wrong subway home. The best way to get under the skin of a new town is to use public transport, but this train was heading for the Bronx on the other side of town. Standing near the doorway of a graffiti-strewn empty carriage, on the off-chance I might recognise something and have to jump off, both inter-compartment doors swung open simultaneously. From one end half a dozen black youths with 'Bloods' written on torn T-shirts emerged from the half light. About the same number of hispanics, all wearing colourful head scarves, postured at the other end. The train screeched aggressively to a halt, to admit several oriental young men all looking like Bruce Lee in fighting mood. Their attentions drifted from each other to me, still dangling from a handrail doing my best to look very nonchalant. Another stop and a bunch of white guys got in gibbering in Russian. There I was, the stranger in town, and the only one

16

with English as a first language. They all looked very lean and fit as if from a West Side Story set. Maybe they would start dancing and leave me alone.

The problem I find with wet leathers in a hot confined space is that they start to steam. Increased agitation as the result of attracting so much attention was making matters worse and by the time one of the larger black guys addressed me, I was doing a convincing impression of a geyser about to blow. "Where you goin' man?" "Just thought I may pop out to Jamaica for a look around," I stammered through a cloud of steam. Everyone except me started to laugh. The vapour build-up was a little like an express train preparing for departure. As the internal pressure increased, jets of mist were released from cuffs and collar.The well-built Blood moved within punching distance, extending his arm. Instinctively, I ducked out of sight behind a sauna cloud. A short stubby finger missed my nose and collided with a subway map immediately above my head. "Two things you got to learn, man. One, you goin' the wrong way and two, Jamaica is dangerous for a lone honky at night." This amused the assembled company even more and I was glad to take their instruction, exiting the train for another platform. Judging by the howls of laughter in my wake, I can not help being a little proud of my contribution to world peace, defusing a potential battleground. Several subway trains, a long walk and, eventually, a taxi were required to get me back to where I started.

An early morning phone call confirmed the Triumph was in customs awaiting collection. The shipping agent said he would send someone to pick me up. After nearly an hour waiting outside trying to keep out of the rain, a big yellow taxi pulled up. The enormous driver, who must have been one of the few cabbies capable of getting into an Oldsmobile and filling it, insisted he had come for me. After half a mile or so he asked where I wanted to go. Now, let this be a lesson. Never get into a New York cab outside the immediate city centre if you do not know how to get to your destination, or it could take hours. Fatman and I quickly established he had picked up the wrong ride. We pulled over so I could phone the hotel and prevent the agent's driver taking off, should he arrive. By this time the monumental flesh-pot had got us lost and had no idea how to get back to the hotel. He stopped three times at petrol stations to ask directions and another hour elapsed before being united with Levi in an airport truck back at the hotel. En route to JFK, I started to take note of traffic rules necessary for survival.

In general, the driving standard is not far short of the British, but sensible rules like overtaking on both sides and filtering right at red lights help traffic flow. They also seem to have more patience and are better at adhering to road regulations. Levi was a very jolly Rastafarian and, like most Americans, showed genuine surprise that I did not know his cousin living in Manchester. He did not believe that London is bigger than New York and no, we do not all live in draughty old castles inhabited by ghosts.

Customs was excruciatingly slow. I had to learn to calm down and not be so impatient, but the desire to get moving was getting stronger with every waiting minute. The problem of shipping a motorcycle from England must have been one experienced previously in the history of USA imports. The Department of Agriculture would not sign the release until the tyres had been inspected for English dirt. So what is wrong with English dirt? Under normal circumstances this would not be a problem, but the shipping agent would not accept the crate once it had been opened. Perfect Catch 22 situation. My Swiss Army knife became red hot removing 54 screws so the inspector could waddle the ten yards from his office, proclaim "Hot damn, it is a Triumph", hand over a bill for $164 and leave me to repack the crate.

As a murky dusk was settling, the Triumph experienced its first taste of New York streets in conditions reminiscent of an English November. The roads suffer during hard winters and there was an inadequate budget for proper maintenance. In home-produced cars with soft suspension, it is not a problem, but dodging rain-filled potholes on a motorcycle, in unfamiliar traffic, was alarming. This was the initiation of an inexperienced English duo in a foreign land. Excitement and anticipation gripped handlebars through sodden gloves. The machine responded to my nervousness twitching with every twist of the throttle. Someone had told me England was basking in sunshine and Brighton had miraculously become sub-tropical. It did not seem fair, but the thought of Marian stretched out in the garden enjoying the sunshine stirred something deep down inside and the emptiness was blurred by more lascivious thoughts of her body glistening with suntan oil.

My youngest daughter Chantie had moved in to supplement the rent and I hoped that two such strong-minded young women were going to get on. They were closer in age than I was to Marian and it felt weird that two of the most important women in my life were sharing a home without me there. What would they talk about on winter evenings? Chantie was prone to talking quite openly about intimate matters and Marian was not afraid to speak her mind. I was their common denominator and would have loved to be a fly on the wall when I was on the agenda – well, maybe not. I was already missing snuggling up to her warm body at night, missing the touch of her skin next to mine. The thought brought a shiver as rain penetrated not very waterproof leathers and I had to shut it out – now it was time to discover America and I was eager to find a dry bit.

Relentless east coast rain drove me south in search of sunshine. Philadelphia, Washington DC and a host of other towns were washed away in the spray from trucks the size of office blocks doing 80mph on Interstate highways with a 65mph limit.

480 miles later, the cloud broke momentarily allowing shafts of evening sunshine to light the way of a novice traveller at the end of a first day's grim riding. I needed somewhere cheap to dry out. My romantic notion of sleeping rough with the bike had disappeared with the last drenching. A friendly local directed me to a hotel and, thankfully, said a sodden crash helmet was not needed around Charlottesville. Minutes later two cop cars and a police Harley Davidson pulled me over with the full treatment of flashing lights and sirens. Typical of the Yanks to over-react. The bike cop took his time to swagger over and inform me, "protective headgear is required at all times in the State of Virginia – Sir." I apologised in a frightfully British kind of way. The cop was looking at the bike registration. The gears in his brain visibly ticking over. "You from Bir-min-ham?" Well, that was impressive stuff. Most Americans had taken my accent to be Canadian or Irish, but this guy had spotted an English voice. "No," I replied, "I'm from Brighton actually." His face went blank for a second. "That in Alabama too?" A brief explanation of world geography was followed by an escort, still with flashing lights, to a bug-feast $19 motel. We chewed the fat for a while and my stills camera saw light of day before he rode off saying, "just wait till I git home tonight and tell Bobby Jo I got me an English one today."

19

The leaden dawn greeted me with two more reasons for depression. Firstly I had foolishly locked my crash helmet to the bike rather than taking it inside to dry out and having poured all night it was quite literally full of water. Secondly, during the early morning bike-packing ritual a weakness revealed itself that I hopped would not plague me the world over. One side of the cast aluminum pannier racks had sheered so Everything had to be repacked to minimise weight on that side until repaired and this was only my second day on the road. Local intelligence pointed me in the direction of Harrisonburg, and, amazingly, a Triumph dealer.

The place was vast and immaculate. Got to hand it to the Americans, they know how to put on a show. Rows of gleaming bikes on a multitude of levels were dramatically lit for greater effect. No one could fail to be impressed with all that gleaming chrome. My problem of broken, badly engineered aluminum, was presented to Vern, Verg and Bob who set about their task with astounding enthusiasm, while I purchased an open-faced helmet. It made me look as if I had a tit on my head, but at least it was dry. Also the bike handling problems were resolved with a gargantuan tank bag. It may have impaired visibility but it stopped the front wheel oscillating in the most disturbing fashion on corners. All tools and spares could sit up front taking much of the weight off the back wheel. Vern's jaw dropped when he saw the amount of stuff being zipped into the multi-level bag. "You won't need all those tools riding a Triumph." It was a real compliment to the British manufacturer, but he did change his mind when he learned my proposed route. They made an excellent job of the repair and charged me a colossal amount of money but it was probably the going rate.

America was going to be a massive drain on resources, but at least it was a gentle introduction to life on the road. The population were in general friendly in a superficial sort of way and more or less spoke the same language. British media portrays the culture relatively accurately and, as I was finding out, there were helpful bike dealers should the Triumph suffer any teething problems. It was a huge gamble taking such an unproven machine, but the respect it commanded was spectacular. That badge was possibly the biggest asset anyone could hope for. Most people claimed to have known someone who once owned a Bonneville, and there were more photographs of Marlon

Brando riding British heritage than there were of the Pope in Vatican City.

The repairs had cost me the best part of a whole day, but there was just time to scale the Blue Ridge Mountains of Virginia in thick fog and rain. One of the delights of travelling the States is that just about every town or major road is a song title. Who needs a map, with the lyrics from sixties musicians to guide you across the continent.

Lexington was a sleepy little God-fearing town in the shadow of Walton's Mountain where everyone seems to be called Jim Bob or Peggy Sue. The pink evening glow cast a startling blush on white timber-clad houses, each with a swinging seat on broad verandahs. Old men in dimly-lit bars puffed on clay pipes while sipping sour rye whisky over a game of dominoes. They huddled round squat tables in a rather defensive manner making it clear the sanctity of the circle was not to be broken without invitation. A dripping leather-clad stranger stopped all conversation. Dominoes in mid-shuffle fell silent.

I ordered a beer. "Where you from boy?" The barman did not move his lips so I turned to face the source of the question. Twenty or so shovel beards all wearing funny hats stared with unblinking expressions. "I said where you from boy?" At 45 years old, maybe I should have been flattered by the remark, but I had an inkling that the guy hiding behind a haystack of facial hair was not being complimentary. Although they had computed a foreigner had invaded their world, my beer was poured and then paid for by someone with a bale of straw stuck to his top lip. I thanked him for the gesture of friendliness, but dreaded to think what might have happened if I had been black or Chinese.

In determined mood the Triumph exceeded the 500 mile a day barrier to Nashville, Tennessee. The Hard Rock Cafe offered shelter, cold beer and friendly company. For the first time I really started missing friends, Marian, my children. Every day was a new adventure governed by a whim, a compass needle and a dose of total ignorance and I wanted to share the experience. That night my notebook revealed the first sign of loneliness.

'England and M seem a long way away. They *are* a long way away. Haven't had much time to miss her yet as there is always so much to do and I'm busy getting my travelling head on. Hope she is not missing me too much. The realisation of how much I love her is a bitter-sweet pill as Christmas and our reunion is an eternity away. It would be wonderful to share this experience with her, but then it would be so different as her clear logical thoughts would prevent me making so many stupid mistakes. Such an old head on young pretty shoulders.'

Travelling alone is challenging and liberating. There is no one to blame if things go wrong, or to confer with over decisions – but nor are there arguments about which way to go with every fork in the road. We had travelled together in South East Asia for a month and enjoyed each other's company, happy to jump on a bus because we liked the name of the destination. You have to be comfortable with a companion in those situations as you are together twenty four hours a day. The penalty for travelling as a couple is not meeting so many people as there is always someone to talk to. I talked to her while riding. Nothing dramatic, just "look at that – mind that truck," or "wouldn't it be nice to have a shag under a vast desert sky?"

3. In Search of Sunshine

A daily routine was beginning to emerge. Up around 6.30am with the sun. Half an hour to pack the bike and start moving – somewhere – anywhere. After 150 miles or so stop for fuel and a bum rest. This part of my anatomy was taking longer to adapt to a new way of life than the rest of my body. Generally I was feeling stronger, but my bum, after spending ten or so hours a day in the saddle was developing painful calluses from the elastic in my knickers. My youngest daughter, in an attempt to drag her Dad into twentieth-century fashion, had given me a pair of boxer shorts which brought some relief . Also my ex-mother-in-law had given me some outrageous flowery cotton shorts that proved to be very comfortable once the airtex lining had been removed.

An important feature of early morning stops was fat-bastard breakfast diners. Eating is taken very seriously all over the States. A Tennessee breakfast typically consists of two eggs easy over (or is it over easy?), hash browns, sausage, biscuit and gravy. The sausage is a burger and the biscuit a bun. If you ask for a burger they put the sausage in the bun. Gravy comes in a separate bowl looking and tasting like porridge with chewy bits. Syrup and blackcurrent jelly on the side – weird but excellent value at about three dollars. One thing I learned early on is never, no matter how hungry you are, ask for a large portion of anything.For a light snack, I went to a Blimpy Bar for a tuna roll. It was two feet long and with the girth of a sumo wrestler. If I hugged the damn thing both hands would not join on the other side. This was a week's food for a Somalian village. Americans must throw away more than the rest of the world eats.

The bulk of each day was spent riding, stopping only for fuel and photographs. Perpetual rain was still hampering any attempt to film. No one had ever single handedly produced a credible film of a round world tour, so I was becoming concerned my cameras were not getting any exercise. By dusk I would be searching sleazy suburbs for cheap accommodation and sustenance. For some strange reason I was still suffering from time lag, so would force myself to stay awake until midnight flicking through thirty or so TV channels of evangelist preachers. Drift off for a couple of hours before getting up at about 4.00am to repack everything in a perpetual quest for better weight distribution. Another hour or so slumber before the dawn invaded once more. Marian had neglected to tell me to take an alarm clock so the curtains had to be left open to avoid wasting precious daylight. She had also forgotten to remind me about a hairbrush so I started most days looking like a cross between Wurzel Gummage and a yeti.

Tennesse sounded pretty dry and Graceland Park Hotel, Elvis Presley Boulevard, Memphis was amazingly the cheapest way of avoiding further cloudbursts and a couple of sunny intervals offered a brief opportunity to start filming. All set up on the banks of the sleepy old Mississippi with more AV technology than Michael Palin, my first mistake was to write a script. Lacking in any theatrical skills, I soon learned the only way of achieving any kind of result was to be totally spontaneous. After about fifty takes, a bucket of batteries and a fair amount of cursing, the first few seconds of footage were making progress until an army of gardeners started cutting the grass with strimmers, prematurely ending my cinematic debut. The Graceland museum was far too expensive and American with its glitzy presentation and 'religious experience' setting, so I headed south once more, not putting my feet down until reaching a flooded New Orleans 600 miles away. I had not seen storms that severe outside the tropics. I had just ridden the length of the United States and been rained on every day. It was never like this in the movies and I was aware progress on mine was not going to plan. A predominantly Vietnamese residential area offered a cheap bed and dry bus ride to the French Quarter for legendary entertainment. Like most towns with a reputation for something, the famous bit is confined to a small area and gazing through a premature twilight brought on by a gunmetal gray sky, the only memorable observation was the multi-cultural nature of a town contained by rivers and marshes. The mighty Mississippi Delta is vast, with more of its fertile wetlands being snatched from Neptune on a daily basis.

The French Quarter is where the town gains its notoriety, clinging on to a recent history with near Hollywood effect. Not so long ago the vast waterway was the only link with the north continent and broad riverboats still dawdle along to the rhythmic pulse of a single paddle. They linger at berth awaiting another assault by noisy tourists wishing to be transported back in time to the days of showboats and steely-faced poker players. Not even streets running with water could dampen the spirits of an ignorant Englishman in quest of fun and live music. Every bar throbbed with sensational rhythm and blues, Cajun or jazz. Between thunderclaps, music moved onto the streets with very competent buskers hammering out their own versions of *The House of the Rising Sun*. A small entrepreneurial shop was doing sensational trade in 'emergency ponchos' for 99 cents, which roughly translated as blue bin bags with arm and head holes and a hood that flopped over the eyes. Hundreds of blue-plastic-clad people were to be seen groping along, bumping into lamp posts or falling into a swollen Mississippi.

While waiting on the steps of Planet Hollywood (a spectacle uniquely American) for the heavens to take breath between storms, a very drunk half French half Cherokee guy fell over me and decided to sit a while to share my beer. Once past the "I'm English" hurdle, he announced to an empty street, "A horse, a horse, my kingdom for a horse." "Richard The Third," I applauded. "No. King Arthur, my favourite European film." It was time to move on.

Leathers were showing signs of mildew, my hands looked as if they had been left in the bath too long and the Trophy pushed 762 miles in about 12 hours to Denton, Texas, in the search for sunshine. I must have been suffering from a combination of exhaustion and boredom when the first terrifying incident of my trip took place. Riding through Dallas, I fell asleep in the saddle. I was dreaming vividly of getting up for work at home, talking to Marian over an early morning cup of tea when I awoke in complete darkness with huge truck wheels spinning only inches away on either side of me. I had ridden into a three lane underpass, and it took all my strength and concentration to ride a straight line back into the daylight.

Texas was a huge disappointment. British media had led me to expect endless horizons of beef herds and nodding-donkey oil wells. The reality was wide open spaces carpeted with assorted crops and an evil cross wind that had me riding at 45 degrees all day. A $19 motel was good enough excuse not to start sleeping under the stars which were almost visible through ominous clouds.

Next to the motel was a petrol station, so I decided to fill up for an early start. An ancient prune-faced woman took my money, inquiring, "You got the cotton in yet in England?" I politely explained that England did not have an appropriate climate for cotton and it is so small the crop would probably not be economically viable. "Well, what about them Italy, France and Germany?" She was surprised to hear that England did not have federal control of Europe and it would fit into Texas several times over. She stood right in front of the bike, legs apart, hands on hips determined to keep the conversation going, but we had run out of common ground. In desperation I pointed at the bunting strewn around in preparation for the forthcoming Independence Day. Small Stars and Stripes flags strung alternately with another I took to be the Texas state emblem were being tugged uncomfortably in the unceasing wind. "What's the *other* flag?" I asked in desperation. "My, don't you folk know nothin'. That's the flag of the United States of America." To this day I am none the wiser.

Escaping Texas for a new state was easy when, more by luck than good judgment, I picked up Route 66 for a second time. The Rolling Stones' lyrics guided me through 'Oklahoma City looks oh so pretty', into New Mexico with classic tall cacti silhouetted against the drama of billowing clouds streaked with shafts of a determined sun. My first day on the road with no rain at all, and an 80mph blow-dry lifted flagging spirits. There were 24 hour fireworks supermarkets in the most unexpected places. Often visible several miles away across semi-desert landscapes, they stood all alone as if waiting for a town to be built around them. I bought some rockets and sparklers, not in honour of the fourth of July, but the fifth, my birthday. Feeling elated by the unaccustomed sunshine, I decided to sleep out without the threat of a soaking. An hour before dusk, I was riding dirt tracks across a good deal of nothing looking for a suitable place to stop and set up camp,

There is an urge in one's survival instinct to sleep next to something. A tree, a bush, a large rock, anything to hide behind or offer token protection. No such luck. As my shadow lengthened, I just stopped, secured the bike and got my sleeping bag out. Fortunately, I had had the presence of mind to buy a bottle of water and a couple of cans of Mexican beer for cleaning teeth and evening recreation. Half an hours' intensive search produced enough fuel for a decent fire. As I was feeling rather pleased with myself for setting up a maiden camp, when out of nowhere a car appeared. The driver was a German woman complaining I was parked across her drive. No amount of scanning the horizon revealed any dwelling and the bit of dirt supporting a dusty Triumph looked very like any other bit of dirt. We had an interesting little chat, after which she conceded to drive round the camp rather than make me move it a few feet to an identical spot. Before her taillights disappeared into the setting sun she did put me right about the time. Without realising it I had crossed a couple of time zones making me two hours younger. Could this be the secret of eternal youth?

The firewood was so dry it only lasted half an hour and to save torch batteries, I settled down to a well-earned sleep in the silence of the desert. Within minutes rustling noises were joined by a curious popping sound. Distant dogs howled, bringing to mind images of werewolves, accompanied by the hum of wind through sparse vegetation. Dawn was a long time coming. This pioneer stuff was going to take some getting used to.

The sign said 'Las Vegas 100 miles'. Not really my cup of tea, but there was a window in my diary that day, so I thought it might be a good place to film Americans in holiday mood. Right on the perimeter of town my progress was interrupted by a rather pathetic little parade. Like everyone else, I parked up to watch. A few cowboys on horses led several hay-ricks carrying painted children against a back-drop of rapidly building cumulus. You would have been forgiven for thinking a volcano had just blown its top in the next town. The sun was snuffed out like a candle as spectators shuffled around looking confused. As the first enormous drops splashed into the gasping dust I asked a leathery old Navajo Indian if this was seasonal weather. "Not in my lifetime," came his reply, and then he gave me the name "Rain Maker." I apologised for dampening the parade and joked that if I could manage a repeat performance in the Sahara there could be money to be made. Tactical error. American Indians do not necessarily share the white American romance with the dollar. "Don't make money – make flowers," he said in all seriousness. My ex-father-in-law taught me one useful lesson. When you are in the shit, stand still. Do not spread it around. Regrettably his words had been lost somewhere on the highway as I asked directions to the strip – Mecca of gambling with the lasers and bright lights that have made Las Vegas so famous. He gave me one of those looks reserved for stupid white travellers.

"You want Las Vegas, Nevada. This is Las Vegas, New Mexico." Well how was I to know there were two of them? This was my cue to ride off towards Arizona, and the Grand Canyon.

No matter how prepared you are for your first sight of a hole a mile deep, a mile wide, that would stretch half the length of England – everyone gasps. Hollywood could not have dreamt up such a set designed to make people feel small. Predictably, the Americans capitalise on every natural asset, but in this case it is to preserve a national monument as well as generating revenue. The sleepy green Colorado River snakes its way through a forest of towering turrets tinted copper and gold. The touristy bit is well orchestrated and not too intrusive, with food and booze in striking distance of well-facilitated camp sites. Without a tent, camp sites are not good value for money and my dirt was only two days old, so I selected a remote part of the rim for personal festivities. I was determined to spend the eve of my 46th year alone and witness a dawn that could be stored forever in a corner of my mind. In party mood, supper was half a dozen cans of Mexican beer and a small bottle of brandy. I had completely forgotten about food, but a camp fire would have been out of the question on the edge of a wood and I had discovered to my dismay, fireworks were illegal in Arizona. It would have been rather exciting to aim a few rockets over the enormous void but I did not wish to experience the wrath of the local constabulary. I did have sparklers and a solitary present from a lovely friend, Rena. As soon as it became too dark to film, I opened the card as the last dying embers of the sun turned Nature's sculpture from ochre to blood red. The card had a pin badge attached with the words 'party animal' emblazoned across it. I opened a beer with thoughts of her pretty face smiling down on my feeble little celebration. The bitter taste of loneliness ran through me with a shudder. "Its my birthday," I announced to the trees fighting back a tear. Someone must have heard as seconds later the stillness was broken by the nearest tree shedding its entire load of fir cones. I laughed hysterically as my anonymous sympathiser pelted me with gifts from the sky. Rena's present was in two parts and so well wrapped, I had to attack the smaller parcel with my Swiss Army knife. Two little ceramic receptacles hardly an inch across with delicate floral brushwork fell onto the soft earth. The other package contained four slim candles that had been welded together in the desert heat. The multi-purpose knife separated them into four roughly equal parts and the stillness of the evening became apparent. Not a wave or sway was detectable from erect flames casting a halos of yellow light over a solitary figure. Time passed as my thoughts were furiously scribbled down into a yawning notebook. As I pulled another can of Mexican sunshine from the ice bag purchased to keep it cool, two things happened nearly simultaneously.

The last candle flickered and died with the grace of a butterfly. Then the ear shattering silence was invaded by a noise that jerked every tendon. The sound itself was not sinister, just the fact that it was the *only* one and not one I was familiar with from other nights spent camping out. This was the first time I had slept next to a forest and everything was different – like the noise of rustling in undergrowth. "It's fir cones falling off the trees," I thought soothing my goosebumps down to a rash of boils. "Yeh, fir cones falling – on animals – like rabbits – wild dogs – grizzly bears – chain-saw murderers." The sound picked up in rhythm and volume. I wished I had a proper weapon. My torch beam was flicking around like a lightsabre from Star Wars and froze on two pinpoints of light. "Shit," I cursed into the inky blackness, "it's a wolf." The white streaked face was undeniable. The spill from the torch beam detected further movement. "Bollocks, there are two of them." The beam twitched back and forth between two passive pairs of unblinking eyes. My brain started racing. "There could be hundreds of them. Whole packs dedicated to cleansing the area of tourists."

A 360 degree sweep revealed that if there were more they had better things to do than salivate over scrag end of biker. Now the next bit is the only reason why I believe there is a superhuman watching over us. Most people would consider a barrage of fir cones dumped on their head a pretty unexciting birthday present. My unwelcome visitors were easily in range and retreated at the first volley. This both delighted and saddened me. Maybe they had only wanted to make friends – but maybe they wanted scrawny old Englishman lightly barbecued. Either way an arsenal of Nature's missiles was gathered to fend off attack. The confrontation and resultant burst of energy had left me a little clammy when a more significant phenomenon struck.

There I was all zipped up for the night in T-shirt, knickers and socks having scraped enough water from the ice to clean my teeth. The ground was firm, but with a reassuring softness from centuries of fallen tree debris, and leather jeans and jacket make a comfortable pillow. I found it also kept the dew off them and if you have to leave in a hurry, you do not want to be groping in the dark for important possessions. Desert temperatures at around 8,000 feet drop like a block of ice after dark. My rucksack, carefully packed for a rapid exit was invaded. A T-shirt was followed by another, then a sweatshirt. An hour later I was lying under a theatre of shooting stars wearing full leathers and crash helmet, cursing the day I chose that light, compact, but crap sleeping bag. My shivers must have registered on the Richter Scale. With the first smudge of orange on the horizon, I was packed up and heading back to the highway. I swear there was more ice in the morning cooling the remaining beer than purchased the day before.

The Canyon had been a great experience despite a few unexpected surprises and was well worth milking to death, so I pulled over for a last photograph. The ground looked solid enough, but loose gravel concealed a steep slope and our first disaster was in the making. The drop was only about three feet and we slid quite gracefully to a halt. The only bike damage was a broken front indicator (big design fault) and a few scratches. Like a fool, I let adrenaline take over and attempted to right the bike without unpacking. There was a clearly audible noise before the pain shot between my shoulder blades. I recall crying out as tendons stretched against the uncompromising weight and the sensation of being beaten with a red-hot poker filtered down my arms. I am not very good at coping with pain, so dropped the bike back into the dirt. From nowhere, a wagon-load of Friends of Jesus appeared and had the Triumph back on the road with one rousing chorus of 'Morning has Broken'. I thanked them for their help and accepted a leaflet called 'Jesus want you for a moonbeam' before riding in a very strange position towards Williams with tears in my eyes. The fire in my back was second only to the thought of failure. 'Could it all be over so soon?' A crushing sense of failure focused my mind on sorting out the problem.

Williams just happened to have the nearest medical practitioner, who prodded, X-rayed and injected the offending injury, with a reassuring diagnosis of a muscle injury and no evidence of spinal damage. He told me to rest for a month and keep taking the painkillers. To properly assess the problem and my riding ability, all luggage was stashed in a motel room for an unladen run to Flagstaff. Despite the pain, this was a joy. I had forgotten how responsive the bike was without its huge daily burden. The town was an absolute picture set in a magnificent arena of mountains and tall spruce. Quite the most attractive American town so far and I regretted not being fit enough to explore in depth. Even at that altitude, the unaccustomed heat gave me a new burst of strength and energy. Arizona to me was the crown of the USA, the jewel being the Grand Canyon. Its undeniable sense of liberty could be attributed to its isolation within the Federal system. A good standard of living is enjoyed by the population who amazingly claim to own more boats per capita compared to the rest of the US, despite being land-locked. Intensive lobbying of the Federal capital in Washington had reversed the motorcycle helmet laws as a civil rights issue. Scenically it offers plenty of pleasant surprises like Flagstaff – and a sign to London Bridge, next to a British GPO phone box, half covered in desert sand. Many who are old enough will no doubt remember driving across that English monument before it was lovingly transported stone by stone to its new location in Lake Havasu City. There was a rumour that the eccentric millionaire thought he had bought Tower Bridge complete with its historic machinery, but had had to settle for the graceful arches more accustomed to spanning the murky Thames. A river was diverted to give the structure purpose and Little England in an American desert was born. The pub I sat in drinking chilled draught Newcastle Brown was reputedly transported from the City of London along with the bridge and various other artifacts. A familiar accent from the other end of the bar said something like "this must be Limey day." I was half-way through apologising for my birth place, before realising the voice was pure Brummie and not the Alabama version. Phil and his Glaswegian wife Sharon had traded the damp cold streets of Birmingham for Arizona sunshine, and were doing rather well at it. His entrepreneurial boss had started a local Yellow Pages and in Phil found an enthusiastic sales representative. A couple of beers later I was bouncing his baby son PJ on my knee and being invited to stay at his house. It is always a little tricky when one half of a couple offers hospitality, but you are unsure how the other half will react to sharing their home with a stranger.

My concern was misplaced as that evening in their spacious home Sharon explained she was used to her husband bringing home weirdoes and admitted she enjoyed talking to other Brits. Phil was very concerned that I did not have any means of protection and insisted we take a ride out into the desert to visit a friend to 'get tooled up'. His `72 Cadillac was left in the garage as I followed in the dust of his big Yamaha. We were introduced to the friend's beautiful Mexican wife, some thirty years his junior and a couple of primary school kids who had inherited their mother's good looks. Every room in their rambling home revealed a loaded firearm of some description, until we sat in front of an arsenal of a dozen or so weapons. After a good deal of deliberation, I parted company with $200 for an ex-police snub-nosed .38 Smith and Wesson revolver. It was disturbingly tactile and small enough to be easily concealed. The five chambers were primed with proper solid rounds, but the remaining ammunition looked a little lame.

A couple of nights later, in the solitude of my Mojave Desert camp, still air was shattered as I familiarised myself with a newly-acquired instrument of death. A couple of sand dunes and stunted bushes felt the wrath of the five sensible rounds in my possession, before it was secreted under the bike seat unloaded. Two parting remarks made by the vendor hung in my mind. Never pull an unloaded gun as you can be sure your opponent will have one fully primed. Secondly, never reveal it unless you're prepared to pull the trigger.

A fluke decision at a road junction took me to the real Las Vegas as the compass needle more often than not pointed at a sheer mountain side or lake, so gut feel had to take over. Mid-afternoon on an overcast day is not the most flattering time to observe the third American obsession in action. The first is the automobile, second eating, and third money, which supports a thriving gambling industry. Animated under powerful spot lights it offers the illusion of excitement and adventure and a vale of darkness, aided by energetic neon and lasers, covers the cracks in a dull unimposing town with all the deception of a theatre stage. The town winces in daylight like a bedraggled circus troop. Outside the big top, cheap sequins are just cheap sequins on threadbare costumes. Everything was superficial – artificial, to whip would-be gamblers up into a spending frenzy. It all seemed a little distasteful, so I kept riding deeper into the desert.

4. Legless in California

I knew California was next to the Pacific, so all I had to do was ride west until the coast was in view. Orientation was determined by the early morning sun warming my back. Not even the compass needed consulting when the sky was clear and I was off to meet a real motorcycle hero. Shortly before my departure from UK, I had been in touch with Dave Barr, a remarkable disabled bike traveller who had invited me to visit for a little advice. In sight of the ocean, I turned right to Bakersfield, an unappealing industrial town and then up into the mountains towards Bodfish. In a few miles, the road rose some three thousand feet out of the smog, through unspoiled country, to the breathtaking sight of Lake Isabella. I phoned Dave from a seedy little beer joint leaving a message with his mother Lucille. He was 'out riding' at the time, but she told me to sit tight and she would let him know where I was. "How will I recognise him – will he be wearing a pink carnation behind his ear?" "When he walks through the door, you'll know him," Mrs Barr reassured. She was right. Dave had presence. I did not know the extent of his disability and in the gloom of the bar, this was difficult to assess as he moved around very competently on artificial limbs. The first clue was a strange length of hinged aluminium protruding from ragged trousers where most people have a foot. He refused an offer of beer. Dave does not drink or smoke and puts his faith in the Lord. My first and wrong impression was we were not going to get on.

In stark contrast to Dave's short haircut and clean-shaven face was Frisco, his riding companion. A tall, lean, powerful-looking man with a long beard and wild hair, although his attitude was far from threatening, but something said it would be wise to stay on the right side of that amiable bear.

We emerged from the half-light of the bar to inspect their Harley Davidsons. Frisco straddled his glittering machine with yards of legroom to spare. Dave manoeuvered his prosthetics over a junk heap that looked as though it should have been in a museum rather than in daily use. He had ridden that 25 year-old bike nearly a quarter of a million miles around the world. From Alaska to the most southerly point in South America, three times through the Great Wall of China and across most hot and cold deserts.

After a scenic ride around Lake Isabella through sumptuous scenery, we descended into Bodfish and Dave's spacious mobile home set in a well-tended garden. Mrs. Barr greeted me, leaving the impression that she was quite used to her son bringing home strange bikers.

I was shown a spotless room and hot shower (bliss), before going over to Frisco's for dinner. While waiting for Dave to get ready, I touched on the subject of his disability with Mrs. Barr as we strolled on a manicured lawn. "He will tell you soon enough," came her reply. He was obviously a man who did things in his way and in his own time.

It is truly astounding how one split-second incident can change the course of a life. The opening paragraph of Dave's book Riding the Edge begins, 'Every journey has a beginning, and mine started on August 29th 1981 in southern Angola while on operations with South African defence forces. Our vehicle hit a landmine. Suddenly I was launched – propelled through the air by the blast. Looking down at the truck from my vantage point several feet above it, my first thought was, I'm on my way to meet Jesus.'

He suffered severe burns, with both legs needing emergency surgery. Nine and a half months and twenty major operations later, Dave returned to active duty minus one and a half legs. That was the real accomplishment of a dynamic character. He had achieved far more than I was attempting on an equally unsuitable modified machine – and no legs! The man's courage and tenacity knew no bounds.

Frisco hugged me like a long lost fiend when we arrived at their ramshackle home which oozed character and the promise of fun. The amiable yeti introduced his pretty wife looking half his age and their two enchanting young children. We sat outside enjoying dinner on rustic tables to animated conversation with Frisco's wife about the injustice to the American Indians. The only building in sight that looked vaguely waterproof was a new timber garage that housed another Harley lovingly restored to concourse condition by Frisco. At least he had got his priorities right.

Before being embraced by the tender arms of sleep that night, there was a revelation and a treat. Crawling into bed I realised that I was in Dave's room, but the feeling of guilt about depriving him of comfort took second place to the joy of my first letter from Marian. 'Dearest Robs, how are you today?' The rest was a mixture of loneliness and confusion. There were no rhetorical questions about why I left her for this foolish adventure, as neither of us had any smart answers. No debate about it being the making or breaking of a relationship. Lying in Dave's bed scanning her well-formed hand, I had no doubts about our direction emotionally – geographically, for me at least, was a different question. Sleep came easily with her final message of undying love.

Not long after dawn I rose for a wander to get my bearings before the household awoke, only to find Dave and Mum had been on the go for hours. Dave started his day with vigorous exercise. "I have less blood, so have to encourage my heart to keep pumping." This sounded like a contradiction to me, but the man had obviously done his homework.

The military discipline had not deserted this dedicated taskmaster and our day together was spent in an intensive business-like briefing. We pored over maps, studying routes, noting addresses and precautions. He could not accept that maps were unnecessary and rejected my theory that a compass would get me there eventually. Studying the bike and badly deteriorating pannier racks, it was obvious to both of us that weight had to be dramatically reduced. Marian's school atlas, laptop computer, printer and suitcase full of other electrical gear were packaged up and sent home. I resented having to ditch the atlas, not so much because it was my only intelligence of a route, but because it was hers. Something concrete that she had owned, fingered and cherished for years. Just holding it made me feel closer to her. Releasing the lap top was less of a wrench as I was not really computer literate, but it would mean Marian would have to interpret my hand written notes and prepare them for publication.

Dave took on the world as a mission. I was doing it for 'fun' and, although his abundant enthusiasm was very encouraging, deep down he must have had serious doubts about my chances of success or survival. His stories and photographs were evidence enough of the apparently hopeless task ahead. Then came our only contentious moment. "You gotta ditch the Triumph. You will get a good price for it here and you can buy a Jap enduro machine far better suited to your needs." "But Dave, you accomplished so much more on an equally inappropriate bike," I protested. "Ah yeah," he philosophically replied, "I know every nut and bolt of the Harley. You hardly know how to say good morning to the Triumph." This was undeniably true, but we had started as a team and we would fail or succeed together.

As afternoon turned to dusk, I was punch drunk with advice and information. We had established a point of contact and he had recognised a kindred spirit albeit hiding behind the ignorance of a ridiculous Limey on a Triumph without a map. I likened my endeavour to having sex standing up in a hammock. Why do things the easy way? My reward was one of his most prized possessions. With some ceremony he handed over a piece of brass about two inches long, a little over half an inch at one end tapering to a sharp point. The metal wafer, slightly conical in shape showed considerable signs of wear. The red and amber Cloisonné design had shed most of its enamel, but the impression was clear. A length of khaki cord implied it was to be worn around the neck. "This is a scale from the dragon's back. It will protect you from attack from behind." That may sound like bullshit, but I figured I needed all the help on offer. He continued, "It was given to me by a motorcycle traveller in Barnsley, England, and kept me safe the world over. The only condition is that you have to pass it on to another motorcycle adventurer when the time is right." It did not sit comfortably with Sundaraj's Hindu talisman, with its sharp point digging into my chest, so instead I attached it to the chain securing my belt bag. This essential piece of luggage contained passport, credit card, money, the loss of which would have meant a one-way ticket home, so needed all the protection it could get.

That night I refused the comfort of Dave's bed and we had a delightful time sleeping out on his driveway, tucked up in our sleeping bags chatting, we watched a fabulous moon rise over distant mountains bathing us in a luminescent glow. Before zipping up, the outhouses had to be checked for rattlesnakes and Dave warned me that if I heard running water in the night it was just him having a piss close by, as such basic needs did not merit the inconvenience of strapping on legs and "If anything happens in the night, run like hell, don't wait for me." Fortunately I am still in the dark why this could have been necessary but, had it happened, I would have been prepared to fight to the death rather than leave a new-found friend. There is a bond, a comradeship felt for those we admire. Dave was on a ten-foot pedestal and I was damned if anyone should try to knock him off. My life had been enriched by the meeting and my chances of survival immeasurably increased.

By 4.30am he was pointing me in the direction of LA. "Ride in peace my friend," were his parting words. "It's tough out there – the roads if you can find them are crap – but you will make it." This last remark was like receiving a favourable exam result. I had passed and if Dave said success was on the way I was buggered if anyone was going to stop me.

Rather than face LA traffic, I found a Triumph dealer in the satellite town of Victorville, one of the dullest places of my acquaintance. There may have been more to it, but all I could find were a few dusty broad streets lined with slab-like concrete shops and the obligatory burger joints. The jovial, rotund dealership owner introduced me to an even fatter young mechanic who condescended to let me watch his assault on the Triumph. Dave's words about my ignorance had hit a cord and I needed to get better acquainted with my travel companion. A quarter of a century ago I could have stripped and rebuilt a Trophy in an afternoon. All I knew about the new one was that the noisy bit in the middle was the engine.

The obese mechanic worked at his own speed, piling on the cost. To avoid having to bend down he used a magnetic telescopic probe to pick up dropped nuts and bolts. He made a pathetic attempt at repairing the pannier racks, but the main problems were worn sprockets and seized chain links, which had been brought to my attention by Frisco. These would take two days to arrive from HQ in Georgia, so I found a cheap Mexican Hotel in walking distance from the dealership and prepared to sit it out. Two days to chill out and get some writing done. The only person who was giving the adventure purpose was David Arnold, editor of CSMA's Motoring & Leisure Magazine. With little evidence of any journalistic skill, he had manfully elected to pay for my serialised story. Fortunately, Marian was capable of reading my writing and was one of the few people who could understand my dyslexia.

The bike was fixed for an outrageous sum and I faced south once more towards Mexico. The only mechanical item beyond his expertise was the horn, after it packed up in all the rain. The mechanic said I could wait another two days for a new one or buy a whistle. Nothing short of death was going to keep me there another hour, so I waved the blubber goodbye and headed back towards Phoenix, then Tucson in Arizona. A deserted camp site was home for a night, ready for an early start through Mexican customs only a few miles away.

Nearly a month had passed since leaving our green and pleasant land. My decision to start in the USA had proved to be a good one despite the excessive cost of bureaucracy, accommodation and bike repair. The last of these was my biggest concern. Both tyres were approaching their sell-by date, but I could not afford to buy new ones until at least the canvas was visible. Everything had to be pushed to the limit. The chain had also shown itself to be the weak link as constant lubrication in arid conditions was essential, however, the adhesive qualities of chain lube attracts abrasive material forming a perfect grinding paste. A no-win situation. Being compelled to fork out huge sums was one thing but not being able to obtain parts at all was a different matter. From now on meticulous daily maintenance would be essential.

My head was spinning with potential problems, most of which I had no idea how to resolve. Mexico was in my grasp, but I was a little unsure which country would be the next. Maybe I should just have thrown my hands in the air and settled for a tour of USA where things were familiar. In a few hours I would be in a country where I did not even have the ability to ask for directions, so would be travelling blind. Despite being gripped by the fear of my own fallibility, the draw of entering the unknown was quite the most powerful force I have ever experienced. The night passed uneventfully, despite a sign saying 'Do not feed the bears'. There was no advice on what to do if they decided to help themselves.

Only a couple of hours after day break the following morning, my stomach was in a knot approaching the modest Mexico border. This was to be the beginning of the real adventure.

5. No Hablo Espanol

White middle-class Americans had warned me time after time that everything changes on leaving the USA. You are entering the seat of all corruption and everyone, regardless of their status, will try to rob you, officially or otherwise. After the treatment by North American customs I was expecting the worst. Armed with my single word in Spanish (el burro – the donkey), I approached the small customs shed hoping I would never need one. To enter the country, no visa was necessary and they had never seen a Carnet de Passage, but stamped the relevant bits and stuck a badge on the bike windshield that had to be removed on leaving the country. This is what I assumed the polite customs officer was talking about, although you are never sure if your only means of communication is ambiguous arm-waving. The entire transaction took about an hour and only eleven US dollars changed hands. Reflecting back on the cost and inconvenience of USA customs, you tell me who is corrupt?

In those first few yards, accelerating away from the raised barrier, the culture shock was not nearly as dramatic as I had been led to believe. Sure, the buildings, cars and road surface were not to their neighbour's standard and the people obviously not as affluent, but my first taste of Mexico was far from the lawless, poverty stricken state I had been told to expect.

On Dave's advice I sought the toll route to Mexico City. This was very expensive but worth every peso when you see the alternative. Immaculate tarmac constructed with the sweat and blood of the poor for the rich to drive on, but we can observe similar social contradictions in just about every country. Cruising at a hundred miles an hour plus, Mexico was going to be a memory in no time at all, but the one thing I had not realised, without the benefit of a map, was the sheer enormity of the country. Very near as long as the USA is wide and with no particular time schedule to adhere to, I could indulge in visiting towns along the route. Mexico is physically a mountainous country and the black ribbon gave me a feeling of isolation as it forged its way through a barren landscape. Just as I started to curse the Mexicans for not building their road on the coast, it plunged to the sea at Guymas. That first sight of the Pacific since entering Mexico was a startling revelation, stretching out several hundred feet below me.

Any excuse for a beer and bum rest, I stopped at a bar to take in a new country. The local population were far too busy with their own lives to give more than a cursory glance at a lost white stranger. Mobile street traders brought their wares into the bars, selling just about everything you do not want. One guy came in playing a guitar. He had seven others strapped to his back. Audio tapes, plastic CD racks, straw hats, bags of brightly coloured plastic things. When they saw my white face they turned away, which was the opposite of what I had expected and experienced in other countries where tourists are considered an easy target. The only people to take any notice were the military at road blocks every few miles. They always pulled me over for a look at the bike as their daily routine was probably pretty dull. Learning fast how best to handle situations, I would shake a few hands and take a photo of some cop astride the Triumph. All good-humoured stuff, but time-consuming.

By the second day south of the USA, the rain had caught up with me, so after a very uncomfortable night trying to keep my pack and myself dry I opted for a cheap hotel outside Mazatlan, a prosperous-looking town on the coast. Everyday events like a comfortable shit and a shower had become privileged moments to savour. The toll road to Mazatlan was the most expensive so far at around £6.00 for the last 80 miles. There had been no fuel at the last two toll booths which caused minor panic. My best reckoning was about 90 miles before a petrol station and I had about 60 miles in the tank. All I could do was hunch up behind the screen for less drag and stick rigidly to 50mph. unable to take advantage of the good road.

Mexico was emerging as a country of contradictions. On one hand it appeared to be passionately clinging to an individual identity, yet it seemed to worship the American materialistic dream. Certainly Americans are not liked and I was at pains to tell everyone, especially the military, "I am not an American Gringo." The social divide is enormous. Every country has its rich and poor with the majority of the population somewhere in-between. Mexico did not appear to have an in-between. Disappointingly, the towns were devoid of any evidence of a Hispanic heritage. Occasionally a new building paid lip service with a Spanish archway or eyebrow window, but in the main architecture was uninspired concrete blocks erected with economy in mind rather than aesthetics. It was hard to fathom whether the destruction of their roots was deliberate or just part of evolution. When old bricks began to crumble and structures became uninhabitable, even for the poor, rebuilding was probably considered easier than restoration.

Capital cities are generally expensive and difficult to find your way round, so I stopped in Toluca for the night, a few miles north of Mexico City, after a gruelling twelve hours continuous riding. Electronic translator in hand, I went to a bar to inquire about a cheap hotel. A young man with a bad limp delivered a cold foaming brew to my table. There were hundreds of different Mexican beers to chose from and they were all good. My excuse for trying so many was severe dehydration. This is a constant problem on a motorcycle even wearing a full-face helmet, as perspiration evaporates immediately. All alcoholic drinks are diuretic and local beers can be quite strong, but this is only a matter for concern when there is a limited supply. That's my story, and I'm sticking to it. The limping youth looked horrified when shown the little LCD screen of my electronic translator reading 'barato hotel por favor,' and did a runner (or at least a hobble), across the road shouting "Padre." An old man with identical limp (maybe there was something in the water, so stick to beer) accompanied him back and started gibbering to me. Slowly my ear became accustomed to his accent and I realised every other word was being spoken in English. This guy claimed to have been an English teacher for 33 years. No wonder no one in Mexico speaks the language.

Staying in Toluca proved to be an excellent idea as an unloaded Triumph was much easier to handle in the manic Mexico City traffic and I had to find a Triumph dealer as the next one was about 8,000 miles and two continents away. At around 12,000 feet it is the second highest capital in the world, so predictably cool, especially during the rainy season. An island surrounded by an unbroken chain of mountains rather than sea prevents lateral growth and every square inch of usable ground is accounted for. Street traders take advantage at inefficient traffic lights selling everything from rubber car mats to condoms. You could do a whole week's shopping without ever leaving your car. The most popular vehicles by far are home-produced VW Beetles. Taxi drivers remove the front passenger seat to make access to the back seat easier and drive around with a flashing blue light on the top. I made a tactical error stopping too soon at a red light. The woman following in a Beetle thought this unnecessary and knocked me off. She made a 'whoops' sort of expression, before smiling sweetly and driving off. An army of ragged street traders came to my rescue, righting the bike and collecting up broken bits of Triumph (pronounced Tree-uumph). Hours seemed to elapse before I pulled up outside massive steel gates. A hand-painted Kawasaki logo was the only clue that I had arrived. The boss' secretary, Lulu, swung open the gate to reveal a tatty yard crammed with bikes in various stages of repair. Quite different from the gloss and chrome of California. Only two Triumphs were visible, both Tigers, and one of them belonged to the owner.

Guillermo Cespedes O. (Willy to his friends) arrived on a BMW Boxer and came over to shake my hand as a dog the size of a barn tried to have sex with me. This was the closest I had come to an amorous encounter since leaving home, so I took it as a compliment. Willy, a good-looking dapper man in leathers, had studied chemical engineering in Chelsea, so spoke immaculate English, which was a tremendous relief. Immediately he had two mechanics set about the Trophy, topping up fluids, changing plugs - and attending to the horn. This had defeated two American Triumph-trained mechanics who had said it was beyond repair. In minutes a smiley young lad who had never seen a Trophy before had the yard ringing to the shrill sound of a mandatory audible warning device. In the USA they replace things, in Mexico they fix them. I like that and Willy was determined not to let me back into the mayhem of Mexico City traffic without a horn.

He and Lulu spent an hour on the phones trying to locate a new back tyre. One was found eventually, but it was on the back of someone's Suzuki. With rampant inflation and grotesque import duty, the nearly new tyre cost a fantastic £200, but I only paid the same price for it as Willy did and a mechanic was dispatched to collect it while we went and had lunch. He paid, and then we strolled round Coyoacan (Coyote) the only piece of old Mexico I had seen in the entire country. Imposing, well-preserved Spanish churches and municipal buildings set in meticulously maintained gardens. It was a joy to see and the Mexico I had anticipated, but the whole point of me being there was to find out what it was really like.

The bike was ready and waiting when we returned to the workshop. He showed me the receipt for the tyre to prove he made no profit from the deal and I asked for the bill for labour, plugs and fluids. He would not accept one peso – such generosity from a stranger was getting embarrassing – and this was one of the cheating, thieving, corrupt Spiks the Yanks had warned me about! I asked for directions back to Toluca. "You will never make it my friend, follow me." He jumped on his Tiger and led me through the city rush hour in an aggressive style of riding unheard of outside that overcrowded place. Willy forced cars apart to let me through and I got a first hand lesson in survival tactics from a native. We finally shook hands at a busy intersection with cars and buses honking in undiluted carbon monoxide. It is unlikely I will ever see that wonderful person again, but he was promoted to the top of my postcard list.

Riding back to my hotel, there was a disturbing movement going on deep in my bowels. Once in the sanctuary of my room I had only seconds to make it to the toilet where I remained in a seated position for quite some time. The TV was visible from my vantage point and I watched most of 'The Poseidon Adventure', dubbed into Spanish, without moving. Lunch had been an unusual treat as most days food only made it to the top of my agenda in the evenings and with a definitely dodgy tummy (maybe lunch was not such a treat after all) fluid was all the body needed. Toluca was a lovely little town and, as the last day off I had had was in California, I booked my room for a second night to explore and try to sort the digestive disorder. My recipe for recovery was to stop eating altogether and indulge in a plethora of beers accompanied by devastating Tequila served as only the Mexicans know how. Suck a lime, lick the salt and down in one – delicious. It did nothing for the toilet troubles, but made me feel a damn sight better.

It was a month to the day since I had departed from the UK and the Triumph had clocked another 9,000 miles. 31 days is no time at all to be away from home. Plenty of people go AWOL for that time, but in my case it was just the beginning, or so I hoped. Curiously enough, the time scale was meaningless as I felt as though I had been on the road half my life. So much had happened, so much seen, but so much more to come. I was wondering if it was possible for a brain to become saturated with the new, making it less exciting. The opposite was certainly the case at that time, as each new discovery, even bad ones, were part of the evolving education as the world revealed itself in front of me. The buzz of everything from sleeping rough to finding a meal each day was the source of insatiable energy and strength. Every day was like being a new-born child full of new sights and sounds in unfamiliar surroundings.

Without powers of communication one lives dangerously on assumption, so it was time to apply myself and learn at least a survival ration of Spanish. Anyone who has the advantage of English as their mother tongue carries with them an arrogance that insists if you speak to foreigners slowly and loudly, as if to a disadvantaged child, they *will* understand. Being dyslexic, new languages are a real challenge, but with the help of my electronic translator, I spent time attempting to understand television. I had learned already to say 'I do not speak Spanish.' What a ridiculous waste of brain power as it was obvious to everyone and time to move on to more useful expressions like 'May I have a beer please.' and 'The vicar has just been struck by lightning'. Despite loneliness due to my lack of linguistic skills, things could have been a hell of a lot worse.

South of Mexico City everything changed as the GNP dropped with latitude. Willy had insisted on the new back tyre as he knew the roads in Central America were evil and, according to him, so were the people. He had seen a lot of the world, but had never been south of Mexico City. Despite this he reckoned he knew the score and most certainly knew more than me. According to him, Guatemala was where the world changed.

We all have irrational prejudices and Willy's was against the people of Central America. Maybe as with the USA, where it is obligatory to hate or despise someone, it is easy to point a finger at a poorer community. The obscenity reaches new bounds when you consider the lack of regard for the indigenous people of America who had their land, buffalo, life, taken from them by the gun.

6. One Big Pothole Can Ruin Your Entire Day

Willy was certainly right about the roads south. Toll roads got cheaper as the surface deteriorated. Rock falls became an hourly occurrence, as the road carved its way through sand-coloured mountains. I could ride round most of them, but the busses and trucks did not stand a chance. From my point of view, the danger started after the clear up as the pock-marked surface soon turned into a rash of potholes capable of unseating the most careful rider, but this, however, was not the worst danger to be experienced on Mexican roads. The biggest hazard, especially riding at night with a pathetic Triumph headlight, was the animals and most of the ones I saw were dead, but they had only got that way from being struck by moving vehicles. Dead horses, donkeys, mules. Deer (big ones), dogs (by the hundred), snakes, and very flat lizards littered the highway as a warning that night riding and road-side camping was not a good idea. I only had one close shave when two pigs decided to cross at the same time. Fortunately the thin one ran faster than the fat one so I passed at 60mph between the two of them.

Finding a way out of Mexico City had been a monumental challenge after leaving Willy, when I had made a huge tactical error attempting to go south through the suburbs. Hour after hour had passed with the bike overheating and everyone giving me different instructions. Manic traffic and incredibly slow traffic lights made progress around the city extremely frustrating and just about everyone had their wing mirrors turned in flat against the car which reduced obstacles while weaving between ranks of traffic, meant drivers were unaware of my approach. Presumably they do this to prevent them from being broken, but it would have been much better to remove them completely and keep them safe in a drawer at home.

I had travelled over 120 miles out of my way just to find a route with the compass pointing south. Annoyed that Guatemala was well beyond my grasp that night and with the threat of a damn good soaking, I rested my runny bottom on a private toilet in a cheap and very dusty hotel. With my miserable diet, I could not work out where it was all coming from. After riding for ten hours with a cork up my bum, I decided it was time to start taking the antibiotics I had purchased at home and have a critical look at what

I was eating. My eating mimes had been producing some rather undesirable results until the electronic translator came up with egg and chips. Fabulous, especially with delicious fresh bread and outrageous fresh chilli. This may sound unadventurous, but if you only have one meal a day, it is important to enjoy it and get enough sustenance for another hard day's riding. In one little roadside cafe, the waiter punched something into the translator in Spanish, but it came up 'scour the bath' in English, so I stuck to egg and chips.

All the locals I met in southern Mexico were tremendously friendly, although this appears to be typical of rural areas in most countries. I even had a smiling police officer on a Harley Davidson escort me to his town limits when I got lost. The first sign of real poverty was the sight of ragged children with delightful faces waving and shouting from the roadside, as I picked my way through the maze of cavernous holes. The people looked different with darker skins and flashing bright eyes. In the more prosperous north and the capital, many affluent locals could have been mistaken for Europeans with pale skins and some even had reddish blond hair.

I had resigned myself to spending one more night in Mexico before seeking Guatemala, but I made the mistake of riding through a torrential downpour about an hour after dark. My tactics were to follow other vehicles through the gauntlet of craters in the beam of the Triumph's inadequate headlamp. Why motorcycle designers think bikers need less light to see by than car drivers is a mystery. One lapse in concentration while wiping a rain-streaked visor and the triumph found the mother of all potholes. About three feet long and a foot deep with steep sharp sides, but full of water so it just looked like a discoloured piece of road. The front wheel bounced on the edge nearly throwing me off. The back wheel went the whole hog scraping the undercarriage and squarely catching the sharp tarmac rim. I wrestled the bike to the edge of the road to inspect the damage. Trucks only a few feet away hurtled by emptying the contents of other potholes all over me.

Willy's two hundred pound back tyre was flat and the wheel was buckled making the bike very unstable on the side stand. I did not have the strength to pull it onto the centre stand and it would have gone over if I had tried to unload it. My only option was to hang on to the bike while groping in the tank bag for a can of Tyre Weld. My disposable torch, given by a friend before leaving, decided it was time to be disposed of and died. In my frustration, it was thrown at a truck that got a bit too close and a few of the following vehicles ran it over, activating the 'on' button making it flash its last signs of life like a dying fire-fly.

Attaching the Tyre Weld tube one handed was a tricky business, but after a good deal of cursing the bike started to rise. I let go, foam squirted out of the distorted rim and the bike went over into a ditch full of muddy water. Fortunately a pick-up truck full of 'barbaric' Mexicans saw it and came to my aid groping around in knee deep water. With a great deal of grunting and animated banter, a very soggy but secure bike was returned to the road for an inspection with my other torch.

There were three men of about forty and a youth of about eighteen who kept calling me 'Gringo'. I took exception to this and attempted to put him right in a friendly sort of way. After more gesturing and arm waving, it was established we needed El Mecanico and they all piled into the truck and drove off in the opposite direction. I had tried to get some information via the translator but they were all illiterate and my pronunciation was too appalling for them to understand.

An hour passed, and the rain was still coming down in buckets. The diarrhoea had ironically made me very dehydrated and I craved a drink. Inspecting a pothole between cars revealed only unpalatable muddy water, then I had a brain wave and got out the 'emergency poncho' from New Orleans. This, laid on the bike, soon gathered enough rain water to bring relief.

I had resigned myself to staying there the night when another pick-up arrived with, yes you guessed, El Mecanico. He was a curious-looking character in his early forties with a skin pigmentation disorder leaving white blotches around his eyes, nose and mouth, giving the impression he was wearing a mask. He, by the light of my torch, confirmed, without any shadow of doubt, the problem was indeed a puncture.

There were only three of us this time and it was impossible to lift the bike three feet into the air to get it on the back of his truck. As he had not got a crane about his person, nor had the presence of mind to bring a ramp, I suggested we park it somewhere safe until *manana*. We approached a tumbledown roadside dwelling in total darkness. Ferocious-sounding dogs darted around snapping at heels as an old man emerged with a stout stick in one hand and a two-foot machete in the other. The bike was secured off the road outside the old man's front door, chained to a post and I demonstrated the steering lock and the alarm. He laughed like a train as the shrill wailing made his dogs bark all the more.

El Mecanico took me to a hotel well outside my budget despite me telling him 'muy barato' (very cheap) and demanded US$20. This I thought outrageous, but four men had got very wet, on my behalf and they had had to come some distance from the town. Begrudgingly I paid up and El Mecanico said he would be back at 9.00am which seemed a little late for a Mexican to start work.

By that time it was well after midnight and I had not eaten all day. Everything I owned was soaked or covered in gooey mud and I was concerned about the bike. The tummy troubles had not abated so I studied the soggy antibiotics bottle label for the dosage. To my horror I discovered I had been swallowing the pain killers for my back by mistake so it was not surprising that the cure had not taken effect. The rest of the night was spent rehearsing a little speech in Spanish for El Mecanico that went like this: "I am not a rich Gringo, but from England, a poor country like Mexico. It is my job to ride the bike for publicity and I do not have many dollars, so tell me how much repairs will cost".

By 9.01am, I was getting worried and considered phoning Willy in Mexico City to explain to the police. They had already had four hours of daylight to dispose of the bike. 9.02am and El Mecanico breezed up on a 600cc Honda of a variety I had not seen before. A little battle-scarred but in good running order. This really lifted the spirits as he obviously knew something about bikes. We rode at 70mph through town with no helmets, my knuckles white on the grab rail.

Thankfully, the Triumph was not as badly damaged as I had originally thought. The wheel was badly distorted, but the tyre looked intact. El Mecanico shot off to get his truck, giving me time to absorb my surroundings. The house was a tumbledown single-storey wooden structure set in bit of a rubbish tip. Four beautiful children, all under ten, played amongst rotting machinery. The eldest must have been telepathic as she disappeared into the house returning with a cracked cup of water. I was thirsty and against my better judgment drank most of it.

El Mecanico returned and got out his tool kit of three Allan keys, all the wrong size and a rusty pair of mole grips. He nearly wet himself when he saw my row of shiny spanners. Before we started I gave him the prepared monologue and we negotiated another US$20 for the work. The wheel was removed and we went in the truck to the vulcanisidora (puncture man) where he and his large lump hammer, with a disturbingly loose head (I stood well back), persuaded the wheel it should be round again.

Amazingly, it all worked rather well. After much banging, sweating and high pitched conversation, the wheel was chucked into an oil drum full of water to prove it. Before leaving I paid up and gave El Mecanico a fake Swiss Army knife for not pinching my tools. These were an inspired purchase at about two quid each and he was beside himself with excitement, opening each feature to study it. The scissors always attract most attention and what they lacked in quality, they more than made up for in novelty value.

At Tapachula, I visited five banks attempting to replenish my cash supply, as a sign said Guatemala was 345km and I needed some local currency. One bank got a bit shirty when I waved traveller's cheques in their faces, but after reading the notice I realised I was in the Department of Social Services. To my surprise, the Guatemala border loomed up in a mile or so as the sign had been for Guatemala City and I was getting very confused by countries that use the same name for their principal town. By obtaining money in Mexico, I had lost out twice on exchange rates, but I had been told money changers proliferated at the crossing, and obtaining quetzales with Mexican pesos would be an easy transaction. Black market money changers always give a much better rate than the banks and there are enough of them for you to play the field. Surprisingly, they all quoted an identical amount and were not too pushy trying to get business.

Feeling rather pleased with the transactions, I was ready to run the gauntlet of officialdom that was to be a constant irritant all through Central America. First the bug man sprayed the bike for 5Q, as if this was really going to stop Mexican bugs crossing into Guatemala, then another five for the fungus man and so on – all recorded and receipted. Kids from five to fifteen were running about wanting to hold my helmet or mind the bike. They stood too close so tended to get trodden on and told to piss off. Predictably this made no difference, so I zipped up all my pockets, demonstrated the bike alarm again to deter the kids from stealing all my gear as I assaulted customs and immigration.

Department after department came and went in no logical sequence and the crowd of kids grew. A man typed out all my details in triplicate on an ancient Remington typewriter. This took forever and the bike alarm went off twice, so I had to run back only to find there was no one within a hundred yards of it. Passport and Carnet stamped, the last of a dozen officials demanded 100Q (about £8.00). I refused, saying all documents were okay, so where is the problem? He got so agitated with my inability to speak Spanish, the bill was halved, by which time I was feeling like the Pied Piper. Why were all those irritating children allowed to roam around customs offices, sitting on desks and fingering paperwork? It had started to rain again with a vengeance, smudging bits of paper as I darted from one office to another. By the end of it water was running out of my sleeves, but with a final 'fuck off' to the kids, the Triumph team were off to discover a very wet new continent. The rain was becoming a real source of annoyance, but I had only myself to blame as I had made two fundamental mistakes.

Firstly, I was not properly equipped with decent wet-weather gear as my perception of Central America had been one of warm, moderately dry countries. Secondly, bad planning had dumped me in the middle of their monsoon season and I had missed the fact that most of it, despite excessive logging, was still a rain forest and there was plenty more to ride through before the deserts of South America.

7. The Thin Bit

The culture shock entering Guatemala was far greater than the USA/Mexico crossing. There had been a civil war raging on and off for thirty years, but I was dangerously ignorant of the conflict. Poverty was far more apparent and the bad roads of southern Mexico were bliss compared to the next couple of thousand miles. Despite the neck of the Americas being very thin, it is still part of the unbroken corridor of mountains that stretch from Alaska to Chile. The scenery changed dramatically with lush tropical rain forest taking over from the dusty barren landscape of southern Mexico as a big blue motorbike joined the procession of overloaded trucks grinding up an alarming gradient. A few hours behind trucks and buses belching dense smoke forced me to adopt a new riding style. In slow traffic the Triumph started overheating, so I had to push harder, taking more chances overtaking. This is where the Triumph proved to be undisputed master. Spot a gap, accelerate like hell, in just about any gear and another convoy of cattle trucks would be a memory.

Frequently, bits of the road that clung to the mountainside had been partly washed away by water that ran in torrents down near-vertical cliffs. This often occurred on the apex of a 180 degree corner so you never had any idea what may be on your side of the road once round the bend. The absence of crash barriers meant there was absolutely nowhere to go except back and without a reverse gear, I was constantly forcing on-coming traffic to give way, and there were some other nasty surprises in store on the roads.

Central American potholes tended to be loners hiding in the least expected places and the only indicator of their depth below the water-line was the amount of gravel thrown out of them by churning truck wheels. At least in Mexico, they had had the courtesy to stay in family groups slowly joining up to hold hands. The second nasty surprise was totes, or speed bumps, generally on the edge of villages, with no indication of their existence as any paint originally applied had long been worn off. Steep-sided, often eight or so inches high, and invisible. Hit one of those at 50mph and you would be launched into the trees, so getting the speed right to tackle them was crucial. Too fast and I would risk serious damage to the bike, too slow and with only a few inches' ground clearance, I would be perched on the top unable to get any traction with the back wheel spinning off the ground. Both cases were responsible for me falling off at some time. Ten-wheeler trucks could take all afternoon to get over some of these and when you consider about 25mph was about all anyone could manage on such a dire road surface, where was the benefit?

Guatemala City looked pretty uninspiring as capital cities go with the usual undisciplined traffic. I stopped for a couple of hours to find a bank, and fell unexpectedly into a tourist office where I foolishly thought a map could be acquired. A very concerned lady told me in no uncertain terms to remove the gold chain from my neck and my two signet rings as they were an open invitation to attack – and "No we do not have maps – Guatemala does not have maps." How the hell can you teach children geography without maps? I was not asking for anything flash with roads marked, just something with an approximate geographic layout of the countries!

Leaving the city I witnessed a grotesque obscenity. There was a shiny bright Macdonald's burger joint with an inflated clown leering down on to the litter-strewn pavement. Darkness had fallen on half a dozen barefoot kids asleep on the walkway framed by the light of the restaurant window. Those kids were more likely to fly to the moon than taste a Big Mac, but the sign represented the best begging patch in the city. The principle of that American dream was to provide cheap nourishment, especially for kids, but in Guatemala it was only attainable by the wealthy.

Tropical storms and perpetual mountain climbing were loosing their appeal, so I followed the compass to El Salvador in the hope things would change. Customs was hell on Earth with civilian couriers fighting for business to lead you through the mayhem and the area was populated by hordes of people with seemingly very little to do except get in the way. I offered a threatening looking money changer a Swiss Army knife to watch my bike and commissioned another energetic courier to guide me through a maze of nondescript departments. He offered to take my passport and Carnet for processing, but I was not going to release them to *anyone*, so I followed in his footsteps through the crushing crowds. Endless tap, tap, tap on defunct typewriters followed in my wake, as I shelled out wads of newly acquired currency and the swarm of steaming people sheltering from the rain were *always* moving in the opposite direction. At the end I felt punch drunk trying to work out how much it had all cost, mentally converting unfamiliar bank notes. In reality it was only about sixteen pounds and two Swiss Army knives, but I felt several years older for the experience. Eager to give El Salvador the benefit of the doubt, I naively rode off in search of better things. My introduction had not been the best and, despite the roads being by far the worst to date, I was eager to find its redeeming features.

Markets on the edge of towns were a common occurrence; however, rather than cleaning the site for next week's market, it just moved to a different patch leaving all the rotting produce for the scavenging dogs that snapped at my heels in heavy traffic. I was glad for sturdy bike boots and leather trousers for protection as I kicked out at mangy mongrels and the bike slid around on stinking vegetables. On one heap of garbage a body was clearly visible lying face down in the filth. It was impossible to tell how long it had been there, but as the dogs were still tearing at the clothing in search of protein, I guessed not long. Passers-by hardly gave the corpse a second glance, but no doubt someone in the country was concerned for a missing father or husband.

By Santa Ana, I had had enough and found a hovel of a hotel just before dark. It was vile and a real-rip off at about five pounds. I was shown a room with a bed, strip light and concrete floor. The man pointed at another door saying it was a good place to store my luggage. I peeped in to see the floor of the cupboard was a foot or so lower than the rest of the room, making a perfect cockroach trap. There were hundreds of them scrambling over dead carcasses trying to escape. The clammy-looking owner told me to only use the *clean* toilet. The broken bowl was near the brim with shit and had obviously not seen water for some years. I dreaded to think what the dirty toilet looked like. The only water for washing in the entire place was a concrete communal tub fed by a hose-pipe. It smelt like rancid butter so I went out onto the dark streets in search of some beer to clean my teeth and fresh bread to eat. Locals followed me along the street calling out and laughing. While purchasing my immediate survival kit from a street stall, the hotel owner pushed his way through a group of youths showing too much interest. He was very agitated and sweating profusely as he marched me back to his heavily-barred premises.

I asked for an ashtray before retiring. "Use the floor," was the answer, but an upturned lid from a chain lube tin did the job. I fell on the bed to write. It felt like a piece of iron. Further investigation under thread-bare blanket revealed it *was* a piece of iron. The words in my notebook scribbled that night said it all. 'Hotel Hospedaje, Santa Ana. 26th July. (only 288 miles today). So far El Salvador appears to be a country with no redeeming features. *Get me out of here - it's disgusting!'*

At first light I was packed and in determined mood to make Honduras by nightfall. An hour later and I was still searching for anything that resembled a road south. Most locals could not be bothered to offer directions and displayed a definite attitude problem. In most countries youths gather round the Triumph asking 'How fast does it go – how many pistons - gears?' All they wanted to know in El Salvador was 'How much?' Naturally they did not receive an honest answer and the dark sinister looks were quite unnerving. Eventually a young man offered to lead me to the Pan Americano Highway. Posh name for a heap of rubble all the way to the capital. I followed in the dust of the guy's pick-up for about half an hour along unmade roads before suspecting he had taken me for a sucker. By the time he pointed the way I was ready to fight for my bike, but he was the only local to show any kindness to a lost old biker and was rewarded with half a packet of Marlboro cigarettes.

My frame of mind may have influenced my opinion of San Salvador, but it seemed to be a festering capital city that hit an all time low in the desirability stakes, with crumbling buildings, garbage strewn everywhere and nothing working.

A policeman approached as I sat dutifully at a red traffic signal. His monologue roughly translated as "Do not stop at red lights as you are more likely to die at the hand of an opportunist passer-by than you are from murderous trucks and buses that have absolutely no regard at all for other road users."

The only saving grace of that hell-hole of a country is its size and by mid afternoon I was preparing for the fight through hundreds of uniformed personnel just to get out. A vast amount of the population of El Salvador are employed by some official body or other and they all want a slice of the cake. Exiting was far more difficult and expensive than gaining entry. By that time

I had learned to keep all documents with rubber stamps to show at the numerous check points in the country. Those officials had not a clue what they are looking at and I got through one department by showing a form issued by the Mexican bug man.

Honduras was getting so close I could smell it, but the surly uniform standing in front of me, stoutly refused a stupid rubber stamp without receiving his wad. He did not wish to see any documents, just cash. When I refused, he physically sat me down between two smelly soldiers and told me to wait. Time passes slowly in times of stress but it must have been twenty minutes before the officer returned to see if I was ready to cough up and when I refused, he made it abundantly clear I was under arrest.

The one golden rule I had managed to grasp, is never loose your rag when faced by a man in uniform. He probably has no power, but risking an El Salvadorian jail was definitely not on the agenda. I had seen their hotel, so just imagine what prison must be like! Keep cool and start trimming fingernails with Swiss Army knife sissors. All eyes were agog as in turn each blade and widget was revealed in a bogus search for the nail-file. Mr. Smartypants was visibly drooling, but only took possession of that piece of Chinese engineering once his rubber stamp had seen the light of day.

The very last was the worst as a fat, young official in a filthy Mickey Mouse T-shirt exposed a large revolver protruding from his waist band and demanded US5$ dollars. I told him there were none left, so he left the room slamming the door. I picked up the tatty strip of paper, mounted the bike and rode the few yards to a piece of string across the road preventing access to Honduras. The smudged ink marks were counted by one, then another, heavily armed guard. All this time I was glancing in the bike's wing mirrors looking for fatty with the gun. My instructions were to return to his office and wait, but they dropped the rope barrier to let me turn round. Honduras was probably only a mile or two down the road across the unclaimed no-man's-land. There was no sign of any military vehicles and I was riding the fastest thing in Central America. The guns looked as if they had not been fired since the civil war started and were probably not loaded. I dropped the clutch and stormed away as fast as the shitty road would let me, swerving round potholes and flying over invisible totes. Being a moderately law-abiding citizen in any country, I am not used to breaking rules especially when in full view of armed law enforcement officers. These things do not come easily and calculating the risk should not have been done on an impulse, yet in effect, I had just slapped authority in the face to save five dollars. I would have been surprised, but terrified nonetheless to have heard gun fire behind me. Who knows what the military orders are in the case of a foreigner attempting to escape the country? And even if there were not any orders, it would only take one over enthusiastic guard to bring down a retreating motorcyclist at close range. Fortunately for me, they were not expecting a white stranger to make a break for freedom and by the time a dilapidated army truck bristling with guns came into sight, I was being processed by Honduras customs. It still took time to get through and there was a lot of shouting going on at the crossing point, but fortunately, El Salvadorian military were not welcome south of their border.

You would be forgiven for thinking adjacent countries would share similar nationalistic attitudes, or at least some common ground, but each one is unique in its own way. We have all been cocky at some time thinking we know the score, but that is a dangerous assumption and, on that particular day, a lesson I was finding hard to stomach.

What a transformation Honduras was. Reasonable road, neat buildings squatting behind succulent palms, friendly smiling people. Nicaragua was only three hours away but this place needed checking out, so I booked into a smart little hotel for a much-needed shower and the chance to wash some grimy clothes. One can only speculate about the dramatic differences between two apparently similar countries. I kicked myself for being so ignorant and still unable to ask questions. That evening, relaxing in a street bar, my beer was poured into a glass and it immediately turned to a solid block of ice. A good-looking man in his early 30's laughed as he saw the look of disbelief on my face. He explained in his few words of English that the beer is kept very cold and reacts with a warm glass. None the wiser, I attempted to keep the conversation going. The translator was red hot as we had a slow conversation much to the amusement of his friends. He was a Nicaraguan doctor working in Honduras and engaged to a 17 year-old local girl and the debate continued, as best we could, about the merits of younger women as Marian is 16 years younger than me. That was my first really enjoyable evening since north of Mexico City. In the morning I would be off in search of Nicaragua, but with the evening sun warming air heavy with the scent of honeysuckle I felt content; who needs El Salvador, Honduras was fab.

8. Thank You God - Whoever You Are

A continent of five and a half countries forms the neck between two huge land masses – and there is no way of avoiding it. The border towns between each country are generally pretty unsavoury as very few people are there through choice. The only residents are those connected to customs, or seeing to the needs of a constant flow of travellers – apart, that is, from the obligatory multitude of kids. Once a military road barrier has closed behind you, there follows a bizarre couple of miles of no-man's-land inhabited often by a transient population of semi-nomads, scratching a living from passing traffic. They are displaced people with no country to call home, building shacks from whatever falls off lorries. These rather depressing stretches fascinate me and I was always tempted to establish how they worked. Who do they pay taxes to? Where does their food come from? Who is responsible for maintaining the road in-between? The answer to the last one is obvious. No one. Those stretches frequently degenerate into churned-up rubble kept passable by the perpetual procession of cattle trucks.

Departing Honduras was the accustomed struggle, but I coped without paying a tout and no one came near the bike after they heard the alarm. Fortunately a black market dealer changed a travellers cheque for Nicaraguan cordobas at an excellent rate and I was stunned to see very few hangers-on and snotty-nosed children as I approached the biggest Central American country. Only one porky youth offered help through customs. His indifference was very appealing and he just looked confused when asked how much, so his offer of help was accepted when he said 'no charge'. He obviously carried some weight (literally as well as metaphorically) as we breezed through without a hitch. He did not ask for any money so was rewarded with a Swiss Army knife that made his eyes pop out. He was genuinely shocked to receive anything and started jumping on the spot with uninhibited glee.

Outside the towns that litter the Pan Americano, Nicaragua has a sparse rural interior with much of the rain forest being replaced by agriculture. The population may be small for its size, but it still has to be fed and crops represent a valuable export. Deforestation is as responsible for changes in climate and weather patterns just like global warming, but as an ignorant observer,

Nicaragua appeared to be doing it with some sympathy for the land. Mature hardwoods such as the noble oak and teak were left fringing fields and possibly benefited from the lack of competition. The most notable feature of most Central American roads were cattle trucks heaving under the weight of prime beef. The animals did not actually have the McDonald's logo stamped on them, but I was pretty sure most were destined to supply the burger revolution. Apparently, provided the space is available, crops go farther than livestock in nutritional value per acre, so the Nicaraguans take advantage of fertile soil exporting coffee, sugar, bananas and cotton, surplus to the needs of nationals.

For some reason the urgency of travel was diminishing and an enjoyable experience becoming more important than just 'getting there'. More out of curiosity than respect, I stopped on the roadside to let a funeral procession pass. All the other traffic pushed its way through, but I could not see the need, so pulled over and removed my helmet. Six elderly pall-bearers solemnly carried the coffin as trucks forced their way past. Those guys looked really old and not far from *their* last ride on this earth. One of the leading ones lifted a hand from the modest casket and touched his forehead in salute at my gesture. A woman dressed in threadbare black, leading the dignified group of about a score of mourners, stopped momentarily, turned to me across the narrow road and made the sign of the cross before continuing her solemn task. There were a few nods from others in the procession and I was glad to have witnessed the sombre event. Being a spectator into the lives of others is, to me, a big part of the travel experience and I had a warm comfortable feeling about receiving a blessing from a stranger.

Less than a mile farther on, I needed all the spiritual help on hand while overtaking a massive tanker with a driver oblivious to a motorcycle along side. The road was raised above a muddy bog on one side and I remember speculating how many vehicles bigger than mine had been swallowed up in that black goo. On the other side, some ten feet below the botched-up tarmac, was a fast-flowing river swollen by seasonal monsoons. The truck was doing around 30mph and I accelerated up to about 50 to get clear of the monster on a road hardly wide enough for four-wheeled vehicles to overtake, so the assumption must have been that the only traffic to worry about is coming from the opposite direction. Level with the cab, the driver, without the benefit of mirrors, decided to avoid a pothole by steering left into my path. Huge protruding wheel-nuts from a front wheel clipped the Trophy's wing mirror, knocking it askew – then one caught the handlebars causing me to involuntarily yank open the throttle and lurch closer to the offending vehicle. The burst of power thrust me forward into its path, scraping his bumper as the bike swerved violently trying to avoid being committed to the watery depths on either side. My body prepared itself for contact with the road surface. In T-shirt and jeans this was going to hurt – if I lived through it. Certainly the bike was a goner as it would be lost forever if it left the narrow road. It is quite amazing how much information the brain can absorb in a microsecond on the brink of disaster. To this day I do not understand how bike and rider survived uninjured. The Triumph and I were still not a homogenous unit, but a few thousand miles earlier that event would most certainly have terminated my travels and probably my life. The incident pushed the bounds of terror far beyond falling asleep riding through Dallas. Completely devoid of any religious belief myself, I will never know if those who do believe can influence the lives of others, but I felt uplifted rather than smug for showing some respect and sharing a little grief at a stranger's funeral.

Nicaragua rises gently towards the south through a landscape curiously reminiscent of England. Tidy tree-lined roads snake through well-tended fields of familiar crops. Litter-free countryside may have been due to sparse population rather than respect for the environment, but was never the less a refreshing sight. I warmed to a country that although recovering from the ravages of civil war, ploughed its energy and grievances back into the soil. The other gratifying surprise was the change in music. From New York to Tegucigalpa (capital of Honduras), bars and market stalls had followed the American dream with sounds of Michael Jackson and even Elvis Presley. Nicaragua pulsed to the rhythm of energetic salsa erotica. Blatant in its sexuality, ostentatious in its liberty, all very sensuous stuff.

The burning question at the back of my mind was why are so many tiny nations in close proximity to each other so radically different in temperament? No doubt a psychologist could offer a sensible explanation, but to me, without intelligence, the differences were dramatic, unexpected and inexplicable.

Progress through Nicaragua, as I had come to expect, was punctuated by military road blocks protecting the nation and creating employment. In my limited experience, the attitude of defence forces is a good barometer of national opinion. Nicaraguan troops admired the Triumph for its novelty value and engineering excellence, rather than its price tag. At every opportunity, they would straddle the beast with flashing smiles, even getting me to hold their weapons while they took their turn. One young officer was so in awe I took him for a little spin for a mile or two. He was still laughing and slapping hands with junior colleagues as I wheelied away for a bit of extra effect. Quite possibly it is a situation of everything being fine until you are on the wrong side of them, but I had no complaints and a slowly developing Spanish vocabulary helped explain the basics of my journey. Most people had heard of England, although very few appreciated how small it is or where it is. "Yes, England is cold and always wet like Nicaragua in the rainy season." This was a total fabrication of course as few places can compete with the ferocity of Central American storms.

Of all the countries visited so far, Nicaragua stood out as being the one worthy of deeper exploration without the pressure of travel against the clock. I would have liked to stay a while to witness a flourishing nation under an emerging political regime. Regrettably, at the time, I was working and the brain could not grasp the concept of leisure time. The work ethic is instilled in the depths of our unconscious very young, so 'days off' had to be earned. The travel experience was proving to be the toughest challenge of my life, but seemed so natural. This was the task I had been born to perform. Nothing was going to prevent its success as the Triumph and I were beginning to gel as a formidable team.

Clouds of tiny yellow butterflies escorted me to Costa Rica leaving a smudge of golden dust on my visor and, for the first time since leaving the United States, I saw a sign written in English. 'Welcome to Costa Rica'. Regrettably the customs officials could not keep the conversation going, but were very courteous in their immaculate white uniforms with high priced travel permits to match. All this administration and accommodation due to the weather, were severely stretching resources and I really had no idea how thin to spread the jam. Back in the UK, it had been impossible to estimate the expense of travel in countries that were still an enigma to me, so I had no idea if my limited cash supply going to last? If you ever contemplate a similar trip, work out how much you *think* you will need, add ten per cent for emergencies – then double it!

Costa Rica, the Monaco of Central America, had excellent main roads and for the first time since since Mexico, I found myself able to squeeze the throttle open on an exhilarating ride through dense rain-forest. Unfortunately this did not escape the attention of the police. The traffic cops in crisp khaki were not armed, so less intimidating than most, but it did not stop one particular young officer asking for the equivalent of £70. I gave him the "poor Englishman" speech prepared for El Mecanico and negotiated a "tourist rate" of about £20 and did not ask for a receipt. After that, I saw speed traps every few miles looking for tourists. The practice must help swell the exchequer and subsidise police beach homes so I took it easy all the way to the capital.

San Jose, looked remarkably affluent with shiny new Japanese cars replacing the aggressive noisy traffic I had become accustomed to. My wrong assumption was that it was on the coast, but actually it is on a plateau in what looked like a vast volcano crater. A smart Yamaha pulled up next to me at the lights and offered to lead me to the coast road. The rider spoke a little English and told me to visit an American friend of his who owned an hotel on Jaco Beach. It would be much too expensive for me, but the owner would advise about cheaper accommodation. After two and a half hours' ride through dense fog on unpredictable roads finding the hotel was easy and I was met by the father of the owner with a pasty, sweaty complexion and I did not notice his gammy right hand until my outstretched gesture of friendship was greeted with his left. Matthew, the hotel owner, was out surfing so I chatted to his racist parents who treated the local "Spiks" like farm animals. They had moved to Costa Rica about twenty years previously from Florida to "escape the niggers." When number one son returned, he practically ignored me as he got the story of my meeting with his friend Pancho on the road from his parents. "Try farther down, you can't afford to stay here," was the sum total of his powers of conversation. The hotel had about thirty rooms in a quadrant round a small swimming pool. Only one was occupied as it was winter (I called it wet) and you would have thought a few dollars through the door would have been better than none, but there was no compromise. A vast part of Costa Rica's economy depends on white North American surfers who can not afford Hawaii.

For a little over £3, I secured a huge concrete chalet owned by a local who was prepared to bargain an out-of-season price. In the private bathroom (that even had toilet paper) all my clothes were thrown into the shower to be trampled under foot while I removed the layer of grime from my skin. The big airy room would have been ideal for drying everything out, but the humidity was not. I went out for a roam leaving the ceiling fan on full blast hoping to encourage a little evaporation. The rather unappealing black volcanic sand turned to sludge under my feet as I strolled along the beach, so, took refuge in a bedraggled little bar.

By chance, the sole party of guests from Matthew's hotel sat at my table. All in their late twenties, Greg was a truck driver, his wife a bank clerk and her idiot, self-obsessed brother training to be a doctor, apparently at a leading American university. The closest he got to constructing a sentence all evening was 'yeah, guess so', and that took about twenty minutes. He also managed 'gimme raspberry shake', and nearly burst into tears when they only had strawberry. It is truly amazing what money can buy. This guy had not got two brain cells to rub together but was to be launched into the medical profession. I was glad to depart in search of a new country.

The tortuous ride over the mountains to Panama was not a particularly pleasant experience. At over 9,000 feet in relentless rain, it was miserably cold, despite being halfway between the Tropic of Cancer and the equator. I stopped to put on another two damp T-shirts and realised I was wearing my entire wardrobe of five T-shirts and one sweat shirt under leathers. At the Panama border, one of the panniers was so badly distorted that I had a hell of a fight to break the air-tight seal. Up in the mountains it had filled with thin cold air, but the warmer lowland atmosphere had created a vacuum. It wheezed like an old man before popping back into shape and to make matters worse, a tube of Nivea cream had imploded, squirting its contents over my documents and cameras. This may not sound like much of a disaster, but it is amazing how little things can turn an average mood into depression.

The ride to Panama City was long, dull and took the best part of two days, more or less in a straight line. There were very few towns and the road only divided once. Predictably I took the wrong fork, but only rode thirty miles before realising my mistake. When there is so much of the world to see, it is frustrating when you have to ride the same road twice.

The sight of the Panama Bridge rising out of the road is rather spectacular, so I crossed it three times for the benefit of the video camera strapped to my arm. Once over the bridge, you are in a new continent. Central America had not been particularly enjoyable, partly because of my bad timing, but it is the only corridor between the Americas, the second of which still awaited me. I knew practically nothing about South America, but Dave Barr had told me of a bike club at an American Air Force base where he had stayed once. I got no change from them, so headed off to the poor area to find an hotel, money and passage to Colombia. As ever the bank was a source of humiliation. I changed a traveller's cheque insisting on 'Dollar Americano' as a load of local currency was not going to be much use in Colombia. The point I had not grasped was that Panamanian currency *is* the US dollar, making my impassioned speech surplus to requirements.

After securing a room, my first evening on the South American continent was spent exploring an interesting city of contradictions. Despite the large population of US military personnel with their 'fuck you' attitude, they were conspicuous by their absence in the town proper. No doubt they considered it too dangerous to walk the streets and could well have been right, but I was not threatened in any way. The city is laid out round a vast bay and the business quarter was still under construction at one headland, forging its way out to sea. Naked fingers of drab concrete pointed at the leaden sky waiting to be clad with tinted glass to cover the blemishes. Panama is one of the emptiest countries I have ever seen, so I could not fathom why they were reclaiming more land for their fiscal centre. At the other end of the bay, the old town revealed the last evidence of any Hispanic grandeur and was sadly, and quite literally, crumbling into the Pacific. Poor locals who inhabited the warren of cobbled streets had neither the means nor the motivation to preserve history. As buildings become uninhabitable they are replaced by characterless tower blocks with intimidating iron gates denying entry. Sure, this happens the world over, but I think it is a shame that one's roots and heritage can not be preserved and utilised, even if we are not particularly proud of them. As night fell, I found an elegant palm-lined square in front of an imposing church. A good place to sit and consume recently acquired bread and tinned pilchards – yummy. All the other benches were occupied by courting couples giggling between open displays of passion. I was a misplaced person and missing Marian horribly. There was so much to tell her, but it was all going to have to wait until our reunion in Bangkok for Christmas, still many thousands of miles away.

Life back in the UK had lost all meaning with the arduous travel. I was in a kind of vacuum with very little knowledge of the affairs of the countries I was passing through let alone of my own country of origin. My daily objectives of mile munching, impromptu survival training and absorption of knowledge were quite enough to keep me occupied. Missing time zones and changing seasons had become disorientating and even if Britain had suffered a nuclear war I would have been none the wiser. I did manage to remember my youngest daughter Chantie was about to have her 23rd birthday, but a 'Happy Birthday' postcard was the best I could do to send messages of love and 'I think of you often'. There had been no contact with friends or family since Mexico City and that had been postcards sent to let people know I was still alive. My next mailing address was Sydney so I still had a long wait before receiving messages from home, assuming of course that I made it that far. There was also another tiny problem that had not escaped my attention. I had to get out of Panama – sounds easy enough when you say it quickly, but south Panama is impassable primary rainforest with no roads, leaving only three ways out.

The Pan American Highway which I had come in on and the only road link between Panama and the rest of the world was not an option because my objective was the southern continent and I had already seen the north. Small aircraft, but if you have to fly a bike out, all fluids and battery have to be removed and carried on board with you. The bike is then chucked on its side and strapped to a pallet which I did not fancy, so I accepted the third option of a boat from pretty young woman in a travel agency. It sounded more relaxing than a plane and at $US166, including cabin and food for the fifteen-hour trip, was quite a bit cheaper.

The Crucero Express was much like a small cross-Channel ro-ro ferry and a welcome break from sitting in the saddle all day. As we slid away from Colon Harbour, I had time to film the rusting graveyard of ships scuttled during the turbulent times of the canal crisis. A score of part submerged wrecks pointed masts in different directions, like a giant porcupine under threat. Each of those rotting carcasses must have had an interesting story to tell, but they were condemned to being pounded by the Caribbean surf with only fish to share their secrets. The pink evening glow gave the scene a dignified serenity against a backdrop of fluffy clouds over distant Panamanian mountains. The country maybe the birthright of the indigenous indians, but they have been squeezed into a barely habitable corner where no one else wants to go. No doubt if the natural riches of the Baring Gap, such as timber and wildlife were easily accessible, they too would be plundered by greedy invaders. One thing I felt certain of was those invisible tribes would never enjoy the opulence of the Crucero Express.

With cabin and food paid for, it was luxury. Most people on board were rich Colombians on a holiday, so the mood was festive and a totally international experience. Swedish officers and Panamanian crew had difficulty communicating, but this added to well-orchestrated chaos. The cabaret was a Russian troupe of musicians and dancers and all the officers did a turn on stage, even the Captain managed a convincing rendition of *Jailhouse Rock*, which was a bizarre sight and even stranger to listen to. I was glad they did not put on a comedian as not many jokes translate into half a dozen languages.

During the spectacle, the security officer came up to me and asked "Are you a Brit boyo?" He was a Welshman from Swansea and only the second person I had met since leaving the USA who spoke English. He too was starved of conversation so we spent a strange but enjoyable evening chatting and watching other officers make prats of themselves on stage. He gave me the only book in the ship's library written in English. He said it was too technical for him but thought Robert Pirsig's *Zen and the Art of Motorcycle Maintenance* would be right up my street. I did not bother to tell him it was about philosophy not nuts and bolts, as he had already inscribed the fly-sheet 'From Roger Crockford – only British officer on the Crucero Express, 4th August '95'.

9. Big Mama Mafia

An impressive storm greeted the Crucero Express docking at Cartagena, North Colombia. As passengers sprinted to the shelter of a small but smart customs hall, a new challenge presented itself to me on board. The Triumph was the only vehicle on the car deck and the access ramp stuck solid a foot from Colombian soil. In a moment of frustration, I unpacked the bike, accelerated like mad up the ramp and jumped to freedom. Getting such a big bike airborne was an interesting experience and one appreciated by the army of customs officials who applauded from the shelter of their office. I wondered how the suspension would take such a devastating impact, but it performed well landing squarely on both wheels and I just managed to pull up before hitting the perimeter fence.

This unusual entrance on an equally unusual cargo did not avoid intense scrutiny by every uniformed individual in town. Word had got around about a mad Gringo on a big motorcycle and they all wanted to get involved. Frame numbers are notoriously difficult-to-read etches in a dot matrix, but they were determined to check that every digit complied with the Carnet to prove it was the bike described. A Carnet de Passage is like a passport for any vehicle and essential for overland international travel. Every page (one for each country) is a three part document recording all identifying numbers and features of the vehicle. All three parts are stamped by customs showing date and point of entry, with the first section removed and retained. When leaving the country the other two parts are stamped with one part remaining at the point of exit. The theory, although I have no evidence that it has ever worked, is that the two pieces of stamped paper will eventually come together to prove how long the vehicle was in the country and it was not sold there. The third piece is just a record of the countries visited. A condition of getting your Carnet fee back on return, is to have a complete set of properly stamped pages. Achieving this often called for a little creativity, as in many cases the point of entry and departure were mixed up and in many places they simply do not have a rubber stamp. Normally, a cursory glance at the number plate is adequate, but Colombian customs were a determined bunch.

Then there was a dispute about its engine capacity. They thought it was 120cc, which is considered respectable for that part of the world. 1200cc was unheard of, so the *cuatro cilindros* – four cylinders had to be pointed out for verification. I had anticipated it may be difficult to exit such a corrupt drug-ridden country, but to be subjected to such close investigation on the way in was quite a shock. Fortunately they could not fathom how to remove the seat so the .38 remained undiscovered. Authorities in most countries had been hell-bent on searching the bike, but no one had yet asked if I had a gun in my pocket. Despite our perception of Columbia as a lawless nation, it only cost two greenbacks to have everything stamped and that was for another bug spray.

With no local cash, but a tank of fuel, my plan was to ride south until hopefully hitting a big town to change money. The clouds parted momentarily, so I stopped at a roadside cafe to take stock. They would not take dollars, but two beers and some bland food were scored for a Swiss Army knife.

I made the mistake of leaving my leather jacket on the back of the bike to dry out and rode off without securing it. I realised my error in less than a minute, but it was nowhere to be seen. Colombian vultures swoop fast and my only warm, near-waterproof cladding had gone. The 'emergency poncho' reacted more like an emergency parachute, so it was better to face the elements in a T-shirt.

The second biggest town in Colombia is an unsavoury, sprawling mass of concrete answering to the name of Medellin. A cockroach-ridden hotel room was secured to escape more ominous clouds that were in the habit of shedding their load on any white motorcycle traveller they could find and, as I was the only one around, was subjected to gallons of water funnelled with great precision whenever the next cover was several miles away.

Finding accommodation could often be irritating as the cheap rooms were inevitably on the top floor. There was never a lift, so several journeys were required to secure belongings. Then the proprietor would insist the bike was taken off the road despite steering lock, chains and alarm. On this occasion the bike had to be ridden up a flight of six stairs where a space was made for it in the lobby.

The next morning started like any other, pulling on damp clothes showing signs of mildew, carrying worldly possessions down five floors to load the Triumph and after a good deal of cursing and manhandling down the steps, the bike was on the street, packed and ready for another day on the road. My next task was to score some pesos, as the so-called universal currency of US dollars was not acceptable, travellers cheques were welcome in only a few banks and credit cards are only used to force entry to other people's homes. Even bars have bars in Medellin. Beer and money are passed through heavy iron grills to prevent locals helping themselves.

The banking quarter looked very much like any other part of Medellin, except the windows had glass and a hefty part of the population were menacing-looking armed guards who could have easily been mistaken for criminals to the untrained eye. One such individual was earmarked to watch the Triumph as financial negotiations can take quite some time. His protest in eloquent Spanish went over my head except for two words, 'No hoy', not today. Well, if I had wanted him to guard the bike tomorrow, I would have been there tomorrow, so I stuffed a dollar into his hand to add to the confusion. The bank was very definitely closed. Pocket translator in hand, the note on a door that looked like something from Fort Knox said it was a public holiday. Great! No money for fuel or food and, worse, a night on the street seemed inevitable.

Railway stations are often good places to find black market dealers and the Triumph was sucking on fumes rounding a sharp bend as my not-so-good day turned into a disaster. The back tyre went down with a bang, dumping me in a litter-choked gutter running with water. So there I was, lying on my back, unhurt but close to tears, while the sky worked up to a soaking of monumental proportions – and it was still only 10.00am.

"You need help?" I will never know if this was meant as a statement or a question. At the time the words came as if from a dream, but I quickly assumed a vertical position to examine the thirty-something owner of the slurred voice. He was better-dressed than most in that part of town and an expensive-looking hair-cut flopped from side to side as he swayed around trying not to spill his bottle of strong Colombian beer. Willy had exhausted his English vocabulary, so Eddie, his younger brother, whose most noticeable feature was a nasty fresh knife wound across one eye, was dragged from another bar to translate as he 'had spent time in America'. In reality, his

English was very limited, colloquial Yank, but good enough to get the point across and better than my pathetic attempts at Spanish.

Willy changed dollars, peeling pesos from a wad the size of his ample fist, while a small army of raggedly dressed people righted the Triumph and pushed it to a closed garage. The proprietor was duly summoned to fix the tyre and fill it with petrol. No money changed hands for those services and it was becoming crystal clear that this family had clout. Several beers and a Swiss Army knife were accepted as a token gesture by the garage proprietor with an approving nod from my new, somewhat inebriated friend.

It is truly remarkable how the fortunes of travel can change. One minute a quick painless death is the best you can hope for – next you are sitting in miraculous sunshine getting drunk with complete strangers laughing at your inability to speak their language. Willy publicly threw his arms round me and announced I was to be a guest in his home. Looking around at some of the homes in that part of town, this was a dubious offer, however it would only be for one night and was unlikely to be worse than a hotel. Eddy led me on his 125 Yamaha to a very posh, fortified apartment block on the edge of town. Entry to the basement garage was through two sets of steel gates, each with armed guards. The rich/poor divide of that unstable economy became all the more apparent when shown the palatial accommodation. Security staff put my belongings in an airy room with five-star facilities.

Eddie introduced me to another seven men sitting around on big settees smoking and drinking. Each introduction started with '.....and this is my brother'. The father of these nine men, very close in age, had mysteriously died many years before, otherwise the regiment of handsome brothers would have probably turned into an army. The only woman was Eddie's exquisite 19-year-old wife, heavily pregnant. Colombia, outside the towns, was proving to be a staggeringly beautiful country inhabited by staggeringly beautiful people.

There was heated conversation between Eddie and Wayne (closest translation), the eldest. "Now I have to talk to Mama," he explained, "she is a manic depressive and has not left her room in two years." Mama ordered me to her bedside. A grey, beached whale with piercing dark eyes studied the filthy white traveller from a huge bed surrounded by plates of half-eaten food. The frilly nightdress beckoned for a closer look. Plump fingers prodded and grabbed at my non-existent biceps. More heated banter and Eddie said she wished to see the Triumph. Several sons escorted her to the garage while the rest jabbered on about her not only leaving her room, but crossing the apartment threshold. All this animated chattering was making me nervous and my brain was working on an escape plan, until Mama waddled back into the room to embrace me. Although short, she practically suffocated me in her ample bosom. Eddie translated as I recovered my breath. "You have no strength to do this thing so you must have courage. Mama says you are family and Wayne is appointed to be your bodyguard in our town." This sounded fine, except I was not aware I needed a bodyguard in their town. Sitting in the best chair with a deliciously cold beer, Eddie's delectable wife fixed my eyes, with a wicked grin. Thankfully, I never understood this look as events took an even more bizarre turn.

Wayne, after escorting Mama back to her room, focussed on me with the same unyielding dark eyes demanding "mokie mokie". Experience of travelling in countries where my single linguistic skill is to ask for a beer has taught me to resort to a slow nod and a gentle smile when faced with an armed stranger making aggressive noises at me. Watch for subtle changes in expression and act accordingly. In this case it paid off and I was handed a cigarette. Two or three puffs later, several people were dragging me off the ceiling and Eddie's wife had her hands firmly established down my trousers. The overall effect of that particular Colombian specialty was rather astounding and my Spanish, or at least some language that I did not understand, but clearly everyone else did, flowed from my tongue.

One looses track of time with drugs that enhance the senses, but after an hour, or maybe a week, Eddie suggested we go for a walk. He, plus spouse, a small dog and I, squeezed into the back of a minute taxi with no back seat, while Wayne sat in the front polishing his handgun. We were dropped at the foot of a heavily-wooded mountain and proceeded to climb. The puppy was given to me to look after as neither of us were equipped for the terrain. The endearing little creature's legs were so short I picked it up for a free ride to the top. Wayne insisted on several more 'mokie' stops in an unceasing torrent of Spanish. He kept tapping my shoulder and delivering an impassioned speech with an unnerving intense stare causing the puppy to drop from its perch on my shoulder. I was convinced my bodyguard was just telling me the manner in which he planned to dispose of my remains and I was doing him a grand favour by staggering up the mountain so he did not have to drag a dead weight.

By the time we reached the summit, I was past caring, but was nevertheless relieved to see a broad flat plateau fringed with stout trees, and a busy market bustling with happy groups of holiday-makers all feeling better for whatever it was they had been consuming. Pungent food stalls billowed smoke into the early evening sky. Vivid colour and shrill voices attacked the senses as the puppy, now bored with pissing and vomiting down my shirt, made a break for it. I set off in hot pursuit, eyes searching between a forest of olive-skinned legs. The dog vanished after a chase that only lasted a couple of hundred yards and it crossed my mind that following the dog had been a bad idea as I realised I was completely lost. There I stood, drugged to the eyeballs, with no idea where my hosts lived, where my bike was and I could not even guess at their family name. By European standards, I am considered very average height, but there, I could get a reasonable view over the sea of black bobbing heads. Wayne was making good progress towards me looking much taller than I had remembered him, until I saw he was sitting on Eddie's shoulders for a better vantage point. I explained that the dog had run off and waited to be summarily executed. Eddy laughed in a way only perfect-featured Colombians can and said that was where they had found it a few weeks previously, cold and starving. Plenty of food and affection had increased its life expectancy. Now it was on its own. White scruffy bikers were not the only creatures to benefit from this family's hospitality. Wayne looked relieved, crossing himself several times before rolling another 'mokie'. Mama would not have approved if he had lost her new son so soon.

The aftermath of an excess of 'herb' is uncontrollable munchies. Normally, I am fortunate not to suffer the sensation of hunger, but on that occasion it hit us all at once and I offered to take them out to dinner figuring it would be no more than an hotel room and their hospitality was worth so much more. They chose a Chinese restaurant where we fell into a bucket of delicious Chow Mein served by an ancient four-foot Mandarin waiter. The bill, after feeding four ravenous people, throwing back the beer and two bottles of crisp local wine, came to a little under ten pounds. Most gratifying and, after a bedtime 'mokie', I found I had discovered a cure for insomnia too.

Brilliant sunshine invaded my room at daybreak and the aroma of fresh Colombian coffee had me searching for the kitchen. It was a large room, with a generous hardwood table (probably of a protected timber) dominating the centre in an inviting sort of way. Three walls were clad in expensive-looking Rococo cupboards, with the fourth revealing the source of the family's wealth. Remember those big sweetie jars when you were a kid that bulged with bulls-eyes and sherbet lemons in little corner shops? Similar ones were stacked to the ceiling crammed full of newly-harvested marijuana. My new found friends were simple farmers earning a living in the only way they knew how.

The day-to-day activities of drug dealers must be fascinating, but Eddie insisted he take a day off from his normal schedule to escort me round half a dozen banks for money so I could buy a new jacket. He kept apologising for living in an economically backward country, and the search for a jacket was pretty fruitless as the only leather ones were outrageously expensive fashion garments for the very rich. In a country suffering from devastating deforestation to accommodate yet more cattle herds, you would have thought they would take advantage of a natural by-product, but I had to settle for a light, not very waterproof, textile job for around £20.

After a moderately successful shopping experience we stopped in a bar for a chat. Eddie's 'American' was returning to him. I asked how he got the nasty knife wound over his eye. On a 'sales' trip to the wrong part of town, two guys had tried to take possession of his motorbike at red lights. Even I could have told him stopping at obligatory traffic signals was asking for trouble. He manfully fought back and in his opinion had escaped very lightly. Wayne had sent people out to search for them as a matter of pride and Eddie was convinced they would not be a future problem to anyone else, even if they were still alive. No one fucks with Mama's family.

He also told me of his time in the USA, where he had married a Texan girl and had had a daughter. So much did he grow to hate his wife that murder was the only way to get rid of her and keep the money. He had kept wolves as a hobby and had hatched a plot to throttle the poor woman, put her in the deep freeze and slowly feed her to his pets. Fortunately for her, he decided against that course of action as it would have been unfair to deprive his child of a mother. This broken relationship was not, however, his reason for returning home. He was fed up of being treated like a third class citizen as, in his opinion, racial discrimination against Hispanics was much worse than blacks.

The evening was spent in the bosom of that welcoming family, laughing and drinking. They said I could stay longer, but it was time to head off on the Pan Americano to Ecuador. Before my departure, Willy gave me a broad-brimmed straw hat to keep the sun off – if I could find any. The last decent sun I had seen had been in the Mojave Desert. Eddie gave me a lock knife with a fearsome four-inch blade to keep me safe and Wayne gave me a bag of marijuana the size of a Coke can to keep me happy. These things they believed were all I needed for a successful journey. Who was I to argue, so I accepted their gifts with pride. This is the bottom line for all ignorant travellers. Unless you really know better, there is no option but to rely on the experience and knowledge of others.

Mama gave me a sloppy kiss and her blessing, which was probably the best gift of all. Since my arrival she had started to emerge from her room, so maybe they had also gained a little from a lonesome traveller. Eddie led me through unruly traffic to the *autopiste* south. We embraced like the brothers Mama had wanted us to be and then he was gone in a haze of traffic pollution. Reflecting back on my ridiculous adventure, the time spent in Medellin always features as one of the highlights. Not just because of the culture shock of being a drug dealer's guest in a notoriously dangerous country, but because of the genuine good-natured people it was my privilege to meet.

10. A Bullet for your Thoughts

Central and southern Colombia was endless mountain climbing on tortuous roads through the most breathtaking scenery. Unfortunately the twisting highway did not allow too much sightseeing as it took all my concentration just to avoid being flattened by a truck, or plummeting several hundred feet down a sheer, unprotected drop. The ride was demanding, but the memories of fun in Medellin had left me in a jubilant mood. I smugly earmarked the experience as a good one for 'down the pub' on a cold winter's night back home, assuming I ever got there, but the bike was not so happy.

On steep downhill sections the Triumph suffered from being ridden on the gearbox as I was concerned the brakes would not last as far as Sydney if the vicious terrain continued throughout South America. Unwelcome downpours would start around midday, so I was always on the road at first light to get as many miles in as possible before bad weather and visibility prevented serious progress. In the sparkling early morning light Colombia revealed the secrets of its natural beauty. First riding in the near dark of the lee side of a majestic mountain – then turn another 180 degree bend to be confronted with a scene to make you gasp. Several times I had to pull over (space permitting on such a narrow road) to absorb the view. Subtropical rainforest in a million shades of green carpeted valley floors to a distant horizon with no sign of dwellings or agriculture. The curious contrast of light exaggerated the already vivid panorama of blood-red earth against equatorial green.

By noon the drama increased as distant billowing clouds turned black against a pastel azure sky streaked with a blush of crimson and I prepared to take on the forces of Mother Nature. Storms could be seen approaching ten miles away and it was occasionally pleasing to see them erupt all around while standing in unaccustomed sunshine. The aftermath of these flash storms was extremely destructive. Rivers of mud and rock plummeted down vertical faces onto an already deteriorating road. Trucks and buses added to the devastation nibbling away at the road edge often causing much of the metal surface to disappear into the yawning valley below. Watching overloaded buses negotiate rock falls and washed-away tarmac was an alarming sight.

Sometimes a passenger would be sent ahead to crawl on his belly to the precipice edge and look under the road surface to see if supporting rock had been washed away. Less of a problem for the Triumph, but slithering around on mudslides was a hazardous business and I fell off on several occasions, covering everything, including me, with a thick layer of sticky sludge. The only good thing about the afternoon rain was being washed clean again before stopping for the night.

Military road blocks also hampered progress through the country. I could not work out why they existed as very few vehicles were searched. Naturally I was a target, but this was more out of curiosity than malice or suspicion. My capacity for carrying anything illegal was far less than the procession of cattle trucks groaning by unimpeded. The only time the armed forces would have been any use, they were nowhere to be seen as I was about to find out. On a traffic-free stretch of road, I was picking my way through another rash of potholes and glanced up to see two scruffy civilians knock a youth of about seventeen to the ground. Each man grabbed one of the boy's wrists with one hand. They both carried handguns in the other and dragged the squirming lad backwards across the road in front of me to a waiting pick-up. I was only a few yards away but they were oblivious to my slow progress towards them, as the boy was thrown into the truck and severely whacked by a pistol butt. Those young eyes showed a terror that still puts shivers down my spine. He knew he was going to die. As the Triumph drew level, the sides of the Nissan obscured my view of a young bleeding face almost close enough for me to touch. Three shots practically burst my eardrums and one of the assailants was rewarded with a spurt of blood splashing his face and tatty gingham shirt. I had just been a fly on the wall witness to a brutal murder and will never know why.

I did not hang around to find out as fear gripped the handlebars and I got the hell out of there, eyes glued to wing mirrors. One blood-spattered face did look up before returning to its gruesome task but paid no attention to a lone motorcyclist. With a churning stomach I stopped and made a potentially disastrous mistake. The .38 that had been concealed from customs officials through a dozen countries was loaded and placed in the centre compartment of my tank bag. Still quivering, with the obscene spectacle fresh in my mind,

I was stopped by a military patrol only a mile or so on.

This was such a common event the routine of stopping, switching off, removing helmet and smiling was second nature. Trying to tell them I had been privy to a homicide was a waste of time and it would have been a mistake to get involved. They were all about the same age as the unfortunate victim who had just had his head blown off. Five of the six were fine, shaking hands and joking, but one was determined to stamp his authority on the situation by demanding documents. He studied an out-of-date Thai visa in my passport for some time before commencing a thorough search of panniers, rucksack – tank bag! Eddy in Medallin had told me the penalty for carrying an unregistered firearm in Colombia is ten years in jail. I asked him what he was looking for. He tapped his automatic rifle just before sinking a hand into the unzipped top compartment. I invited him to look in the bottom one and indicated the middle zip was just to attach the two together. This was dangerous stuff. God only knows how the gun was not discovered, but it was returned to its original hiding place at the first opportunity.

All fears of suffering a repeat performance leaving Colombia for Ecuador vanished with a wave from officials on both sides of the barrier.

I had already seen the devastation caused by gross deforestation and in northern Ecuador it is total. Barren mountains completely denuded of all vegetation erode at a rate that can be measured daily. Legions of grubby men fight a losing battle to keep the road clear of mud and rock falls and fields have been reduced to dust bowls with not a plant in sight to prevent infertile soil being systematically washed or blown away. In Colombia, the indigenous Indians in their colourful heavy ponchos with startled wide-eyed babies slung on their backs had been friendly and happy. They may have not been well-off by most people's standards, but marijuana grows wild as only weeds know how, determining the mood of locals. No such luck over the border, where sullen Indians huddle together wrapped in brown blankets and the obligatory bowler or trilby, regardless of sex or age. The most common form of transport was a donkey, so fuel stations were few and far between.

Vast stretches of road made from loose cobbles were taking their toll on the bike, vibrating everything, tearing tyres. This was a really punishing test for the Hinckley factory. The already-bald front tyre kept losing pressure, making handling difficult. At every opportunity I had to stop to reinflate, but as there was no leakage overnight it became obvious that the appalling road surface was causing the problem. Nuts and bolts were checked every evening as part of a daily maintenance routine along with lubricating and tensioning a sad-looking chain. Apart from the obvious dangers, night riding was out of the question as front and back bulbs had blown with the vibration and I had already used the spares.

The Pan American Highway divided with no indication of which way was Peru or which way were the hostile cold Andes. The compass rather than instinct won and the pitted road soon became more pits than road. After only a dozen or so miles the snow-capped mountains were casting a shadow over the rapidly deteriorating path ahead. By this time we were only managing about 15 mph, feet dragging in mud and drying puddles for some stability. At the first opportunity where the track was wide enough, I laboriously did a fifteen point turn between twiggy hedges.

Picking my way back through puddles of indeterminable depth, I became aware of two men standing behind the scrubby thorn bushes that skirted the road on my right. Had I seen them on my way up? I was not sure, as it took a fair amount of concentration to remain upright on that terrain. Maybe all the revving and wheel spin from the turn had attracted their attention, but soon they were level only about twenty feet away, still partly obscured by the shrubbery. Normally in such a remote part a gesture of friendship would have been appropriate, even a few words of recently-acquired Spanish, but my hands were too busy and a full-face helmet is not conducive to conversation.

The taller one with a weather-beaten face under a broad-brimmed hat raised an arm to point at the ridiculous white man fighting to keep vertical. He was telling his *amigo* the silly bastard on a big bike is lost, I thought. The next few seconds were the longest of my life. The ear-shattering bang and windscreen fragments hitting my visor happened simultaneously. "What the hell was that," I said out loud attempting to fathom two apparently unassociated incidents. If a tyre had burst, I could not see why that would cause the windshield to shatter. I needed to stop to investigate and if I had a problem, the two guys only a few yards away may be able to help. I did not relish the idea of being stuck in such a remote spot and the tall one was still pointing at me so surely they would come to my aid. Even riding at a jogging pace through mud and rubble, care has to be taken with the brakes to prevent the wheels locking up, but despite the terrain, the bike handling had not apparently changed. "What's going on!" The answer came with a second explosion, which seemed like light years later, but in reality was only a few pounding heart beats after the first. The noise of a handgun pointed in your direction is fantastic and quite different from when pointing in away from you. When the blatant facts of the situation are unwelcome, the brain takes longer to compute information, but by this time I had worked out that the person who I had thought might be a savior was pointing a pistol at me, not a finger and the first bullet must have narrowly missed my left shoulder. The second shot confirmed my suspicion that not only was I a target, but the bandit's aim was getting better. My head suffered the sensation of being kicked very hard just behind and above my right ear by a determined man wearing hob-nail boots. The velocity of a bullet travelling at twice the speed of sound colliding with a robust crash helmet wrenches the neck so much my head made contact with the handlebars as I was launched forward by the impact. A vague memory of 'life flashing before your eyes' was followed by an instant of semi-consciousness and then blind terror.

Adrenaline tried to take over, but curiously enough the part of my brain still functioning pleaded caution, so I avoided doing a wheelie into the nearest mud-filled ditch, and instead managed to accelerate away from the brink of disaster. All the senses become sharpened in life threatening situations. Eyes are forced wide open to avoid blinking as that is all the time needed to make a fatal mistake. My hearing was slightly blunted in my well-fitting crash helmet, but I felt convinced I could hear the sound of my assailants breathing. The smell and taste turned from the unfamiliar odour of cordite to undiluted fear. Touch becomes amplified as sinews stretch with inhuman strength. The bike skipped from side to side across the wet grass bisecting a cart track in danger of becoming a bog. Had I dropped my trusty steed, I could probably have righted it with one hand.

The next mile (or was it two?) went on for a lifetime. There was no acute pain, just a deep base-note throb following me. After the initial shock one's instinct for survival has the ability to convert agony into positive energy as pheromones block nerve endings that even prevent prey suffering when attacked by predators. My vision became blurred, but probably due to tears and a steamed up visor than anything dramatic. My shaking limbs still responded to every bump in the road as the hideous truth of the matter sank in. I had to stop to check the damage, confirm my head was still where it used to be, ensure I was still alive and not riding as a headless chicken runs.

Despite jelly legs, my composure when checking the side stand was on firm ground and switching off ignition, was not what may have been expected from someone who had just collected a bullet in the head, but I remained calm and rational Only when the bike was safe did I practically fall off into the waiting quagmire. Numb, quivering fingers took an eternity to undo the chin strap and wrenching the crash helmet off took a concerted effort accompanied by a good deal of cursing. My reflection in a wing mirror revealed nothing as the wound was too far back and my expression made me feel detached from the image, as if looking at a stranger. Gentle probing with quivering fingers found hair matted with drying blood and then I noticed a soggy stain on the helmet lining. It was obvious my injury was minor and had probably been caused by fragments of fiberglass being forced through the foam padding of my helmet.

My fear gently subsided into relief and then anger. A complete stranger had tried as hard as he could to kill me. This was not an absent-minded accident or negligence that brought death knocking, but a deliberate attempt to end a life – and I wanted to know *why?*

Theft of a motorcycle and my meager possessions seemed a pretty weak motive, but then I could have strayed onto someone's cocaine patch, or maybe it was my bad timing again and this was the tourist-hunting season. The other burning question begged to know if this was likely to happen again. There must be other countries where opportune armed bandits are prepared to take a pot shot at a lone biker and there was the possibility I would have to cross the odd war zone. Maybe it was time to take the hint and head for home – unless I wanted to make the trip in a wooden box. By the law of averages, it must be unlikely to be shot twice on any trip. Conversely, the same law would say the chances of surviving two attacks is remote.

I am fortunately of that generation that has not experienced war first hand and doubt if I would not have the courage or conviction to face a conflict. However, the fascination of guns has been with me from childhood, although their appeal is purely aesthetic, like a gearbox or other well-engineered piece of metal. Never before has the realisation been so evident as to their designed function. A knife, it can be argued, can have a wealth of functions, but a gun is undeniably an instrument of death. In a couple of days I had experienced two unrelated incidents of guns being used in anger. I hoped they would be my last.

I forced my battle-scarred Shoei helmet over a throbbing wound before riding off with ears ringing and an awareness of a dark vignette at the top of my area of vision. Was the visor dirty or was it progressing blindness? The fear of armed bandits pursuing was the only answer I needed so got the hell out of there.

There is one question that still nags me while suffering the irritation of insomnia. Why was there not a third shot? The guy practically had the rest of the afternoon to put a third bullet in my back. If only my Spanish had been better I could have returned to ask him. Did he run out of ammunition, or fall in a ditch trying for a better shot? And what of the conversation with his companion? "Bet that put the wind up the bastard," or "That's funny, I could have sworn I got him in the head". Months passed before I was able to put any detail to that traumatic experience as fear of my own vulnerability buried the severity of such a hostile and unprovoked attack. The irony of the incident was my good fortune to be shot in the head. Had the assailant targeted another part of my body I would have been killed or at least lost control of the bike making it easy for him to finish the job with a knife or blunt instrument. Had I just had a lucky escape or was I unfortunate to have been shot in the first place?

Ecuador, for me, never held the magical beauty of Colombia just a few miles away, however from that day on my eyes absorbed the naked rusty mountains with a new affection as the realisation of human frailty smacked me in the face – or should I say hit me in the back of the head?

11. The Long Yellow Line

By Quito, I was beginning to think Ecuador was close to El Salvador in undesirability. Rain fell in buckets – it was freezing cold, yet the town practically straddles the Equator. Every major town has a focus area for the rich to live and play in, but all I could find, cruising sodden streets, were ugly concrete high-rise buildings of much the same colour as the sky. An intricate network of wires and cables connecting the apartment blocks swayed in an unwelcome chilly breeze. Premature twilight brought on by total cloud cover made me decide to stay the night rather than push on to the outskirts for cheaper accommodation. When I stopped at a hotel that looked well outside my budget, the bike had clocked less than 300 miles in ten hours' riding, but then I discovered the best thing about that desperate country. The sucre (local currency) was suffering from rampant inflation with three thousand to the pound. Four star luxury was a little over a tenner, but the phone call to Marian cost another £15 – just to hear *my* voice on the answerphone. I was so disorientated. Working out time zones for a numerical dyslexic is more difficult than exchange rates, but at least she would know I was okay after such a long silence. I did not mention I had been shot in the head.

South of the capital, Ecuador reverts to a recovering tropical scene, that at any other time of year would have been a pleasure to ride through, but the rain persisted and the bike needed careful nursing. The poor thing was simply not the machine for cross-country use and I was beginning to think failure was inevitable if the vastness of Peru and Chile demanded the same level of stunt riding I had experienced in the last couple of thousand miles.

Finding Peru should have been easy. Just follow the compass south. On a road that changes direction every few yards this is a hopeless task, so I had to resort to asking locals. They either lied, did not understand, or just did not know. As a consequence, I spent a whole day searching for a way out. What I had failed to grasp was, although Peru is undeniably south of Ecuador, there are only a couple of places where crossing is permitted. The drop in altitude became evident as the brakes got hotter on steep downhill sections and the atmosphere got appreciably warmer. At dusk I stopped in a strange little town satisfied I was within striking distance of a new country. Pick-up trucks driven by young men cruised town with more than their fair share of pretty young women riding in the back wearing very short skirts for a devout Catholic country. They all tried to look very nonchalant gripping the tail gate as the trucks jerked through the traffic.

After checking room prices and paying in advance for the privilege of sharing my bed with a good deal of insect life, I stepped outside to start unpacking the bike only to find it had attracted some unhealthy interest from three disturbingly fit looking young men. One sat side-saddle chatting to his mate studying the controls. The third guy, much shorter and less threatening, was picking at my pack secured to the back seat. I tried smiling and making friendly gestures pushing number one off the seat, after making 'fuck off' signals to 'fingers' assaulting my luggage. It became brutally apparent these guys meant business as the one at the front stuck a knife blade into the ignition switch making it perfectly clear he wanted the keys. This was the first eye-to-eye conflict I had experienced in a foreign land and I was at a loss to know how best to react.

Number one gave me the cue. Ever since Willy gave me the lock knife in Medellin, and showed me how to use it, it had remained in my left jeans pocket with a leather thong attached to the handle dangling outside. Hanging next to it from my belt was the remote alarm switch. A dirty finger stabbed at the alarm switch with an inquiring prod. I purposely mistook the inquisitive move and in a well-rehearsed movement (this was no time to make a prat of myself), four inches of Colombian steel glimmered in the dull streetlight glow. They froze. I waited for one of them to pull out a bigger knife so I could run like hell with a valid excuse for deserting my travel companion. Fortunately they got the impression this gringo was prepared to fight for his belongings, so started fidgeting, then smiling. The opponent's knife was pocketed and a dignified departure was made by all – but me. I suddenly realised I was shaking violently through undiluted fear and my assailants must have thought the behaviour threatening rather than cowardly.

On the only Ecuador border crossing to Peru, there is a disgusting little town where random market stalls are set up to disrupt traffic. In my relief to see a decent piece of tarmac in front of a very hot Triumph, the throttle wanged open all the way to the Peruvian barrier. Feeling smug, I sat while customs sorted their way through my impressive pile of documentation. After cutting my teeth on Central American bureaucracy, I felt I had cracked the system and could not see why Peruvian administration should be any different to anywhere else. Another golden rule of travel is never make assumptions about a country you have not experienced. They are all different.

A taxi slid to a halt in a cloud of dust outside and within seconds the smart elderly uniformed passenger was waving a finger under my nose and being very abusive. Apparently, I had passed another check point a couple of miles back, but the barrier was open and I had been going too fast to be stopped. I paid for his taxi ride back to the office, and we sat down to the official formalities. His only English was 'Welcome to Peru', so we really got on like a house on fire and a packet of Marlboro later, the Triumph kissed the world's best road surface outside Italy. A continuous yellow painted line stretched to a distant horizon that never got any closer, even at 130mph. The fuel consumption of a 1200cc bike loaded to have the aerodynamics of a public toilet is frightening. Fortunately, the Peruvians not only had had the brains to build most of their road along the coast, but they also provided mud-hut villages - with fuel! My sense of speed diminished very quickly and I was glad for some long-overdue thinking time through the barren desert under perpetual cloud cover.

The feeling of travelling in limbo was a strange one. No one knew where I was, including me for much of the time. I had absolutely no knowledge of activities back home. Hour after hour of solitude on the road every day gave time for introspective thought. What am I going to do when this is all over? Returning home, poor, old and jobless was not the best of prospects, but there was plenty to go before then. My immediate concern was what happens if the very bald front tyre blows out at speed?

Peru is a vast, diverse country and much of it is almost inaccessible, but a good road link north to south is essential for trade and commerce and I hoped the excellent black top would stretch at least as far as Chile. The Peru I saw was the place that stopped the rolling waves of the Pacific at a beach that goes inland about three hundred miles – and then the mountains start. Sometimes the mountains do make it to the sea and the ride round steep bends with a bit of grip was exhilarating. Frequently the ocean disappears for hours as the road meanders inland to a fantastic lunar landscape of perfect crescent sand dunes, slowly marching towards the country's artery. Although it was cool and totally overcast, this part of Peru was in the grip of a severe drought, which is a seasonal occurrence that the population seemed to take in its stride.

I contemplated sleeping out again as the desert between towns was completely deserted. The only problem would be getting on and off the road as most of it was elevated a foot or so above the shifting landscape. The Triumph would have sunk to its axles and, with only half a dozen vehicles a day, I could have ended up staying longer than intended. In fairness, it was so cheap that sleeping out could not be justified. The other problem was water. Very few things in bottles did not contain alcohol and I still had not found a tap that worked, so what did the locals use for cleaning their teeth? I found the answer at the first Peruvian pitstop where my daily ration of about a gallon was drawn from a well in the kitchen and given to me in a plastic bucket. I had considered bottling a bit for the road, but holding it up to the light revealed it had the texture of thin soup, so stuck to the beer. One quickly learns economical use of water, which dictates the order in which things are done. Wash body, then hair followed by some clothes. The remaining residue would be used to flush the toilet.

When the road meandered inland and into the mountains, you have no idea how far you are from the sea, my second navigational aid. Keep the big blue yonder on your right and you are heading south, so it was always reassuring to see the foaming waves even though it was much colder on the coast than in the mountains. Sea mists fed the cloud cover, but when there was a rare burst of sun the place really lit up, so I decided to find somewhere to chill-out (literally) for a day and get some writing done.

Hundreds of miles of fabulous virgin beach passed without so much as an attempt at attracting a tourist. Curiosity rather than anything else pointed me down a small dirt track to Ancon. It was a purpose-built village for rich Peruvians to come and sail their yachts and reminded me of Cornwall. I took the liberty of riding on a broad brick paved walkway along the small marina. The only person I saw, on account of it being out of season, was a white guy in a peaked sailor's cap. Frank was Danish, spoke perfect English and had run Ancon Sailing Club for many years. He took me to a two-bucket-a-day hotel and promised to see me in the morning. While unpacking the bike with a considerable audience, both pannier racks fell to the floor. The big boxes must have just been hanging on by the locks for miles. In fairness to the manufacturer, they are not recommended above 80mph because of excessive drag and that day I proved them right.

Determined to catch up with CSMA Motoring and Leisure articles, I rode the brick pathway to a charming square surrounded by shops and cafes. Street lighting was good and few people were around to tell me off for riding without lights. Outside was as warm as inside the only open out-of-season restaurant, so I sat writing in solitude after ordering egg, chips and bread. A gang of half a dozen kids arrived on roller skates and started admiring the bike. Within minutes I was towing them all round the paved square behind the bike to a chorus of shrill squeals of delight. I was afraid this would annoy immediate residents but they all came out for a look and a laugh. The youngest of the bunch, a girl of about six with a twisted leg, could not keep up with the swishing tail of friends, so had pride of place on the bike behind me. To see her bright smiling face was all the communication needed between foreigners.

Fortunately Frank knew a creative metal worker to fix the disintegrating cast-aluminum pannier racks. Five of us worked most of the day resolving the problem. Very few things in Ancon are new. Every nut and bolt was recycled from a scrapheap of rotting vehicles, rust removed, threads recut. Mild steel straps were cut from the sills of a dead truck, drilled, filed and bolted into place. Amazingly it worked and the panniers clipped on as well as if they had been new. After paying him the few solas for a hard day's work I also gave the jolly moon-faced engineer one of my adjustable spanners that he had coveted all day. When I removed it from the tool pouch, out popped a headlight bulb to light me all the way to Chile.

That evening, Frank declined to dine with a conversation-starved biker, but did say if I finished my writing that evening, he would post everything for me in the morning. Going back through my travel notes took forever. So much had happened since my last piece just over a month ago in California. More countries than most people visit in a life-time and still less than a third of the way round.

Lima was another disappointing capital that looked like a replica of so many others. Traffic pushed its way around at a grinding pace and I struggled to find a landmark to make the city memorable. It would have been rewarding to have found a feature or area to refer to in future conversation, but without any knowledge of what to look for, even if it did exist, I pushed south again towards the more interesting rural countryside. The overwhelming sense of loneliness was the only excuse I needed for a fast run to Santiago and a ship to Australia for a little Spring warmth. On reflection, Peru is one of the countries I have promised myself I will visit again to explore properly. I loved its emptiness and longed to head into the rain forest in search of a lost and ancient culture, but a sign just before the Chilean border said Santiago beckoned, only 1,250 miles away. Two days' ride if the roads remained good.

Once through Peruvian customs there was the opportunity to spend my last sol on fuel before having to score Chilian currency, so I would not lose out twice on exchange rates. I was always pleased when I got the fiscal transactions right as I was accumulating a sock full of coins and notes that were useless outside their country of origin. What I had failed to grasp in this piece of no-man's-land was there was *another* check point before the Chile border. A polite but insistent customs officer took me to a tiny cafe next door, where a large surly woman of about ninety broke off from making coffee to meticulously copy down my life history from rapidly accumulating documents. For this service she charged one sol. They had all been used, so my last US ten-dollar bill had to be used to give her the stupid sum. Of course, the change was given to me in Peruvian shrapnel no one would touch outside the country leaving me penniless.

The immediate change between the two major Pacific coastal countries is almost imperceptible. The road is not quite as good; the centre line changes from yellow to white, but the endless desert horizon is the same - until Arica, the first town to appear out of the barren Chilean desert.

Gone were the little suburban shanty towns, replaced with smart, low-rise apartment blocks. Smartly-dressed people drive cars with lights, paint and everything. Wide palm-lined avenues run between prosperous-looking shops. There had to be a bank to change a traveller's cheque. There was a closed one as it was Saturday but, never mind, it reopened on Monday.

There did not seem much point hanging around Arica as with no money. I was condemned to going hungry for two days and sleeping out, so it might as well be somewhere further south. With a tank full of petrol, I decided to keep riding and find a camping spot near the next decent sized settlement.

The desert became less and less interesting, turning into a flat, stony landscape that stretched in every direction. The distant Andes were hardly visible, blending into an unbroken grey sky. Unlike Peru, where towns have developed along the country's lifeline, indeed exist because of it, in Chile there is not a village, truck stop, or tin shack for two hundred miles. Occasionally a signpost would invite vehicles to divert off the tarmac onto dirt tracks to access towns. I had the feeling they could not be very significant if they did not have a proper road to them. I was beginning to feel rather desperate, switching to the reserve tank with no sign of civilisation. Okay, this may have not been a hot desert at the time, but there was not enough moisture to sustain any vegetation, so how long was I to last without water? To make things worse the road climbed dramatically for several thousand feet and a fantastic head wind was adversely affecting fuel consumption.

In desperation I followed a dirt track off to the right that announced Pisagua was only twenty eight miles and the Triumph ridden carefully should get there. Also my rough reckoning told me it must be on the coast as the Pacific had been out of view since entering the country.

The road seemingly terminated at a 2000 foot cliff. On the billiard-table-flat plateau it was impossible to gauge the altitude. Looking over the sheer precipice, a dirt track had been etched out of the cliff side, twisting back on itself, often with hefty overhangs. From the amount of loose rubble lying along it, there was obviously very little traffic and not a dust cloud in sight to indicate any other vehicular activity. With not enough fuel to get the bike back to the highway I had no choice but to try. Carrying so much weight made downhill riding much more difficult than uphill. Second gear all the way. The front brake just made the wheel lock up on the eroding track, so I had to slide the back wheel round each perilous bend, throwing loose rubble over the diminishing drop.

There were, of course, no crash barriers to prevent plummeting to the

Pacific, Not that there ever had been any on the perilous Pan American carving its way up perpendicular mountains. Every mile or so, macabre little shrines marked the spot where vehicles had fallen to their deaths. Strangely, most appeared to have fresh flowers on them, yet the nearest habitation was sometimes a hundred miles away or more. Frequently the number plate of the unfortunate vehicle was used as the horizontal bar on a cross marking the spot. I got used to judging the severity of a bend by the amount of crosses silhouetted against a uniformly overcast sky. On one particularly severe spot I counted twenty two crosses using number plates indicating that was the number of vehicles to have suffered an untimely death. Looking over revealed a scrap yard of twisted metal some 800 feet below. In the case of buses there would be just one big cross and lots of little ones with the names of each passenger. Filming them was a constant reminder of the fragility of life.

From about five hundred feet up on the track, Pisagua revealed itself and my heart sank. A tiny village of one tatty street straight out of a spaghetti western. The closer it got the more worried I became. The last couple of hundred yards and the only straight bit of the road was set at about thirty degrees running into the dirt street. Fortunately, there was no sign of life as stopping half a ton of bike and rider would have been impossible.

Exploring the ghost town on foot took about five minutes. Neat little clock tower, but the clock did not work. One hotel (closed, but the most respectable and only brick-built building), a few timber-clad shops and single-storey dwellings mostly boarded up. There was a police station of sorts at one end and I contemplated asking for a bed in a cell until finding it too was deserted. Spooky stuff!

Stuck without food, water, fuel or money, I straddled the bike outside the hotel wondering what the hell to do next. Three tiny children appeared from nowhere shouting and dancing round the bike. Kids of that age are so uninhibited and these may have thought they had discovered an alien but they were not deterred. If there were children there must be adults I reasoned and sure enough, the chirpy, laughing voices were interrupted by the sound of big bolts being shot and the impressive carved wooden doors of the hotel swung open. Siesta time was over! My dilemma was explained to a very sympathetic host who agreed to change a travellers cheque and let me take my pick of hotel rooms. As it was out of season I had the run of a fabulous old colonial-style hotel with high ceilings, tall carved doors to every room and creaky wooden staircases. A room with a view of the ocean was secured for about six pounds, which included dinner. The vista also let me gaze upon the village, but this did not add up to more than an eye full.

Pisagua depended on a few fishing boats, but had a very low-key tourist trade for those who wanted to get away from it all. The next problem was petrol. The proprietor purchased a little under a gallon from a fisherman, as apparently everything for the village arrived by sea, hence the state of the road. Attacking an uphill gradient is less demanding than downhill, so I felt confident that, at worst, we would make the highway to Santiago before running dry. With petrol and pesos my chances had improved immeasurably.

The early evening was spent attempting to capture the place on film and, after a giggly chat with some teenage girls, a couple of cans of pale but strong *cerveza* – beer were purchased from a closed shop. I sat for an hour before dark on a kid's swing drinking the beer, watching pelicans and seals feeding on the shore. The three original children enjoyed the company of a white stranger who was prepared to play silly games on a swing or build sandcastles and with little kids a verbal dialogue is not necessary to have fun.

After a splendid candlelit feast (there was no electrical power) of fresh fish, I was issued with a good-sized bucket of water and retired to a comfortable bed to write and enjoy a last beer before facing Chile again.

Back on the tarmac, sitting at a constant 50mph to conserve fuel, I overtook a pickup truck towing a boat. In the back of the truck were two large plastic drums. One must have been water and the other could have contained petrol, but probably two stroke for the boat's outboard.

They stayed in my wing mirrors until the Triumph coughed and I contemplated spending the rest of my life in the middle of one of the world's most barren deserts. There was just enough time to dismount the bike before flagging down the truck. A man in his forties accompanied by his son stopped, siphoned two gallons of precious fuel from their tank but would take no payment. He then insisted he follow me to the next petrol station about fifty miles on to make sure I made it. I gathered he was a diver for something and would have been considered poor by western standards, but he would not let me pay to top up his petrol tank. His only word of English was 'hospitality', for which both he and his son received Swiss Army knives. They were more than happy with their end of the deal and it was so little for me to give for their generosity. We all drive past broken-down vehicles every day and do not stop for fear of 'getting involved', interrupting our status quo. We can learn a great deal from those who have very little material wealth to give. The more we have, the less we are prepared to share it. Learning is one thing, putting the education into practice is quite another. If knowledge is not put to useful purpose, it is wasted and I hoped the often painful lessons were making me a more tolerant and less prejudicial person.

Lack of fuel stops were severely hampering my progress to Santiago, as detours off the road were necessary to obtain vital petrol, less vital food, water, bed and beer. Travelling abroad is always a question of 'when in Rome'. Abide by their rules and, if you do not like them, do not go there. Under different circumstances, Chile could have been a delight, just like Peru, but the crushing sense of isolation drove me on in a depressed frame of mind to find a country where I could talk to people.

Antofagasta presented itself only about six hundred miles from Chile's capital for another untimely stop. Regardless of my desperation to get to Australia, I was determined to see as much as possible. The likelihood of passing this way again was not on the cards for quite some time.

Imagine a giant has taken a handful of shabby buildings and scattered them randomly over hills that face an awesome ocean and you will get the picture. Having established a bed for the night, I set out to explore. In these situations make sure you have a card or the address of the hotel written down, or you may never see it again. Walk on a block system, turning left at every opportunity until you return to where you started. Then you can be more adventurous, increasing the block as more landmarks become familiar. About thirty six hours had passed since eating the last crust of bread on the roadside, so I fell into a respectable looking restaurant for sustenance. The translator did not help in interpreting the menu so I took a chance and was rewarded with an impressive pile of seafood. Outside sat a group of well-heeled Chileans facing the cold in woolly hats and heavy coats. Their kids ran amok through the restaurant and street getting under everyone's feet, but there was no annoyance shown by waitresses or pedestrians. This was the way of life of comfortable Chileans, but I preferred the attitude of poor children in Pigagua any day. Travel is a bitter-sweet experience and that night I was missing a glass of wine and a cuddle in front of the telly with Marian.

Two more hard days' riding through mountains on unpredictable roads and I was glad to find Santiago as night fell in freezing drizzle. The desert had turned to sparse olive-green vegetation in the last five hundred miles and it had become evermore evident that Chile was experiencing a severe winter with all the rain falling in the wrong places. My next objective was to cross the biggest ocean in the world and I had little idea of how to achieve this – but, as always, that was tomorrow's problem and there were a few more immediate ones to work out before then.

12. The Big Blue Bit

Cruising the streets of Santiago looking for a cheap bed was a nightmare. Everywhere quoted ridiculous sums starting at US$150. It was dark, raining and three degrees centigrade but, despite this, the bike started to overheat badly in dense traffic, so the tick-over was dropped and the ignition turned off at every opportunity. Naturally this stuffed the battery and I was close to tears at lights on a dead bike when a very smart local offered help. I attempted to explain the problem in dreadful Spanish, but in times of stress I resort to speaking 'foreign' using any words that spring to mind. 'Kaputt electrico' did the trick and he started flagging down taxis looking for jump leads. No joy, so he pulled out a mobile and phoned the police, insisting he waited with me to explain. Lovely man. Apparently he owned a big Kawasaki. We stick together, us bikers, even though we do not speak the same language.

Two foot patrol men turned up but did nothing but have long animated conversations on mobile phones, until an armoured bus arrived with a dozen or so tough-looking cops. I would not have liked to be on the wrong side of them. The multitude of uniforms benefited from the arrival of three police motorcycles, a Boxer and two strange off-road Hondas. With most of the Santiago constabulary gathered round a dead Triumph, it would have been an excellent time to rob a bank on the other side of town.

They offered to push, but as everything had cooled down, I tried the starter for the last time and the beast burst into life. There was quite a roar from the assembled crowd as I shook the hand of my saviour and followed the three-bike escort to the cheapest dump they could find at US$36 a night. Shit-pit hotels come with the job, but expensive shit pits are most disappointing, even if water was available from a tap and not a bucket. Cold, wet and hungry, I fell into bed hoping my friend Derrick Lello, who had arranged my transport to New York, had also faxed his Santiago sister company warning of my arrival.

Bless him, he had and to my great relief his agent, Jamie Letelier, greeted me at his office in perfect English. Only the second native to speak English since leaving Texas. With astounding enthusiasm, he applied himself to the task of getting one old biker and a Triumph to Australia. Unfortunately a boat had just sailed and it was to be another month before the next meaning I would not be reunited with the bike for six weeks. The only alternative was to ride to Buenos Aires, but the Andes were closed for the winter. The other insurmountable problem was cost as Chileans are not great travellers and there is no tourist trade infrastructure. Gone are the days of banana boats picking up cargo and passengers, so the cheapest formula was for me to fly and the bike travel by sea. The whole package, including crating the bike, cost a fantastic £2,000. I could not afford to stay in Santiago one day longer than necessary. There was something in the curious mix of that orderly city that made it fantastically expensive. My flight was arranged via Tahiti and New Zealand to add to an already colourful passport and give me one last day to explore.

I am not really a big city fan, but Santiago was clean and buzzing with economic optimism, despite a revalued Peso and whispers of authoritarian corruption. There were more buses per capita than most places, all in dedicated lanes to ease traffic congestion and a splendid new metro underground further helped the flow of commuters. I preferred to walk the two miles through bustling streets as public transport can be tricky when you are unsure of where you want to be and I was perfectly capable of getting lost on my own. Santiago certainly presented itself as a city going places in the world economy.

Most of the architecture could be loosely described as modern and just about every significant building was graced with larger than life bronze castings. The national hero of Chile is an Irishman by the name of O'Higgins. Banks, parks and streets are named after him. His father was affiliated to the Spanish court in the early 18th Century and after an English education, the young O'Higgins returned to Chile to rebel against his father and the Spanish government by liberating the country. He then did the same in Peru. This real Che Guevara character is now immortalized in statues all over the city and his birthday is a national holiday.

All packed up and ready to escape to a new continent, I descended the four floors loaded with luggage and heard Annie Lennox singing *A Whiter Shade of Pale* on a radio somewhere. Shortly before departing England, Marian had bought the CD to listen to on our Saturday morning lie-ins. They had been very special times, eating breakfast in bed, chatting, making love.

Hearing the song made me burst into tears and I had to climb the million stairs back to my room to recover my composure.

To kill time, I indulged in South American egg and chips that the fat waiter understood in one. My Spanish was improving – just as I was about to leave. He was the only fat person in Santiago and insisted on singing to me very loudly from the next table while I tucked into my last meal on Chilean soil.

At the airport, customs arrested me as I no longer had possession of the Triumph. Well, it was not exactly hand luggage and, if it could have travelled with me, it would have been in the hold. Yet another Catch 22 situation reared its head. I was unable to travel with the bike, but not allowed to leave without it – and the plane was practically taxiing up the runway! Fortunately Jamie came to my rescue once again. A very special man whom I have sadly lost contact with.

Sprinting through the metal detector, in a bid to catch the flight and two armed police pulled out guns when alarms started ringing and lights started flashing. I had forgotten to stash the Colombian lock knife in my pack, so I had it confiscated, but would be able to retrieve it in Sydney. Once on board, feeling rather clammy from all the stress, the captain announced our arrival time on Easter Island. I was supposed to be going to Tahiti. The bastards had put me on the wrong fucking plane! Sod it. I was not going to get off. Fortunately it was only a stop-over and eventually a warm balmy night welcomed an exhausted Englishman with his head in another time zone. My watch said 9.00pm, but local time was 3.00am and I could not work out what day it was.

Those two days in Tahiti were my first completely recreational time since leaving home. Nothing to do but sit on the beach outside a fabulous hotel (all included in the price) and chat to locals about the French exploding their evil bombs just off the coast. Why can't they do it in Paris rather than pollute – destroy – part of the ocean next to that idyllic isle?

There was a time when I spoke enough French to have a conversation, but with my brain somewhere in South America, locals were bemused by my attempt at speaking to them in Spanish. At dinner on both evenings there, dusky Polynesian dancing girls with half coconuts covering their breasts swayed rhythmically to traditional music. How do they move like that? One could sympathise with the crew of The Bounty mutinying. I would have joined them.

Two days R&R in fabulous sunshine restored strength and flagging spirits for the next stage of a voyage of discovery to New Zealand, which I knew in my heart was going to be a delight. After crossing the date line en route to Auckland, I was even more confused about what day it was and resented losing twenty-four hours of precious life.

Youth Hostels may sound like a contradiction for someone of 46, but they provide cheap, very adequate accommodation. Most of the other people were young Japanese backpackers, who either did not speak much English or were just unfriendly, cooking vast pots of noodles. There is something about that tongue that sounds aggressive even though they may be telling jokes. Curiously enough, although New Zealand is an English-speaking country, the feeling of isolation did not diminish. This was probably because the travel team had been split up and I was reliant on trains and boats and planes to get around. This does have its attractions, but with the bike, the options were limitless.

My objective was Christchurch on South Island to meet a friend of Marian's who had looked after her for a while when she travelled New Zealand. I could rent a car for about £20 a day, but fuel was expensive, camping out without the bike did not occur as an option and it was still winter. Internal flights were cheap, but that is no way to see the country, so a train ticket was purchased for the following morning, leaving a little time to explore a most attractive and compact major city.

Auckland is a town of clean, wide streets with sympathetically designed low-rise buildings. Kiwis were friendly and their apparent slow pace of life gave them time for a chat. The Youth Hostel was on the edge of the Asian quarter with a fascinating mix of Chinese, Japanese, Korean, Thai and Vietnamese shops and restaurants. This bleeds into a tidy little Red Light district with a few low-key strip joints, massage parlours and escort agencies. Everything was closed as it was Sunday, giving it a slightly spooky feel like a deserted fun fair. Pubs appeared to be the only entertainment and there were plenty of them selling excellent Guinness. The UK pub culture leads the world, but NZ comes a close second.

A neat, three-carriage, but painfully slow train travelled the length of North Island to Cook Straits for the ferry. There was not a great deal to do but count sheep munching on abundant lush grass. After a million or so that got dull, but it was too cold and uncomfortable to catch up on sleep. The ticket man told me the ferry took about four hours depending on the weather and that day a force seven was blowing. "Is it really that far?" I asked. "Nope, the ferry is really that slow."

South Island strolled past through undulating fields with a dramatic mountainous backdrop. The single-track railway rattled along next to an angry Pacific, foaming against an isolated land and I began to realise the considerable length of both islands. We tend to think of NZ as being the little island off the coast of Australia, but that infectious country has a very strong and individual identity. Although similar in square miles to the British Isles, it is more or less in a long North to South straight line – and practically empty. I have always admired the stout New Zealand attitude towards nuclear pollution and looking at the country it is easy to see why. A more unspoiled landscape you could not wish for and quite rightly, it is fiercely protected.

Starved of conversation, I threw myself at the first vacant seat opposite a woman attending to a juvenile who had apparently just learned the art of blowing raspberries.

Neither of us were aware if it at the time, but this chance meeting was to affect the course of my travels.

Sue Al-Sobky was of English birth but had spent many childhood years in New Zealand and most of her working life in Dubai, where she had married an Egyptian and had a son, Omar. He was eight, precocious and hyperactive. A suitcase full of toys amused him while Sue and I chatted about the meaning of life. There is something remarkable about encounters with strangers on trains. You can be almost intimate as it is almost certain that you will never meet again. I did detect a sadness in her face, but perhaps it was just tending to such an inquisitive, intelligent child that sapped her own abundant energy.

We were of similar age and middle-class upbringing, but had led very different lives. Immaculately dressed, flames of neat strawberry-blond hair framed a face that still held the prettiness of youth, but with eyes that displayed the knowledge and experience of age. She sparkled with laughter at my appalling jokes and, although the Middle East was not on my travel agenda, I took her business card with the promise of a postcard or two. My new friend was a high-flier who commanded respect. We parted company on Christchurch Station as I staggered off under the weight of a bulging rucksack to meet another stranger.

Less than a year after Marian and I had moved in together it had been her turn to see a bit of the world. We were both a little afraid of the word 'commitment' and her pre-arranged travel plans would have been a convenient excuse to separate if the relationship had not worked out. During her time in New Zealand, she had made friends with Peter Miller, who made a bee-line for the only person on the platform carrying a house on his back. My fortunes of travel had changed with the meeting of two exceptional people in an exceptional country. Peter showed me a warm bed – and bliss, a bath. His wife, who he had absolutely doted on, had died only a year previously, so maybe our point of contact was loneliness, but it did not matter. I felt comfortable, secure and wanted in Peter's world. A clairvoyant had told him he would not spend the rest of his life alone. No one needed a crystal ball to see that a sprightly man in his mid-fifties, financially secure and with a real lust for life was an attractive proposition.

He invited me to phone Marian. What joy to hear her voice again. The timing was superb as she had invited some friends round to watch the last video footage posted in Peru. She had become a little depressed when viewing the footage of my crash helmet with a bullet hole in it, but was glad to hear I had not suffered severe injury. Those time-lag phone calls from far off places were always a little awkward, especially when it is someone else's phone bill. "I love you and can't wait for Bangkok," was about all I could think of saying. I hoped the hesitation in her voice was due to geographic not emotional distance.

Two days was all I spent in that likable man's company, as Australia beckoned and I wanted an update on the bike's progress across the biggest blue bit in the world. There was sufficient time, however, for Christchurch to get under my skin and not just because Brighton Beach was only a few miles away. Attractive litter-free squares are skirted by an interesting mix of stout stone and brick buildings, possibly not as old as the architecture implied. There is something satisfying about the familiar and that town handed me everything on a plate. Shops for contact lens cleaning fluid - with the label in English. A hair brush – and best of all, a nearly-new leather jacket from a pawn shop for £25. My enthusiasm for the place prompted Peter to suggest I phone Saatchi and Saatchi to inquire about the possibility of future work. The MD, an Englishman, gave a greasy leatherclad an hour of his time for a very positive chat with no promises, but 'keep in touch.'. Peter drove me to the airport where we had a hug and have remained friends ever since.

13. Buses and Backpackers

Forty days of unbroken sunshine were terminated by the arrival in Sydney of a bikeless biker. Fortunately for me, my ex-brother-in-law Mark resided in that energetic cosmopolitan city with his Thai girlfriend Lakana and their delightful daughter Dominique. Mark was the first person I recognised in three months on the road. The last time we had seen each other had been several years previously when I was married to his sister. He was visiting his homeland with a girlfriend and his short visit turned into a two year stay in our family home.

They were extremely welcoming and said I could stay in their comfortable Coogee Bay apartment until the Triumph arrived. It was a tempting offer and it would have saved money, but the thought of staying in one place for a month, with not much to do, defeated the purpose of being there.

Mark had a degree in paleontology, but chose to earn a living as a self-employed bricklayer, which to my good fortune meant his work schedule was flexible and gave him a little time to support my cause. The other benefit was I could partly repay his generosity by elevating myself to the status of bricky's mate – which, I am proud to say, I am damn good at.

With Dominique strapped firmly in the back seat of his VW 'combie', we investigated outrageously expensive bike hire companies, then started to look round for a bike to buy until mine arrived. This sounded like a good plan as it could be sold a month later, but it would have left Mark with the problem of finding a buyer as I continued my journey. This did not seem fair, so I decided to explore the East Coast by public transport. A ticket to Byron Bay was secured leaving me a couple of days to explore Sydney and, with Mark's guidance, get acquainted with some local beers.

Sydney is a thriving, affluent city contained to the east by the Pacific in a succession of idyllic beaches arcing between headlands. Even Bondi was relatively unspoiled and a well-tended pathway formed a popular coastal walk between stretches of silver sand. The only area of the entire city to blot out sunlight with tall buildings was the financial quarter, but even that was tidy and ran at its own pace unlike the frantic high-stress trading markets of

London or New York. People always had time to stop and chat, especially in bars and cafes.

Lakana could not do enough to make my stay enjoyable and she introduced me to the bustling Chinese and Thai markets fringing a classic Chinatown. She and her two radiant older daughters, Oie and Joy, worked at the Coogee Bay Hotel and conveniently managed to adjust shifts so Dominique always had a babysitter. They made an enchanting but contrasting group – three typically petite Thai women with a blond all-Australian girl of two, ahead of her years physically and intellectually. Lakana had bravely moved to Australia some fifteen years previously when Oie and Joy were not much older than the new family member. Her husband was killed on active service preventing evil Kamer Rouge troops advancing from Cambodia. So numerous were the deaths to the cause that the only notification she received that her loved one had perished was a phone call from the authorities who had not time, or presence of mind, to sympathise. Australia gave her the opportunity to depart Bangkok to start a new life in a foreign land. She had left behind the family whom she was not to see again for more than a decade. Such courage.

Before striding north on the backpacker trail, there were a couple of welcome days to rebuild my strength. I had not realised the punishment my emaciated body had suffered through the Americas, so relished spending time catching up on writing, cold Guinness and best of all, cheese sandwiches. I sent thirty eight postcards at enormous expense to friends at home, some made en route and others I hoped to meet in the near future.

The overnight bus spat me out onto the cold, deserted streets of Byron Bay at 4.00am. Fortunately, I had left most of my heavy gear in Sydney, making my progress round that very pretty but tiny town to a Youth Hostel relatively easy. Byron Bay has developed from the relatively new industry of back-packer tourism and supplies its demands brilliantly, attracting an international set of travellers to its acres of immaculate beach, set in surroundings notable for their natural beauty.

The biting wind inspired another bus ticket to Hervey Bay, the farthest point north possible in a day. The Greyhound bus drove through the grotesquely over-developed Gold Coast Surfers Paradise and the superbly laid out town of Brisbane, following a well-trodden hippy trail. There were many places worth stopping in to explore and I became more frustrated that travel was dictated by a bus timetable rather than a whim.

Hervey Bay was a sprawling, less attractive version of Byron, but after agreeing a deal with the proprietor of the Colonial Backpackers Resort, I decided to stay a few days to explore the area as there were no pressing engagements in my diary. The town capitalised on two natural phenomena to attract tourists. One, especially in Spring, was whale watching and the other, Fraser Island National Park, the biggest sand island in the world.

Man has used and abused whales since the beginning of time. Thankfully, only a couple of countries persist in the bloody slaughter of graceful intelligent creatures that show nothing but friendship and curiosity towards fellow mammals. I spent a fabulous day filming gentle monsters swimming so close with their young that an outstretched hand would touch them. They choose those warm waters to spawn and prepare their offspring for the wrath of the northern Pacific. Parental care and tolerance of juveniles was obvious. Hunting those splendid creatures, even though one could feed a village for weeks, is blatantly unfair as they show no fear of man and their inquisitive nature compels them to investigate.

The same applies to the bottle-nosed dolphins dancing through sparkling surf with a permanent grin on their faces. They love to play with boats, just keeping ahead of the prow, darting from side to side with all the precision of the best synchronized swimmers. Hunters never had it so good killing such large animals that have no means of fighting back. Their only defence is speed and agility in the water, but without the knowledge that they should be taking flight, they present themselves to the harpoon with all the trust of a young child. With their proven intelligence, it is surprising the word did not get round to swim like hell in the opposite direction on sight of any boat.

The second attraction took a little more organisation back in the succulent wilderness of Colonial Backpackers. Fraser Island was rescued from the grasp of commercial loggers and sand miners. Whales are not the only beneficiaries of a change in conservation policy and another natural resource has been saved from annihilation. In both cases they still have economic worth and are capitalised on for the pleasure of tourists in a controlled ecologically acceptable manner. The island is the largest heap of fine silver sand in the world, held together by the roots of virgin tropical forest. There are many rare, protected timbers sought after because of their straight-grained strength and resistance to sea water.

Groups of half a dozen are encouraged to rent a four-wheel drive mini bus to 'do' the island. A disturbingly fit and energetic young man called Rob and I visited the off-road centre to watch an instruction video about 4X4 driving on soft sand tracks through the forest and across dunes. The east coast beach was treated as the only highway with normal road rules applying - when the tide was out. The briefing was thorough with as much time spent on the conservation of the island as the vehicle.

There were a couple of prohibitively expensive hotels on the island, but we were supplied with two bulky ex-military tents and cooking implements for more basic but fun accommodation.

Our party was made up of three blokes called Rob and four girls who were not. I was awarded the name 'Don Rob' being more than double the average age of the group. The mature and very likable co-driver became RJ and the third gangly boy scout, who said 'cool' just a bit too often, remained plain Rob. There was Gayle, a fun-loving Yank, who enjoyed my abusive banter about Americans, and three rather solemn Israeli girls just out of national service, who were a little over-sensitive about their country and religion. One meets rather arrogant travellers from the Promised Land all over the world, doing their thing after compulsory military service.

The evening before our departure we went shopping for three days' provisions. The Israeli girls were kosher vegetarian (they eat raw carrots and rarely drink) so the three Robs shopped separately for sausages, burgers and booze. Gayle, the Jewish American, indulged in both camps.

No sooner had we driven off the tiny ro-ro ferry on Fraser Island and a schedule for the trip was put together by the Jerusalem girls, with all the complexity of a military manoeuver.

On our first evening, after collecting a stack of firewood, the dilapidated tents were pitched, one for the boys and a rather more crowded one for the girls. After weeks of sleeping out, the tent held no attraction for me, so I rolled out my sleeping bag next to a magnificent fire under a clear sky.

Sausages cooked on sticks can be pretty disgusting as inevitably the stick catches fire, depositing the banger in glowing embers. By the time they are retrieved, they are unrecognisable, but washed down with enough warm Aussie white wine and beer, no one really cared.

All over the island, the most evident indigenous animal was the noble dingo. Short sandy coats and attractive canine faces, they have the appearance of well-kept domestic dogs. Tourists are encouraged not to feed them as they can be bold and theft is an easy meal.

During the night, I awoke to find one foot firmly grasped between powerful jaws. Another took hold and started dragging me towards the sea. So powerful was the grip on my foot, escaping the confines of my sleeping bag was impossible. Two more dogs ran back and forth around my head snarling. The experience was far more physical than the wolves at the Grand Canyon and there were no handy fir cones for defense. Handfuls of sand worked nearly as well and an extinguished stick from the dead fire was retrieved for protection. The consequence of the attack, apart from a badly ripped sleeping bag, did not become apparent until the following evening.

Surprisingly, Fraser Island has two freshwater lakes. Sea water is purified as it seeps upwards through the sand. An hour's drive and a five kilometer walk brought us to Lake Wabbi hemmed in on three sides by dense forest. Our walk through lush vegetation had revealed all sorts of timbers and plants new to me, but I neglected to take samples for later investigation. The fourth side of the nearly rectangular lake is a huge sand dune that rises to about 150 feet out of the cool water, reflected green from towering trees. Climbing at 45 degrees through soft sand is hard work but the unbroken view of billowing olive tree tops was worth it. The feeling was similar to looking down on clouds from an aircraft.

Once at the top, the idea was to run full tilt down the slope into the lake. Great fun, but as the sun began to set, the five kilometer walk back to our transport was a lot less fun. I could see that if we got lost, staying in one place was our only option until daybreak. There followed a 20km night drive through soft sand and massive deep ruts that would flip any normal vehicle. Very uncomfortable for the passengers getting thrown around with all the camping and cooking gear, but the schedule said camp on the shores of Lake

McKenzie so there was to be no compromise.

Pitching inadequate tents in the dark was a bit tricky and, although we missed it, rain had fallen heavily, making fire lighting with wet teak even more difficult. After an hour we had a real furnace going that was to last the night, but then in the flickering light the theft was discovered. Rob opened the cool box to find three pounds of sausages and a pack of burgers missing. Those clever dingoes that kept me busy in the night were just a decoy while their friends opened the sealed box, removed anything that smelt good and then replaced the lid. No doubt the beans and spaghetti would also have gone if they had had a tin opener.

Young people's appetites are ferocious. They had been stopping all day for snacks, but still managed to completely devastate supplies in one meal. RJ was getting irritated with two of the girls as they took so long to do anything and they demanded rather than requested things. I asked him to make allowances for people communicating very well in their second language and they would mellow with time and travel, or go home as ignorant as they left. Their attitude towards me was rather patronising, but they were attempting to be complimentary. They persisted in telling me how much older I was than their parents, yet was fitter and enjoyed 'young people's' activities. Fun is not an exclusive right that comes with youth. Just the opposite in my opinion.

The opportunity of a free bus ride back to Byron Bay prompted my departure from Hervey Bay. I was feeling naked without the Triumph and wanted to get back to Sydney to check on its progress across the Pacific, but still had time to explore a bit of Australia away from the coast. On recommendation, I checked into the Arts Factory and the sight of my press ID once again produced a favourable result when negotiating a price.

The curious complex covers about an acre, with most dormitories and recreational rooms surrounding a swimming pool. Every available wall is painted with colourful but not very good murals. They offered me a 'wagon' on the island for a couple of quid a night. Narrow wooden walkways span the few yards to a patch of ground surrounded by a lake. Fortunately the water is not very deep so those who fall off the slatted path when pissed or stoned can wade the distance. A dozen or so sturdy canvas structures fringed the island, pointing at the lake. Stretched over metal hoops, they give the appearance and were about the same size as traditional Western chuck wagons without the wheels. Very comfortable and private, with the added benefit of waking to a wonderful view of the lake. The wild life could be a little noisy at night, but so much better than traffic.

The place was a hippy paradise with second-generation backpackers maintaining a tradition of guitar-playing and dope-smoking. Bronzed young men strutted about in sarongs carrying didgeridoos trying to look 'cool'. Women are far less pretentious and make better company as a rule. Living among people slightly younger than my children is not as exciting as one may imagine, as they have less to offer and an unappealing 'bin there, done it' attitude. One guy in his early twenties asked how old I was, to which I replied "fifty six," adding a decade to my real age, just because the same questions were getting tedious. "Amazing, you don't look a day over fifty." Well, I could not blame anyone but myself for that one, but he was more offended when I asked how many years before he was allowed to drink in pubs. There is a magic age when people stop wanting to look older and try to look younger. Everyone is different and I did not care too much as long as body and mind did not let me down.

After a couple of days of not having much to do, I was getting bored with sitting around writing, so hired the cheapest car from 'Rent-a-Dent' to look around. The area immediately inland was rather dull until falling upon Nimbin, hippyville extraordinaire. Some years previously, a group of travellers had taken on the might of a big logging company and won the case to preserve the area from devastation. The result was a community living in one short street of timber clad houses growing marijuana for a living. The police had turned a blind eye for years, but had just built a little police station next to the Rainbow Cafe where growers sold their wares. The building did not look as if it had ever been used, but a notice on the cafe door saying 'no police without appointment', showed a good deal of restraint by the local constabulary. 'When in Rome....' and all that, so I purchased a little weed to smoke that night while camping out on the nearest deserted beach.

By the time I had found a suitable secluded spot for the night it was dusk and predictably I had forgotton to buy food, but had a couple of beers.

A joint was rolled in a crimson sunset glow with the warm sea lapping at my feet. Before it was finished, I had had enough so popped it down a little hole in the sand that formed a perfect fit. Some time later, the remains of the joint popped out again and a very stoned crab struggled to the surface and staggered into the sea.

In the haze of dope and beer, I got to thinking life could be a damn sight worse and who ever the genius was who put that scene in front of me together deserved a whole bunch of brownie points. Waves are such a clever idea and a lovely way of finishing off the wet bit before the dry bit starts. White foamy crests out of the blue churn soft sand about for children to play in. So considerate. In semi-darkness, I scribbled down some thoughts on the matter. 'Had the brief of designing the meeting of sea and land been given to me, the water would have be contained in a transparent membrane rising vertically, following the coast a bit like a giant fish tank, so we could see all the beautiful things we are destroying. Small islands a few feet across, would be surrounded by the membrane towering towards the sky. The resultant tube would be home to multicolored butterflies. To avoid overcrowding, spiders capable of clinging to the membrane sides could catch butterflies with fishing rods.' At that point I became hysterical but had to write it all down to see if it was as funny in the morning.

One more night in Byron Bay was all I had before the bus back to Sydney and it was spent at the Railway pub, the busiest meeting place. I had enjoyed many interesting conversations there with a huge cross section of people. Peter, a classical ballet dancer who had danced the world for some major companies, until his knee cap was removed by a Greek taxi driver in Athens. He will never dance again. Georgie, a Swiss boy dying of a terminal lung disease determined to spend his last year travelling. A Belgian in his late twenties called Ziggy, a Thalidomide victim with stubby hands protruding from his Tee shirt. Lighting a cigarette was a major challenge, yet he had seen most of the world and spent a couple of years on the road in China. His only regret about his condition was not being able to play the guitar. Brave people who were downgrading my trip to the status of picnic in terms of effort and endurance.

14. 'On the Road Again'

Back in Sydney, customs announced the arrival of a battle-scarred Triumph. Everyone said the authorities would be strict about cargo from South America, insisting on steam cleaning and probably a detailed search. I was also concerned about the state of the front tyre as I did not believe they would release me onto Sydney streets riding on canvas. As in the USA, the chatty agriculture department woman had no means of opening the crate so the Swiss Army knife took over. I had learned that in such situations, the best strategy is to ask as many questions as possible about anything other than motorcycle import. Get them on a hobbyhorse about family, politics, their job – anything to distract them from the task in hand. This can be time-consuming, but they are more lenient if doubts are not put in their minds.

After a cursory inspection, I had to get a taxi to the nearest bike shop to buy a new battery before riding behind a Coogee Bay bus. This little trick never fails even though you generally have to follow it round the houses, stopping at every bus stop, but there was no particular hurry and it was probably still quicker than getting lost.

A Triumph dealer was very thorough with his service, knocking spots off his Californian opposite number. New front tyre, back brakes (amazingly all the nursing through Central America had saved the front pads), filter box, plugs, fluids. I stayed to help strip and clean carbs, adjust timing and change valve shims. No one could guess when the next service would be, so preventative work had to be done, although the Triumph was showing little sign of mechanical wear from its ordeal so far.

A day was spent trawling embassies for visas and one more night before heading West. A pile of mail arrived from friends and family, some of which had been sent on from Dave Barr in California. What bliss to sit and read out-of-date news but, most of all, to scan pages of Marian's well-formed words over and over. Only nine weeks before we were to see each other again for Christmas in Bangkok.

Dominique had her third birthday, so I hunted the shops for a suitable present. China town, surprisingly enough, could not provide dragon finger-puppets, so I opted for a complicated pop-up book and copy of A. A. Milne's

When We Were Very Young. The old classics still hold their appeal and on my baby-sitting duties I would half read, half act the poems to make her laugh. *The Bad Sir Brian Botany* was her favourite. Mine too at her age.

We were all invited to a barbecue at the opulent home of Mark's boss, another Pommie. Trevor had managed to hang on to his strong Birmingham accent and, having built a successful construction company, was a lesson in what can be achieved in Australia with hard work. He had not long since suffered an expensive divorce and rather than sit and mope, he had celebrated by going to Thailand at the age of fifty to find a new wife. He found Dym (whom he called Tim) about half his age and who spoke very limited English. No doubt Lakana's connection made sure Mark was never short of work. As a condition of the marriage, Dym had brought her eight-year-old son Yort with her, who had turned into the all-Australian boy, never removing his baseball cap and only eating burgers, while Trevor insisted on meat and two veg and Dym only ate Thai. Meal times were complicated events.

Dym had just revealed to her new husband that she had two younger daughters whom she wished to bring over – with her mother. I think Trevor was a little confused about who he had married and what it was all going to cost. On the surface it looked as if the man had been well stitched up, although it was a symbiotic relationship, with Dym providing sex on demand. What I would have found unappealing with such a partnership is the lack of a good conversation and a laugh *after* sex.

At dawn the following day, Mark led me to the best road out of town behind his Yamaha 1100 – and then he was gone. A knot of excitement gripped my stomach – the Triumph team were 'on the road again'. That song by Canned Heat flooded into my head at some time on most days and had been a real inspiration to keep moving. With a rekindled sense of adventure, I headed into mountains cast blue with the breath of gum trees. Australia may be the smallest, flattest continent, but the interior is vast and the mountains gave the impression of being pretty high on that bright cool morning. Good roads meandered through villages with neat low-rise brick buildings reminiscent of Wales.

With the dust settling and Sydney some 450 miles away, I descended to the orchards and vineyards of Griffith. The air was heavy with the scent of citrus fruit and the makings of fine vin rouge. Most of the population may be third generation Australian, but they choose to converse in Italian, the tongue of their recent ancestors. Close your eyes, and the smells and sounds are pure southern Europe.

The Trophy pulled up outside the first bar to let its rider wash the dust from his throat after a reasonable day's ride. Half a dozen hairy bikers in well-worn leathers scrutinised my every move. One went out to inspect the overloaded bike as no branding was visible with the tank bag in place. He returned saying, "don't punch him guys, it's a Trumpet." I dread to think what would have happened if the bike had been from a factory of the rising sun and it was reassuring to see the respect commanded by the badge of a British legend.

They were Black Uhlan, proud of their German roots and enjoyed the reputation of an aggressive chapter of Harley riders. More ZZ Top beards than you can wave an oily rag at blew in the wind as a convoy cruised through town with a Pommie bastard in tow, ready to enjoy their unique style of hillbilly hospitality down at their club house. After rather too many beers, most of us sank into unconsciousness rather than sleep.

The following morning, I nursed my hangover all the way to the suburbs of Adelaide before striking north for the Great Interior and my first experience of bush camping.

When sleeping out, especially without a tent, many precautions have to be taken and survival rules followed. Unfortunately I had no idea what they were so was making it up as I went along. Set up camp well off the road, keeping newly-acquired machete close at hand to ward off intruders, reptilian or mammalian. Roll out sleeping bag on the right of the bike in case the side stand loses its footing in the night. On that note, share a traveller's observation. Regardless of the country of manufacture, or side of the road ridden on, the kick stand is always on the left. My theory is that is the side a horse is mounted from.

From the beginning, a 'no tent no map policy' had been the source of grief and joy. Getting wet had been depressing on rainy nights, but at least a quick get-away would be possible in an emergency. As predicted, getting lost was almost a daily occurrence, but the reward was an alternative world far from the tourist trail and a compass was enough to point me in the direction of the next country – well, most of the time. On leaving Sydney, Mark had given me a road map but I lost it in the Black Uhlan clubhouse and it was far more interesting not to know the name of the next town.

Once the fire had died and bread with 'tasty' cheese had been consumed, there was little left to do but swat mozzies and contemplate the Southern Cross in an ocean of stars. Loneliness can be a very liberating feeling. Without contact with any other human being, all I had to worry about was the next day on the road. After nearly five months, waking up each morning wondering where the hell I was had become the norm. First tricky task was to find clothes, as they were the same colour as the dirt they lay in. Clean teeth with the remains of last night's flat beer and return contact lenses to eyeballs, attempting to remove a crust of desert sand from their surface. Check fire was well extinguished and collect up or bury any rubbish. That first morning presented a bit more of a challenge as a near gale force wind during the night had scattered my measly possessions over a good deal of South Australia. With the strength returning to my shoulders after the enforced break, I was ready to take on the magnificent, shimmering Stuart Highway.

One of the great pioneers of Australia was John McDouall Stuart, an engineer of remarkable tenacity, who first forged a path across that barren landscape in 1860. He was beaten back by hostile natives just short of his goal of the Northern Territory, but his legacy lives on. For the best part of a century, the red ribbon of earth was systematically washed away in winter and blown away the rest of the year, until a seven-year project joined Darwin to the south with a black line probably visible from the moon on a clear day. Fifty meter road trains using the road must also be visible from a considerable altitude. They are uncompromising when on the move as it takes forever for them to get up to speed and then stop again.

The strong crosswind persisted to Coober Pedy, an opal mining town of some 1,500 souls. The constant buffeting made progress hard work and overtaking road trains dangerous. Riding on the lee side of the monsters brought a little respite, until being nearly blown off the road after passing the cab. All in all, the road was not proving to be as much fun as I had expected and, to make matters worse, two bike problems presented themselves. The

£200 Mexican back tyre had lost pressure and shed all its side rubber from riding at 45 degrees for two days. Secondly, the fuel tap crumbled in my hand turning it from reserve. Even twisting the control flange with pliers did not release all the available fuel, so I kept the two spare tanks topped up, further increasing weight.

Continuing with the back tyre in that state would have been extremely dangerous if it blew out at speed. Also, a bike parked on the roadside while getting the tyre fixed would have been an open invitation to theft. One of the many things not available in Coober Pedy (surprise surprise) was a back tyre for a Triumph, but a local garage arranged to have one put on the night bus from Adelaide.

I checked into a cheap hostel and spent the rest of the day exploring the rather weird town suffering from a grit storm that attacked every bit of exposed skin like sandpaper. In the strong wind, it was difficult to appreciate a temperature of 38 degrees.

Most people in Coober Pedy were miners looking for that 'get rich quick' opal discovery. To escape dramatic changes in temperature, they choose to live underground in 'dug-outs'. The principle is easy. Find a hill, bulldoze a flat slab on one side and start digging. Some sink well below ground level and are, by any standards, sophisticated homes. Even the parish church is underground. There was a story going around that one dweller started digging a new bedroom when his wife became pregnant and discovered such a rich opal vein he could afford to retire to the east coast.

By far the most interesting place to visit is an elaborate museum hewn out of Mother Earth as a testament to the remarkable achievements of the pioneer John Stuart. All very riveting stuff, but after a couple of hours I found the underground existence a little claustrophobic and was glad to face the red dust tornado outside. Wandering round a large building with no windows, no natural light at all, becomes oppressive for those uninitiated in the art of subterranean living.

The morning brought a new tyre and change in weather. The temperature dropped 30 degrees and freezing rain turned dirt roads into a quagmire of crimson mud. Confused barefoot aborigines shivered on the streets in minimal clothing clutching the ubiquitous 'tinny' of VB beer.

Although their livelihood is protected in most parts of the continent, their quality of life in white man's settlements is generally sub-standard. This could have been self-inflicted to some extent but, like American Indians, Africans or the population of the Indian sub-continent, they were perfectly happy until greedy pale faces came to rule by the gun.

Out in the elements once more it was immediately apparent how much the ailing back tyre had been affecting performance and I discovered the best tactics for coping with a raging storm is to attack. When the wind veered north, charging at 110mph headlong into the teeth of the cyclone was the best choice, but fuel consumption rocketed. Matters were frequently made worse when local meteorology shifted the gale 90 degrees to the west. A full-face helmet presents considerable wind resistance from the side and I was compelled to keep stopping just to face the other way for a while to let my neck recover. I developed a technique of hanging my bum and most body weight into the crosswind to keep the bike upright.

A combination of fatigue and fuel feed problems meant stopping at most roadhouses that occur every hundred miles or so. At one, a very sensible, well-packed BMW Boxer sat outside streaked in mud. Time for a hot coffee and chat. Hermut was in his mid-thirties and even scruffier than me. He was so exhausted he kept dropping into his native German just when his English was getting impressive. He had camped out in his excellent little tent, but had only managed half my mileage that day and had not got the strength to continue. "Give me za hills of Buvaria any day - it is warmer zan dis desert."

We were both heading north and the prospect of a travel companion for a while, especially one far more experienced than me, was quite appealing, but I was resolved to press on for some better weather. Another 150 miles and fading light said it was time to stop. I had not seen a live kangeroo, but dead ones littered the road. Hitting such a big animal could be terminal, so night riding was out of the question. Avoiding *one* may be easy enough, but generally his friend would be right behind.

Since reading *A Town Like Alice* as a child I had always wanted to visit the desert town. Who would want to live in such a remote place? The answer is, very few people and it proved to be a terrible disappointment. Much smaller than expected, travel shops promising adventure in the wilderness rubbed shoulders with tourist shops selling didgeridoos probably made in Taiwan. The route bisecting Australia was turning out to be a dreadful mistake. Either coast would have been far more interesting.

I sent a couple of ridiculous postcards depicting whales leaping through the surf saying 'Welcome to Alice Springs'. The nearest sea was not much short of a thousand miles away. I pushed on towards sub-tropical Northern Territory. Yet again, the bike handling started to deteriorate. My brand new tyre was going down due to the defective valve, and for some reason very few road houses had air pumps, but a road train driver came to my rescue as they carry compressors on board. As we sat inside over a 'thank you' beer, a donkey walked past the window with Wayne's hat in its mouth. That hat had travelled on the back of my bike a very long way and, frankly, I was rather upset about having to retrieve a half eaten chewed up mess from the donkey's mouth.

15. Wizard of Oz

There is no speed limit on the Stuart Highway north of Alice Springs. It is where they run the famous Cannonball Road Race, but I could not take full advantage of it because of the ailing back tyre. Thankfully, the temperature increased every mile and I started shedding grimy T-shirts until the high humidity had me sweating wearing only one. Spontaneous bush fires erupted on both sides of the road often reducing visibility to a few feet and the flames licking the verge were hot enough to singe naked arms. Although the sight was dramatic, they sweep through the trees at such a pace very little damage is done to upper branches and it keeps the undergrowth in check. Some plant species depend on fire to induce germination when the ground is free of competitors, so nature is left to its own devices in growth control.

Another striking feature of the landscape is fascinating termite mounds frequently taller than a man. Millions of tiny white ant architects construct the most elaborate homes resembling miniature versions of the Grand Canyon. The population is so dense they form their own forests amongst the trees in a sea of manufactured stalagmites. Occasionally a whole field of 'magnetic' structures break the horizon. They form blades with the long edge running precisely north-south to give the flat sides maximum sunlight. Aborigines have used them for generations to navigate across otherwise featureless landscapes.

A combination of bike problems and long-awaited sun, at last, took priority over mile munching. This was the Australia I had come to see. At a fuel stop, a gang of sixteen German bikers pulled over for a rest. At enormous expense, they had air-freighted their Japanese single or twin cylinder enduro machines to Perth. They had three months to travel Australia, but despite their machines being built for the job, not one had been off a bitumen road in the first eight weeks. I asked one of them if he had considered purchasing a bike in Perth and selling it at the end to save costs, but he had not thought of that. He proudly announced he had a Triumph Triple at home, but did not consider bringing it as it would not have put up with the conditions. I felt like punching him after what my Trophy had been through and, worse, what it had to come.

Dave Barr had given me the address of a couple who lived near Darwin and had helped him on his travels. Even though I had sent several cards to warn them of my imminent arrival, these are always tricky times when you have no idea what sort of welcome you are likely to receive. Not many people get excited about the prospect of a stranger turning up on their doorstep asking for help, but Dave had said the Walkers were good people who had happily shared their home with him when he had had bike problems in the Northern Territory.

Just a few miles inland from the north coast, a sign to Humpty Doo stood out like a beacon. The Triumph veered off to a little shopping precinct in search of a post office. My only information was a PO box number, but I figured that, in a rural community of about 3,000, the post master would be a sensible person to ask.

While standing there, looking like only a lost English tourist can look, the taller of two locals interrupted their conversation to help. I took a flyer and asked if he knew Slim Walker. "Yep, he's standing right next to you - anything else?" The second of the pair fitted neither of these names, with an impressive beer belly protruding between shirt and shorts and he was supported by a single crutch of the Long John Silver variety. He presented a peculiar spectacle, but possibly not as peculiar as me. Neither of us had any notion of what to expect and on that first meeting I guess the revelation was mutual. Slim had been practically crippled some three years previously when a minor knee operation following a motorcycle accident had gone badly wrong. The resultant traumatic bone infection was so severe further surgery was not possible for years. Staggering about on a crutch for so long had devastated his hip and other knee joint. He obviously put up with great discomfort, but I never heard him complain.

After establishing I was the Pommie he was expecting, the instruction to follow his ute (pick up) seemed easy enough - that is, when it was visible through the cloud of red dust from the dirt road. On either side mango plantations brimmed with heavily-laden fruit. Trees were resplendent with bourgainvillia adding to the explosion of colour. The sun shone – it was blisteringly hot and I caught sight of a live kangaroo hopping across the road, proving the liberal number of dead ones scattered over the highway were not just for the benefit of tourists.

When Slim pulled off the road, rippled like a river bed, it was to five acres of carefully planned jungle. Capability Brown would have sold his mother for those trees. He had had to plant for his grandchildren, but in the Northern Territories less than a decade is needed to reach horticultural maturity. Linda, Slim's wife and the visionary behind the garden, welcomed me to their splendid home. Like most houses in the area, it was constructed in alloy panels with leafy verandahs and patios nearly doubling the floor area. A small swimming pool with no straight sides sat comfortably in a sheltered oasis of its own. Fireballs of puce, vermilion and flame orange erupted from succulent shrubs in every direction. Not a great deal was needed for peace of mind in Linda's version of a tropical paradise and once the beer bill was paid, feeding two colossal but affectionate bull mastiffs was probably the next biggest expense. Linda doted on the dogs and they were more efficient than a door bell. Unwittingly, I made a grave, insensitive error by patting one of them just after it had been rebuked by its owner. Social faux-pas are the easiest way to piss people off, even apparently little ones. Uninvited guests should attempt to make themselves invisible to let their hosts get on with their lives. Watch where people sit to relax or at table to make sure you do not elevate yourself or sit in *their* chair. Smoke only if they do and do not hog the bathroom. Basic social skills, but this can be confusing as every culture is different. Mistreating someone's pets in a negative or positive way is possibly the biggest gaffe of all and I had just jumped in with both feet trying to be 'nice'.

A fabulous meal of massive fresh shrimps and crab appeared from nowhere after I had shed several layers of dirt in the pool. Linda just smashed them up with a hammer for us to scoop out the tender meat and wash down with ice cold beer. That may have been a typical evening with the Walkers, or extraordinary as there was someone new at their table, but their hospitality to a stranger was astounding, despite me being slow to learn Northern Territories etiquette. To avoid becoming a permanent spare part in their home, I immediately started making plans to move on.

Darwin shipping agents did not advise taking the bike to Indonesia as it would have to be crated and the authorities there do not like importing vehicles faster than the police cars. This was a little disappointing as I had wanted to go there and have been told it is brilliant riding, although island hopping can be difficult and expensive. Singapore was the only sensible solution so I booked the bike on the next ship out. This left me a few more days to ride around a bit more of the North Coast before surrendering the Triumph to customs once more.

Most of that part of Australia was totally undeveloped, although beach-front plots were being sold to people wanting to take advantage of all that natural beauty. No doubt the area was destined for development, but at that time a deeply rutted dirt track had to be negotiated before finding the sea. Secret places, with practically no access to prevent discovery, make you feel like a real explorer privileged to witness beauty reserved for the few. As Australia is so vast and the population so sparse, it offers such treats by the score and I was pleased to have found my isolated spot on the beach to camp for the night. The sunset was like a furnace, with distant storm clouds adding fuel to a flaming horizon. Smoke from bush fires exaggerated an inferno slowly extinguished by the sea. I watched, totally captivated, from my carefully selected 'deserted' spot.

"G'day Mate. Just thought I'd pop over and tell ya, that's not a good place to camp - salties 'll ave ya." Owen went on to explain that salt-water crocodiles are ferocious killers and, since the rivers had become overcrowded, they have taken to lunching on tourists enjoying the body temperature sea. These are the most successful eating machines on the planet. Descended from dinosaurs, they can live in fresh or salt water and can run across the land as fast as a man. Once they have a good hold of a foot, they drag their victim into the water, roll them until drowned – then supper time. Owen's face wrinkled into a disarming smile. "...... just thought I'd mention it as I saw a fifteen footer last night just where your sleeping bag is now. You'd be much better off on the grass higher up – where all the snakes are. You hungry? Me mate and me were just about to throw some roo tail and ram's bollocks on the fire. Interested?" Well, you can not go refusing invitations like that, can you?

Owen's camp was only a couple of hundred yards up the beach, but well away from the sand. A big van with a refrigerated trailer formed a backdrop to the camp with a couple of 'bivvies' laid out in front of a camp fire. Bivvies are a splendid arrangement of sleeping bag and small tent combined. Waterproof, mozzie proof and very comfortable, but much too bulky for me to carry. The flickering fire revealed a wrinkly old man working at an enormous frying pan in the flames. "That's Cuz. He doesn't say much. Saves his strength for abbo girlfriends. Tinny, Mate?" Owen said with a chuckle, as he threw me a can of cool beer.

Cuz (Cousin) was seventy but looked ten years older with a toothless grin and body as wiry as a blackthorn. Leathery, matchstick legs protruded from baggy shorts, with an equally baggy AIDS Relief T-shirt completing the fashion statement. Owen, on the other hand was nearly sixty, but looked a decade younger. Solid, powerful shoulders supported a fresh face with sparkling pastel-blue eyes. Tufts of blond hair peeped out from the sweat-stained rim of a leather bush hat. He had left his wife and decided to 'get some living in', so he travelled all over Australia selling kangaroo tails to Aborigines. The money was not important, but it gave him a motive to travel around. Fluent in two Aboriginal dialects, he had great respect for the indigenous people who had taught him to survive in the bush. "Hell, even Cuz's Mum has a bit of abbo in her – quite frequently, so I'm told."

Owen's ancestors were among the original Botany Bay pioneers and he was proud his new great-grandson was eleventh generation Australian, still living on the family homestead in Carnarvon. I told him of the one in Wales, still the ancient site of royal investiture as it was in the days of Owen Glendower, the wizard Welsh king. He was fascinated by the story of the fearsome warrior doing battle with Bolingbroke, later to become Henry V, and decided it must be his heritage.

Not for the first time 'when in Rome ....' applied, as a near vegetarian Pommie tucked into delicious kangaroo tail and ram's testicles, before partaking in the traditional Aussie activity of drinking yourself into oblivion. The sultry night air made it too hot for sleeping bags. "What do you do if it rains," I asked him. "Turn over and get the other side cool," was his truthful answer.

To Owen, life in the bush was the natural thing to do and maybe, if he had been thrown into the middle of Times Square or Piccadilly Circus, his survival skills would have been sadly lacking. The outback was his home, a place that may seem hostile, even alien to most city folk, but I loved it and was eager to learn more. This was the very reason for taking on the adventure in the first place. The very reason for not carrying a map. No cartographer could have found me that idyllic spot with an encyclopaedic bush guru. He laughed at my ignorance and naïve questions, but without mirth or superiority, and always gave me a truthful answer. More than once my response to his answers was "You're kidding me." "I never joke about the dangers out here – that way you could end up killing someone. You may be a bit stupid and only a skinny little Pom, but that's better than being a *dead* skinny little Pom."

My mind was a sponge absorbing every bit of fascinating information from a real life 'Sundowner' and I desperately wanted to spend more time in that knowledgeable man's company. They were heading south to Katherine and he recommended a ride around the area. "Will I be able to get a shower round there as I'm caked in dust at the end of each day?" "No worries mate, go and see Edith."

Edith Falls was a welcome relief and the most devastating shower provided courtesy of Mother Nature. A swim in the lake got my temperature down to boiling point after riding slowly on rough roads all day. The engine heat was singeing the hairs on my legs and then the bike got stuck in a rut and fell. On the way down my right shin made contact with the red-hot exhaust. Severe blistering was prevented by applying a cold beer bottle at every opportunity.

Katherine Gorge was a little too organised for my liking, but beautiful nevertheless. I kept riding to where the dirt track divided and the flip of a coin took me to an empty camping park where the road terminated at a shack doubling as a pub. The only other customers were two middle-aged German hunters with an Aussie guide. They were there to shoot buffalo that, although not indigenous to Australia, roam wild in some areas. In long flannel trousers and military camouflage jackets they were having trouble coping with the heat, despite travelling in an air-conditioned Nissan. One of the hunters boasted he could shoot a bull from a quarter of a mile away. Bloody hero. Where is the fun in that? Give the animals guns to shoot back and really sort the men from the boys.

"Your shout Pom," came a familiar voice from behind me. "Cuz is off with one of his lady friends, so thought I'd track ya down before dark." I never did discover how Owen knew where to find me. "Ya may not look like much of a meal for a croc, but it would be a shame to loose a proper adventurer." This I took to be a staggering compliment. "Unlike the fat Krouts," he continued in a loud voice glancing at the hunters. Hunting for pleasure he considered to be obscene, upsetting the status quo of Australia's fragile ecology.

I purchased a 'slab of tinnies' for the evening entertainment and we retired to his camp by the side of a gurgling thermal spring. Stark bollock naked, we bobbed about in a warm, crystal-clear thermal spring, drinking beer until the sun went down. "Snakes 'll be out soon and you could get bitten treading on one in the dark," he explained. As many as a third of Australian snakes are venomous and potentially lethal if not properly treated in an hour or so. Northern Territory is notorious for black or brown monsters up to six feet in length, some of which have been known to attack unprovoked. He gave me advice as to what to do if bitten. "Probably won't do ya much good, but at least ya have a better chance than if a salty gets hold." Reassuring stuff!

On our way down for an early morning dip, Owen showed me fresh crocodile tracks in soft mud, explaining how he knew from the size and shape that they were only 'freshies', (freshwater) beasts a few feet long. "That was lucky," I said, realising we had been camping only a few yards from all the night time activity. "Luck," he laughed, "rely on luck, and you're croc tucker."

My travels had been enriched and made a little safer by a chance meeting with a charismatic character and I had one more night out in the bush to enjoy before returning to the sanctuary of Linda's magnificent garden. With Owen's words still ringing in my ears, I spent a day riding through fantastic tropical rain forest in Litchfield National Park stopping periodically for a swim in lagoons fed by waterfalls. Not far away, Lake Bardon showed no signs of human activity, so I set up camp determined to use the tiny camping cooker and billy can purchased in Sydney on Mark's advice. In near darkness I found the meths bottle, followed the instructions, but there was no way the thing was going to perform so I built a substantial open fire to heat my beans.

The problem with the cooker was identified in the flickering light. I had filled it with water, not fuel as the bottles were nearly identical. These little incidents were, more often than not, caused by my own stupidity, which made me angry, but as in this case, were also the source of great humour. It is too late to say 'if only', too late to curse the gods for not making me think a little harder before acting. Once the damage is done, the only thing to do next is find a solution. Nevertheless, it is amazing how profoundly depressing minor problems can be and how elating it is when you get something right. By the time I had got a roaring fire going on that particular sultry night, there was still plenty of time for more to go wrong.

The night air was so still cigarette smoke rose vertically without wavering and then the bugs came out to feed on the blood of an Englishman. The worst were sinister-looking sand flies, green in colour and about the size of a house fly, but with a ferocious bite. They approached with a low buzzing note – the B52's of insects. Wait until the drone stops, then start slapping every bit of exposed flesh before being clamped by merciless mandibles. Fortunately they were slow and generally got swatted for their trouble. The cloud of mosquitoes was worse and drove me under my sleeping bag, made into a rudimentary tent with only my nostrils peeping out. In fading torch light, it became apparent I was in the middle of a vast swarm blotting the stars from view.

In high humidity, on a sweltering night, I sat by a raging fire, covered in a thermal sleeping bag – sweating buckets. What would Owen have made of *my* bush craft? The thought made me laugh hysterically, spilling beer all over my quilted shelter. The front line mozzie attack eventually moved off leaving only a couple of million stragglers, so I threw off the protection to let them get on with it. I would have to manage on the blood they left behind. The high-pitched whine of gossamer wings became so familiar, I could identify individual insects and became intimate with family groups hell bent on a banquet. On a trip to the water's edge to retrieve cooling beer, the swarm moved over the lake making the surface boil with jumping gold fish looking for supper. A startling sight in torch light, as reflected flashes of gold illuminated the turbulent water.

Sleep did not come easily with thoughts of crocs and snakes, even after the aerial wildlife moved off in a welcome breeze. The potential dangers had prompted me to keep both machete and .38 Smith and Wesson close to hand. While drowsing, the breeze picked up momentarily, blowing a piece of string across my face. I jumped about three feet vertically, cocking revolver in mid flight and nearly amputated my willy with the machete. What I had neglected to do was locate the torch, so I stood a good chance of shooting my own foot off trying to hit a snake that did not exist. Even in the hands of experts, guns are dangerous things and it was clear I either needed to ditch the thing or learn how to use it with relative safety

16. Another Stressful Day in Humpty Doo

In the comfort of the Walker's home, I had a little time to prepare the Triumph for its passage to Singapore. Whilst stowing the handgun back under the seat, Slim inspected the bullets provided with it. They were just target rounds that would not shoot their way out of a cardboard box. I had carried the thing half-way round the world and it was about as effective as a one-legged man at a bum-kicking party. Shouting 'bang', at an attacker would have been an equal deterrent. He told me to go to a sports shop in town to buy some proper rounds. Incredible though it may seem to an Englishman, from a country populated by ballistophobes, anyone in Australia can purchase ammunition over the counter for just about any firearm without showing documents of any description. This will inevitably change as the world becomes a more violent place with guns at the root of the problem. Australia will never rate with the USA for gun-related crime and new legislation is severely curbing ownership of any firearms. However, the masterful Slim Walker had identified my dangerous ignorance of handguns and set about decreasing my chances of self-inflicted wounds. With the patience of a saint, he let me accompany him to his gun club. He possessed two .45 automatics and a .45 revolver. Knocking targets over using a high-tech laser sight was easy, although I was painfully slow compared to his performance. Slim's expertise was appreciated and made me a little safer in possession of a firearm.

After telling him about Owen's advice regarding crocodiles, he suggested I took a boat down the Adelaide River to see them in the wild for myself. Flat-bottomed tourist boats carry twenty or so croc watchers down the muddy river, swollen by the onset of the rainy season. Crocodiles are versatile enough to take advantage of any new source of food and have developed an impressive jumping technique to feast on fruit bats resting in branches of mangrove trees that overhang the river. Fruit bats grow to be the size of a domestic cat and make a tasty morsel for even the biggest opportunist croc. Killing both freshies and salties in the wild has been outlawed, unless one has hold of your foot, but the Australians have turned a natural resource into a passive form of commercial enterprise by taking advantage of the bold salties' considerable hunting instincts.

They have become accustomed to the chugging boats and are more than happy to perform for tourists to be rewarded with an easy meal. Lumps of meat dangle tantalizingly on a booms a few feet above the water. Monsters up to twenty feet in length, weighing as much as a ton, slither from muddy banks and stealthily snake their way through the water. One almighty flick of an awesomely powerful tail easily thrusts unforgiving jaws a few feet out of the water for an easy breakfast. Their agility and ability to learn is quite remarkable for a reptile with more brawn than brain.

Slim and Linda invited me to visit their latest real estate acquisition at Dundee Beach, not far from where I had met Owen a few days previously. The ute was packed up and a trailer carrying a sit-on mower the size of a combine harvester attached. For Ben and Miggy, the two dogs, this was a maiden voyage, so Linda volunteered to sit with them in the open-sided truck behind the cab. For some miles she suffered grit and stones thrown up by the wheels on bumpy dry dirt. Localised storms indicating the onset of the rainy season had churned a rough road into a mud bath and Slim demonstrated his considerable driving skill negotiating lakes of blood-red sludge, attempting to give Linda a more comfortable ride in the back.

Eventually he steered off the road into a rough driveway that cut a swathe through virgin jungle terminating abruptly at the Timor Sea. A sea-view glade had been forged into rampant bush where we stopped to rescue Linda and dogs, all three of whom were encrusted in dust and mud. Fresh water had to be collected from a communal pump, while Linda, unperterbed by her ride, prepared an impressive fire from the lifetime's supply of dry timber lying around on the plot.

I took my chances with the salties and went for a swim to shift a day's grime. It was the only time in my life where sea water has been significantly above body temperature. Linda threw half a cow onto Dante's inferno while we sat back sucking beer and watching a perfect orange orb sink gracefully into the ocean in true Hollywood tradition. All over the world, people's tempers are being put to the test at traffic lights in every major city, leaving me wondering *why?*

We all have our own thesis on what normal is and a good deal of it, like commuting to work with millions of other people, is unappealing. What

I was doing for 'fun' may be very unappealing to many people, but it is remarkable how 'normal' it felt and I was beginning to worry about my ability to slot back in to the rigid structure of contemporary western society when it was all over. The popular conception of normality had been a way of life for me for nearly half a century. The experience of travel was profoundly moulding my attitude to life and I was resolved to embrace the re-awakening – change the rules – move the goal posts – anything but jumping back on to a bandwagon playing unplatable music. The how, when and where would have to wait, as the Triumph was stowed in a container and I was off to a different, but familiar culture in South East Asia. But, not for the first time, I had placed myself in someone's debt and there was no real way of showing my appreciation for their tolerance when Slim drove me to Darwin in readiness for an early morning flight.

Some twenty years previously, Cyclone Tracy had interrupted the Christmas celebrations of the 14,000 inhabitants of Darwin by completely flattening the town. Planners had taken advantage of a clean canvas and created a new image from scratch. It does not take long to absorb that tidy, well laid-out town and predictably the last evening was spent in a pub reflecting on Oz – a very enjoyable milestone in my journey of discovery. I had seen the East Coast, ridden its length through a desert wilderness, met some exceptional people, but not really scratched its surface. After the rigors of Central America it had been easy travel with time for a little introspective thought about the meaning of life. Australia represented more than a new stamp in my passport. It was the first time I had really appreciated that this whole travel experience thing was as much about discovering myself as our fascinating planet. It was more than just something that happened because I got bored one afternoon, it had real purpose and was giving me an understanding into the minds of those who find salvation within themselves. I have never subscribed to any religious doctrine, just the opposite, but travel with its integral and inevitable education presented a plausible 'belief', although I was still struggling to define what *that* 'belief' was all about.

A youth hostel was home for a night with only the sound of geckos barking to break the silence. A bullfrog joined in, sitting on the window ledge puffing out its almost transparent gossamer membrane like someone chewing bubble gum. They do look perilously vulnerable puffing out a bulbous balloon twice the size of their heads. I was grateful to that bullfrog for reminding me of all the magnificent wildlife, much of it unique, that I had been privileged to witness on a vast isolated island. It had all been new to me and a world away from one of the most crowded islands on this planet.

Although Singapore's religious community is not dominated by Christians, the night streets were ablaze with illuminated Christmas decorations the night I arrived. Any excuse to feed a buoyant economy and whip up more visitors into the shopping frenzy. I was ten years old the first time my father walked me round the streets of Old China Town and the Indian quarter. Bugie Street was the most notorious red light district in the world and a lively tourist area. My ex-wife had brought me back to the island thirty years later and there was not a building other than Raffles Hotel that I recognised. Lee Kuan Yu had created his own vision of a thriving cosmopolitan city without a plant or brick out of place. A few crumbling streets still remained as a token of Singapore's oriental heritage, but even these were due to be rebuilt for the benefit of tourists rather than the local inhabitants. Bugie Street had just reopened as an immaculate and very respectable market overflowing with touristy restaurants and bars.

Compared to the Singapore of my childhood, I was now in a characterless town where even the possession of chewing gum is a caning offense and people are employed to sit under trees with baskets to prevent leaves from fouling the footpaths. That last bit is a lie of course, but the bit about chewing gum is true. Apparently, when the subway system and pride of Singapore first opened, someone prevented the automatic door closing by placing a lump of the evil goo on a door jamb delaying a busy rush-hour train. An emergency debate in Parliament voted overwhelmingly to ban the substance and shops were given 24 hours to shift it from the shelves. Wrigley went underground. Most water sports are prohibited anywhere near the harbour area (so take your fishing rod for a long walk to avoid prosecution) and smoking is banned in open-air taxi queues. One person standing by the road is permitted, but two people constitutes a queue, so put the fag out.

They claim there is no prostitution or drug abuse, but the hangman's noose is in regular use and a caning machine has taken over from Chinese jailers to ensure impartiality. It is, however, a bustling, energetic, twenty-four-hour community of mixed races and religions living in relative harmony. Moslem, Buddhist and Hindu temples are comfortable neighbours with Christian churches or synagogues. Although the official language had just changed from English to Mandarin, everyone could communicate well with an ignorant old biker. Massive government controlled eating markets ensure everyone can buy an excellent meal for about a pound. To keep prices low, the vendors do not pay taxes and the competition is strong. Despite being the only white diner, I took advantage of them at every opportunity. The frantic pace was very stimulating as I fell into a bowl of excellent fish wan ton to the rhythm of a hundred chattering woks.

By far the best value-for-money accommodation in Singapore are small Chinese guest houses which, although they tend to be a little sparse, are always spotlessly clean. After checking into one at random for a few dollars, I rang yet another of Dave Barr's contacts. Luckily for me, he had accumulated a shed load of names and addresses of sympathetic people prepared to lend a helping hand, but I was a little unsure of his perspective. The only thing we had in common was a desire to travel on motorcycles and it would be a fair assessment to say that we were not out of the same pod. Slim Walker commented on how different we were, so what was the next one going to think of me and, frankly, how happy would you be if you let one in and were then bombarded by a string of uninvited house guests?

Ben Lackey was just as Dave described – a good-time Yank of about fifty with an affinity for bikes. His home was an absolute showpiece of elegant and very expensive-looking furniture and objects d'art. The showpiece in his sitting room was a beautifully painted and maintained Harley Davidson. Getting it in and out whenever he fancied a ride must have been quite an operation as the wheels and tyres would have to be meticulously cleaned before riding it across a pale beige shagpile carpet.

He was very helpful and knowledgeable about Singaporean ways as he had been a resident for six years. There was one more day before my bike was to arrive, so Ben said I could stay at a friend's house who was away on

The Bike Attracted Attention The World Over

Getting up in the morning, always with an audience: Rajasthan, Northern India

How many cylinders? Kenya, East Africa

There Are Some Interesting People Out There

I thought I'd pulled, but alas a lady boy: Bangkok, Thailand

Friendly cop: Central Mexico

Bath time: Nicaragua style

The bodyguard, the dealer, the wife: Medellin, Columbia

Two generations of Triumph Trophy: Penang, Malaysia

The team that bought my smashed up bike to Delhi

Robbie Wasn't The Only Thing On Two Wheels

'Taxi, Sir?':
Southern
Mexico

She thought she had
discovered an alien in
a space hemet:
Pisagua, Chile

Motorcycle
sound system:
Columbian style

Absent Friends

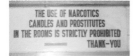

The notice outside my bedroom:
Bangkok, Thailand

Robbie and Marian reunited:
Bangkok, Thailand

How many sarongs does one
person need? Marian:
Koh Samui, Thailand

Robbie, Simon Jones and the first glass of champagne.

business. A four-bedroomed mansion in the heart of the city was all mine. Americans abroad certainly live well.

Customs were efficient, but I was very disappointed to find my bike on the quayside with a flat back tyre and my crash helmet with the bullet hole in missing. Of all the things that could have been stolen, that was a surprise. I wonder what explanation the thief made up for having a helmet with a bullet hole in it. With some difficulty I managed to get the tyre reinflated and used my spare open-face helmet to ride behind Ben's car to a Triumph dealer. Harry Lee, the rotund and very jolly Chinese dealership owner sat us down for a chat and coffee while my bike was attended to by his mechanics. Whenever the touchy subject of spending money was on the agenda, I would get a bit fidgety speculating about the cost, but Harry's relaxed attitude was infectious and I was in for a lesson on customer relations, Singapore style. The pavement outside Harry's dealership doubled as a workshop, where two young mechanics performed with blinding enthusiasm and speed to keep labour costs down, pushing pedestrians into the road while preparing my bike, and Harry, with his perpetual reassuring smile kept my pulse rate under control. I think Harry spotted that I was not one of his wealthy Harley customers, so the bill was also a pleasant surprise.

He had some interesting views about Triumph's aggressive marketing approach and was not impressed with the way they conducted their business. Singapore probably has more bike dealers and workshops per square mile than anywhere in the world, many selling luxury bikes to a cash-rich society, yet, according to him, Triumph's uncompromising attitude has prevented penetration into a potentially massive market. In many parts of the world, especially the Far East, motorcycles fall into two categories. Small capacity machines (the Honda C90 being the world leader) are used as work horses and big ones are purely for the recreation of the rich. Singapore has more than its fair share of wealthy, aspiring bikers and, although Triumph have a range of very appropriate products, Harry did not think they had a hope in hell of selling any if they stoutly refused to consider nationalistic differences. For example, because of the lack of space, dealerships are inherently very small, so can not carry much stock and need to order smaller numbers of machines than in other countries. Also, he suggested Triumph encouraged him to carry an unnecessary amount of spares as well as branded clothing inappropriate to their climate. This may have just been his hobbyhorse for the day, but he was quite adamant at the time.

I was finding Singapore with its control-freak administration a little claustrophobic and crossing the causeway to Malaysia after only a couple of days, was an absolute joy. At the border there is a sign saying no locally registered vehicles are allowed to leave the country with less than three quaters of a tank of fuel. Petrol is about half the price in Malaysia, like most things, so without this rule being strictly enforced most motorists would have are happy to drive an extra mile or so to save a lot of money on a tankful, which was precisely what I was doing.

If you ask anyone to reflect back on their lives, there will always be a period of profound change or awakening. To those a generation older than me, it would probably be 'The War'. To others it may be the birth of children, finding a faith or time at university. With the mixed blessing of a military childhood (you get to see plenty of places, but it buggers up your education) *my* turning point – period of realization – was living on the Malay Peninsular as a developing child. The place was a revelation – a feast to young eyes eager to absorb everything new, from the colour of the people to the geckos on my bedroom ceiling. Malaya, as it was known then, was in a period of transition from British rule to independence and violent power struggles, between the appointed government and disgruntled terrorists, proliferated to add to the excitement.

Returning to a place after an absence of many years, I am always surprised how many things have changed, but more surprised by how many things have remained exactly the same. One dramatic change to Malaysia since my boyhood years is the fantastic motorway infrastructure, possibly the best but most confusing in the world. Motorcycles, mostly Honda C90s, are so numerous that dedicated motorcycle lanes are provided with crash barriers to keep two-wheelers safe from cars. Little detours divert bikes around toll booths making travel cheaper and special safe areas are provided under bridges for bikers to shelter from the rain, which were particularly useful to me as an unseasonable monsoon hit.

A damp trip to Kuala Lumpur was essential to claim the Indian visa I had arranged in Sydney, but had not been able to stay long enough to collect. All Indian administration seemed to run on a different time scale to the rest of the world and even trying to fathom their hours of opening was quite a challenge – once I had found it in that booming capital.

KL suffers from the same rebirth as Singapore, presenting a concrete jungle equivalent to any major Western capital. Skyscraper hotels and business centres make a statement about a flourishing economy, but have destroyed most of the evidence of the muti-cultural society that I knew and loved as a child. But Malays, Chinese, Indians and Europeans continue to live cheek by jowl, with each nationality fulfilling a niche that evolved over years of British rule and has been maintained since independence. All residents have to be fluent in Malay, although English is taught to a high standard in schools. The Chinese also speak their own dialect, Cantonese or Hokkien for instance, and Mandarin, their common language. When you are aware children are skipping from one tongue to another, without taking a breath, it is impressive to a monolinguistic westerner.

With considerable devotion to duty, I managed to score a vital Indian stamp on my passport, but to my horror found out it would only have cost me half as much had I purchased it there rather than in Sydney. I could have off-set that against staying locally while it was being processed giving me more time to savour Malaysia. Although I had visited once since childhood, when my wife brought me back for a fortieth birthday present, this experience was very different. We did it the posh way in those days in featureless four-star hotels that grace skylines the world over. Internal travel was by air or air-conditioned hire car. On this occasion I was in the elements amongst locals that did not wear a waiter's uniform. I fell in love with the place all over again as youthful memories flooded back with every sight, sound and smell. To me, I find smell quite the most provocative sense when it comes to kick-starting a distant memory and I was being treated to a childhood full of them.

For once, time was on my side. It was mid-December and there were nearly two weeks before meeting Marian in Bangkok for Christmas, so I had a little time to indulge. The East coast was under three feet of water (there seems to be no happy medium with me and rain) so I kept the sea on my left heading north to Thailand, but could not resist the futuristic causeway from

Butterworth to Penang Island. In the last decade or so, much of the coast has developed into a tourist paradise for the well-heeled, but I was delighted to see most of George Town, the state capital, had not changed much in the last three decades.

Chulia Street is backpacker city with cheap guest houses providing rooms to Western travellers for a few pounds. I was resolved to stay for a couple of days to sort out an increasingly painful problem with my right hand. The strain of holding the throttle open all day, every day, had damaged a tendon in my wrist. A doctor in Darwin had gaven me some painkillers and anti-inflammatory cream and told me to rest it for six months as tendons take forever to heal. I was not in a position to take his advice so had to ride the length of Malaysia holding the throttle open with my forearm. I had even tried bandaging my hand to the twist grip, but any flexing of the wrist sent stabbing pains up my arm and across my shoulders. Continuing without a short rest would have exacerbated the problem, potentially terminating the adventure, so it was a good excuse to sit still for a couple of days with an arm in a sling.

Unlike the eastern Australian resorts, Chulia Street had a far more diverse cross-section of travellers. I admired the couples accompanied by their very small children. Life can be complicated enough for a young parents but, on the move, without the convenience of Cow & Gate and Pampers, they were working hard to give their kids that lifetime memorable experience.

There was an interesting conversation in every cafe and a warm welcome in every bar. Outside the Hong Kong Bar, I noticed a big twin squatting in the street with a helmet slung over a handlebar. Protective headgear is compulsory in Malaysia, although this was often interpreted as a woolly hat or a small wok tied on with string.

Seeing any bike above 125cc was rare and I was looking at a gem, so I went in to find the owner. Bill Townsend was an Aussie, a little older than me and with one of those faces permanently creased up in a disarming grin. Some years previously he had ridden his 25 year old Triumph Trophy to Penang from Sydney and stayed. He had bought a washing machine and ran a one-man laundry at his own pace. A couple of days in his company did body and soul a tremendous amount of good as depression was setting in about my ability to keep riding. We discussed at length the problems I was going to have entering Myanmar (Burma) because of the vicious war with Thailand and his information was that, even the Bangladesh border was closed. I had visas for both countries and it was the only land route to India. On his advice, I reluctantly checked out shipping agents to see if it was possible to jump a vessel to the subcontinent, but they all went via Singapore and there was no way I could sail with the bike. Despite newspaper reports of renewed conflict, I was determined to attempt crossing Myanmar. A young Burmese refugee said it was possible and gave me his family address in Rangoon, saying they would help if I ever got there.

I had always known Myanmar would be difficult, but I desperately wanted to go, not just because it was the only sensible overland route to India, but I had read enough to know it is a country of mystery, ancient culture and great beauty. My Father had fought his way across that forbidden country escaping Japanese soldiers during the last world war. Maybe I felt it owed me something. Now the vicious Myanmar political regime was at war with Thailand and there was severe unrest on its Bangladeshi border. The potential problems and dangers were too numerous and enormous to contemplate, but something irrational drew me to that country and I suspected being 'forbidden' had something to do with it. The possibility of danger was *frighteningly* tantilising and I was eager to learn more about the suppression of the people. I despirately wanted to walk the streets of Mandalay and I might never get this close again, so I was set to give it my best shot. Ever since being the target of a Columbian bandit, the expression 'best shot' had taken on new meaning when it came to calculating a risk but, before throwing myself at the mercy of Myanmar troops, my thoughts were focused on reaching Bangkok to see Marian and getting my wrist back into shape.

Two days of writing in a notebook with my left hand was all I could afford before bracing a slowly recovering wrist for the ride north to Thailand. Regrettably, all my efforts to become ambidextrous were in vain as the journal was lost. This may sound like a small detail, but it upset me as those spontaneous words were my only record of events apart from video footage.

17. Nit Noy Mao Felang

Once across the Thai border, I could not resist taking off my crash helmet, just because it was legal to do so. A liberating experience like skinny dipping – the fragment of cloth covering one's wedding tackle should make no difference, but it does. Also, because the roads are a long way from Malaysia's standard, traffic travels at a far more leisurely pace.

I was determined to follow the east coast, keeping the sea on my right this time, as it was a part of that beautiful country unknown to me. After Hat Yai, an unappealing town, I got hopelessly lost riding unmade roads looking for the coast. It was pure assumption that a road existed, but that part of the country is so thin, getting back to the Bay of Bengal from the South China Sea should not have been a problem.

I stopped in a little hamlet of wooden dwellings to get my bearings and a crowd of a dozen or so Thais emerged from a house to investigate. None of them spoke a word of English but we had a good laugh as I drew pictures of the seaside to tell them what I wanted. A large glass of mehkong fire-water whisky was offered and accepted as the bizarre graphic conversation developed. One phrase stuck in my mind. '*Nit noy mao felang*.' A little bit mad white person, I was later to discover. The one word most Thai people do understand is 'bungalow', used to describe holiday beach huts. Once this was established, finding the sea was relatively easy.

The road terminated at a small fishing village also used by locals as a holiday resort. There was only one hotel that looked much too expensive, but thankfully a woman who spoke Englishstepped from the crowd that surrounded my bike. She found me a splendid room for a couple of pounds and she asked if we could have a chat later in the evening. She was a school teacher and, as very few Westerners visited the area, she wanted to learn about European traditions and cultural differences between our nations.

One subject close to the heart of most Thai people is their monarchy. Pictures of the King and Queen hang somewhere in most households and the monarchs command a reverent respect, although they have no more political power than the British Royals. The King's birthday, a national holiday, was approaching and it is their version of Father's Day. She was surprised to hear that we hardly pay lip service to an imported American event that was invented for commercial reasons rather than paternal love and that we do not regard the British monarchy as being the guiding light of our nation.

The one piece of information I neglected to ask was the name of the village we were in. This ignorance was compounded up a good deal of the east coast as road signs were written in Thai script and no one spoke enough English in exclusively native resorts for me to ask. Despite verbal solitude and geographic ignorance, they were enjoyable days feeling my way north enjoying impromptu hospitality from locals in holiday mood. Unlike Malaysia, which is predominantly Moslem, but with a huge religious and cultural mix, Thailand is almost totally Buddhist and the people demonstrate their pacifist beliefs with an open show of friendliness. To them I was a curiosity as pale faces were a novelty in that part, especially ones on big blue motorbikes. Groups of laughing holiday makers would leave their beach parties to stop my progress, always with the obligatory glass of pungent mehkong. Sparkling bright-eyed children with wind-chime voices enjoyed a ride on the back of a British legend before the owner became too inebriated. It was difficult to refuse such enchanting faces.

With Bangkok in my sights and thoughts of Marian's imminent arrival, I had one more night before assaulting the most unruly traffic in the world. Roadside restaurants are generally good places to enquire about accommodation as some of them rent rooms. The pretty young waitress was of no help, but she sat next to me anyway to compare the colour of our arms. Mine were darker than hers which she didn't understand until I removed my watch to show normal white skin. She ran to the kitchen giggling and it sank in we were being watched. She returned dragging a rather embarrassed friend and indicated in no uncertain terms that I was welcome to stay the night with her. They probably just wanted to know what colour the rest of me was.

After dark, feeling exhausted and with a right arm about to seize up completely, I found a town with towering posh hotel blocks lighting up the night sky, all promising fun - in German. Voluminous whiter-than-white Europeans strutted the streets in loud shorts and 'kiss me slowly' hats, and bars claiming New Zealand, Australian, German or even Italian management lined the narrow streets.

I dropped into one at random to find a drunk Kiwi, claiming to be the owner sitting at a table. My understanding was that, only nationals were allowed to own businesses in Thailand. Foreigners were permitted a 49% shareholding, making them less than equal partners. The establishment was about to go bust, but he did not care as they could live with his wife's family in the north. He did not speak one word of Thai and boasted that his pregnant wife was kept in check by the fist.

He called to her for more beer and cigarettes and told me it was her birthday, insisting I attend a party later in the evening. Flattered by the invitation, I agreed as it was potentially interesting, and went off to find a cheap room to clean up. The problem of a present reared its ugly head, so I wrapped a Swiss Army knife in tissue and taped a couple of sparklers (purchased in New Mexico) to the package for extra effect. Granted the present was not up to much, but I hoped the presentation made up for it.

Three hours later, the Kiwi was still in the same chair, drunker than ever, with half a dozen other whites. The wife brought out food and beer for all (no wonder the place was going bust) and retired to the kitchen. After a couple of hours of hearing the guy telling the assembled company how great he was, I ducked into the kitchen, lit the sparklers, handed over the meagre gift and left. Less than a minute later (so the sparklers did not last long), she ran down the street to thank me for the thought, with genuine gratitude in her eyes. It was the only present she had received that day. Pity it was not something a little more exciting.

Ambling back to my three-pound-a-night room, sparkling laughter rippling on the night air attracted me to another establishment for a last Singah beer before bed. By contrast, and this is an observation not a nationalistic remark, the Italian co-owner spoke to his native wife in Thai and served at the bar while she waited at table. They had built the business up over four years and the books were 'looking healthy'.

Feeling uplifted by the change of attitude, I took up a fly-on-the-wall position to absorb the scene. The town is probably the nearest *felang* resort to Bangkok so the street was awash with pink blubber and beer bellies. Many tourists fly into the capital, buy a girl (or boy) and spend their holiday sitting around waiting for bed-time. One tall Scandinavian-looking man went to put his arm round his petite Thai 'girlfriend', but missed her completely so much was the height difference. With often only a dozen or so words between them, time must pass slowly and one wonders if inflating the economy is adequate compensation for the spread of AIDS.

After six months on the road, I was looking forward to a holiday. Many people would consider that the adventure so far had been a holiday, but body and soul were crying out for some unstressed rest as I forged my way to the fastest city on Earth.

Bangkok traffic flows faster than Mexico City, or any other city for that matter. Three-wheel, propane-driven 'tuk tuk' taxis weave alarmingly in and out of traffic queues, and I was quick to take advantage as they cleared a path for a lost Triumph. More than half the vehicles are bikes, generally 90cc Hondas that have undergone some severe tuning. They are used as family saloons (carrying up to five people at a time), taxis, delivery vans and police chase vehicles. When lights turn green, the smell of burning rubber and high-octane fuel stings the nostrils. The smoke from a couple of hundred bikes all doing a grand prix start seriously reduces visibility and the noise in a street of high-rise buildings is mind-numbing. After an hour or so of fruitless searching, I paid a bike taxi to lead me to Khao San Road, a haven just north of the river, bursting with life and totally dedicated to the needs of white backpackers.

Getting the bike off the packed road was essential, so I found a guest house with a forecourt and booked a spacious room in preparation for Marian's arrival the next day. Seeing her again after so long, in that alien place, was going to be a surreal experience, even though we had travelled extensively in South East Asia together before. Our reunion room had a nearly square double bed, with a full-length mirror running the length of it. Outside, a notice read: 'The use of narcotics, candles and prostitutes in the rooms is strictly prohibited - thank you.' Well, this was Bangkok after all.

The city changes pace after dark. Restaurants and bars spill into the streets, exacerbating traffic and pedestrian congestion. Prostitutes, drug dealers and market traders sell their wares amongst a sea of blond hair and pink faces. Staying anonymous is practically impossible as everywhere you sit down for a quiet Singah, someone will come and talk to you. A young wide-eyed Maori called Hemi was one such person who had seen me arrive on the bike. He had just had a mystical experience, and needed to tell someone.

In an adjacent street, an old Indian man in saffron robes had approached him and put a piece of paper in his hand, but did not allow Hemi to look at it. No money changed hands, but the Guru told the young New Zealander some revealing things about his life and predicted three things that would happen to him in the near future. The boy was still a little sceptical, so the Guru asked the name of his mother. It was a long, complicated Maori word. "Open the paper," said the old man. Written clearly, with correct spelling, was Hemi's mother's name. "Now you may make some wishes." Hemi thought of three and the Guru told him to look at the palm of his other hand. The number seven had magically appeared in ink. "Ah, so you are allowed seven wishes." Hemi was so impressed he gave the mystic all his money, leaving him nothing for the evening, so he asked for some of it back. Half was returned on the promise that after the second good prediction came true in 28 days, he was to send US$50 to an address in Kashmir. Not a bad party piece.

Hemi wandered off to tell someone else of his mystic experience and I was invited into a conversation with two men in motorcycle leathers. So far I had only met a handful of bike travellers, so two in one night was a bit overwhelming. We had all approached Bangkok from different directions. Theo, a Belgian, had just crossed the Middle East, Pakistan and India on, unbelievably, a 1947 350cc BSA. He could do anything to his bike, except remove the crank, with a tool kit that fitted into his pocket. By contrast Sjaak, a Dutchman, had ridden his Honda Fireblade of all things, across Europe and Russia. Honda were so impressed with his effortsthat, they had flown him and and his bike to the factory in Japan, 'where three men in white gloves rebuilt my filthy bike for free', then flown him on to Thailand. Triumph had not so much as given me the time of day. So typically British. For the first time a new generation Hinckley-produced bike was being put to the ultimate challenge, but still the manufacturer seemed irritated instead of pleased. I had staked so much to fly the flag around the world and the stony silence from Triumph was beginning to make me think my critics with Japanese allegances were right.

Credit, however, has to be given to the exceptional engineering. I had punished and abused my Trophy 4 halfway round the globe, over some of the toughest terrain the world could offer and its big pulsating heart had not skipped a beat. My biggest worries for the next ten thousand miles or more were tyres and chains as road and climatic conditions were going to deteriorate dramatically. Both of my two new friends thought my choice was misguided and Theo said Africa would be an impossibility on such a machine, but fuel was only a few cents in Iran. Not all bad news then.

At least I had made it halfway round and with Marian's imminent arrival, it was time to take stock. What had been learned, was I a better person for taking on half the world? There was never anything to prove by this adventure, but I had just survived (barely in some cases) six months on the road travelling through twenty countries and if there was no gain, where was the sense in carrying on? These mostly rhetorical questions were committed to a growing journal, which was always a good barometer of my mood.

'20th December – Khao San Road, Bangkok

I've just met two guys who are far more experienced travellers than me and they don't really have any satisfactory answers as to why we do this thing. It's not just about an education – I could have learned most of it and more from books, or just observed it on television – the passive way of travelling. My perception of travel, some 20,000 miles ago was one of spectating not participating in the people's lives that I have drifted through. A fly on the wall – as invisible as the voyeur watching television – but how can this be true if I was physically there? There is a forensic theory that it is impossible for someone to enter a room without leaving evidence and no matter how small or insignificant the evidence may be, the person can not avoid leaving their mark. This is the difference between experiencing and observing and this is what makes this adventure a unique education. It's the 'taking part' that makes the difference. I could spend my life circumnavigating the globe, but each lap would be totally different, and partly because the marks left behind would be different. The time traveller plunging backwards could not 'take part' for fear of changing the future. Tread on an ant and watch the mutation evolve into an ant that treads on people. It's about footprints on the moon. Bless them, the Yanks made their 'giant step for mankind', but now that virgin celestial orb is tainted by man, with an indelible impression on its surface – and probably a heap of discarded garbage.

I hope I have not left any disfiguring scars. It is better to be benign than make a mess of trying to be beneficial. My contributions to countries and strangers' lives have been pretty insignificant, unless someone gets stabbed with one of the many Swiss Army knives I have liberally scattered across a big chunk of the world.

Half a year sucking dust and other people's exhaust fumes in places that have presented both astounding beauty and devastating ugliness. I tell people I'm doing this for fun – what the hell *is* fun? I am exhausted beyond belief, but have never felt stronger. Not just physical strength, but an inner strength, deep down, that keeps the sinews pumping in the teeth of adversity. I feel ready to take on the world – or at least the rest of it, but one day all this will end and I don't want it too – but that is something to wrestle with in the future, because today is Marian day minus one and the minutes are passing so slowly as I sit scribbling in my diary. Time to get pissed.'

Regrettably, I did get pissed with dire consequences, as three seemingly terrible disasters happened in about an hour. Firstly, I lost my Zippo lighter, with the 'Trip of a Lifetime' engraving. Then I noticed a light-fingered individual had removed the gold chain from my neck that had been there for twenty five years, I cursed myself for not having taken th advice of the tourist guide in Guatamala. That was a blow, but worse was the momento on the chain. In Penang, I had met a talented young Englishman called Steve Butterworth, who made a living delicately carving and piercing out the detail on coins. The one I selected as a conversation piece was on an English ten pence piece, depicting the Queen smoking a joint. The loss of all three items was profoundly upsetting. With so few personal day-to-day possessions, losing anything caused an irrational reaction. Was it an omen of Marian's arrival? Was the 'Trip of a Lifetime' at an end? Another twenty-four hours would provide some answers.

18. My Christmas Cracker

It was Marian Day! What should I do? How should I prepare for such a momentous occasion? I had secured a room, should I fill it with flowers and lay on the champagne? No answers were forthcoming and the anticipation was getting painful. Six months without her to touch – to hold, but not many hours had elapsed during that time without her invading my thoughts, my dreams. I had warned the chirpy woman in the hotel reception I was expecting a couple of friends to arrive. Imagine my joy returning to the room – our room, after a hot day fighting bureaucracy at the Pakistani embassy, to find the place strewn with Marian's belongings. The familiar rucksack spilling clothes, washbag, towel, books. I picked up a sarong she had bought on our last trip to Thailand and held it to my face, then deciding that was a silly thing to do, ran into the mayhem of Khao San Road to search for her and her travel companion, Rena.

There are certain memories in everyone's life that always remain fresh. Moments to be locked away deep in a drawer of the brain to recover and enjoy at will. Watching your children being born – losing your virginity – the first jump off a thousand-foot cliff with nothing but a piece of sailcloth over your head – seeing a pale travel-weary face beaming at me from the Hello Bar. The thought of that first kiss, first touch, still makes my toes curl up. Marian and I were together again and Rena was the icing on the cake.

Our time together over that memorable Christmas period was a blur of days and nights merging together as the three of us soaked up western tourist destinations. We must have appeared a curious trio. Two pretty, almost Germanic-looking young women accompanied by a weather-beaten old wrinkly. Rena was far from being a spare part as Marian and I became re-acquainted and we were good enough friends to share a threesome sleeping bag when the necessity arose, but something had undeniably changed between two lovers who had spent six months apart and Rena was to be the foil to take our minds off the serious stuff of 'where do we go from here?'.

All relationships evolve and had I spent the last six months with Marian, our relationship would have changed. We may have learned to love each other all the more or learned to hate each other. As it happened, we had spent half a year apart and I was expecting to pick up from where we left off – as if the separation had never happened – and we were the same people that we were then. Neither of us had been in a time vacuum. She had spent the last 182 days doing new things without me – so had I, and I felt like a changed person.

Curiously enough, the situation was almost a repeat of a reunion a couple of years previously when it was Marian's time to see the world. We had lived together for less than a year when she left on her tour starting in New Zealand. Rena had joined her later in Thailand, then I had made up the numbers for a month just before Rena returned to England. One of their favouite resorts was Koh Samet, a delightful little island basking in the Gulf of Thailand. Marian took me there after Rena's departure, and one of the waitresses who recognised her asked why she had ditched her friend for her father. After that, whenever I saw the inquisitive young woman, she would giggle saying, 'You boyfen not Fadda.'

There is something about the Thai language that prevents native speakers from finishing their words in a foreign language. Post Office becomes 'Po Offi', guest house, 'ge how'. The economy of speech even reduces ice to 'i'.

During that first and fairly short separation, we did not make any firm rules about celibacy, we never really talked about it. 'What happens, happens, but when we are together, we are very much together'. She was better at accepting my 'unfaithfulness' than I was her's, so on that occasion, I was more of an emotional wreck than on the repeat performance. Marian's rampant promiscuity, as I saw it, while travelling had been the source of the only significant row we had in all the years we spent together. The penalty for my irrational jealousy and hypocrisy was a bitter pill, but one that had to be swallowed if we were to move on.

On our second encounter under Asian skies, the trio deserted Bangkok to revisit Koh Samet for a dose of relaxation and fun. This was a good enough motive for getting severely hammered on mehkong and Coke on our first night. Never do this before an important day – like one where getting up or speaking is critical. The potent brew has the power to numb brain cells at an alarming rate, but Coke and a bucket of 'i' cools the fire to lure you into a false sense of security. It is only when taxing tasks like standing up are performed that one appreciates its strength. During one rather inebriated session, Rena invented a new card game. The 'player' selects a card at random and without looking at it, gives it to the 'dealer'. The 'player' then asks three questions with strictly yes/no answers. After that, the 'player' has one guess to the card selected. We played ad nauseam without success, until in one round we all got it right. We could never play again lest the magic moment of harmony be destroyed.

We deserted leafy Koh Samet for a boat trip to the tranquillity of Koh Chang, one of the biggest but least developed islands close to the Cambodian border. Progress is inevitable, but I was disappointed to see a strip of tarmac replacing the dirt track Marian and I had experienced on our last visit. Holiday beach 'bungalows' proliferate in most Thai coastal resorts. The range spans from a palm leaf ridge tent construction for a few pence a night to quite sophisticated brick-built structures with bathrooms and verandahs for a few pounds. The standard ones are constructed in bamboo with palm leaf roof, squat toilet and open water tank. A bucket dipped into the tank flushes the toilet very efficiently and doubles as the shower. Firm but comfortable double beds are draped with mosquito nets and, with often limited electricity supply, the space is made all the more intimate in candle light.

Rudimentary beach cafes serve mouthwatering food and drinks where primary jungle meets fine sand and lapping waves. An idyllic recipe. The only problem with such hedonism is finding a motive to move on. Regretably, Koh Chang was booked up for Christmas, so we had to return to the steamy capital to find another beach destination for our celebrations. Also I was eager to gain intelligence on the war with Myanmar and enquiries around the city indicated that there was still one crossing open to that troubled country at Mae Sot. Visas were acquired at considerable cost for Burma and Bangladesh in the hope I could still access India overland. In the mean time, the girlies booked overnight transport to Krabi on the South East coast where we had been told there would be accommodation over the Christmas period. I was to follow on the bike the next day. It was only just over 600 miles, but indifferent roads and no map meant a sixteen-hour ride stopping only for fuel. That was the longest period of time spent riding in one day for the entire trip. Perhaps the added incentive of a couple of extra hours with Marian drove me blindly along unlit roads searching for potholes in the inadequate beam of a Triumph headlamp.

We secured a couple of excellent beach huts and the on-site restaurant paid lip service to a Christian celebration with fairy lights on a twiggy branch under the palm thatch. We spent Christmas Eve enjoying a buffet dinner of grilled fish, chicken and rice with the sensation of warm sand between our toes. Christmas day was similar, swimming, drinking and wrestling with a barracuda in Thai curry for lunch. What bliss. I was falling in love with Marian all over again, but she was putting up barriers despite intimate walks on the beach holding hands. One of the joys of beach walking in that part of the world is an Aladdin's cave of beautiful flat and conical shells. Neptune's bounty to be enjoyed by tourists and hermit crabs. It can be spooky to reach out for a shell and watch it run away before you can get close.

On Boxing Day, I took Rena for a bike ride round a rubber plantation where I showed her how to strip the bark and collect liquid white rubber in a half-coconut cup. It never fails to amaze me that someone found a method for collecting sap (the same the world over) and then put it to so many uses. The Malaysian industry went into severe decline when synthetics became more viable for the tyre industry. AIDS helped turn the tables as natural rubber is preferable for condoms and surgical gloves.

That night, plagued again with insomnia, I sat on the hut verandah, naked save for a sarong draped about my shoulders. The sea shimmering in bright moonlight was so tempting I went skinny dipping. The light was too bright and possibly the wrong time of year to experience luminous microbes lighting up disturbed water. My first encounter with the phenomenon had been in Kuantan, eastern Malaysia on a cloudy night. Splashing sea water excites plankton into a bright green sparkling luminescence. Swimming underwater generates more light until your body glows like a kinetic neon tube. I wrote 'Robbie' in the wet sand, and managed to get to the second 'b' before the 'R' faded into darkness again.

The only partial success that night in Krabi was watching footprints fade as I ran through the gentle surf. Solitude had been the norm for six months – and I was beginning to enjoy it. Returning to our bungalow, I threw myself in the hammock strung on the verandah for a last cigarette to savour the moment. "That's funny," I thought. "I'm sure the packet was left on the table." A full thirty seconds elapsed before realising I was on the wrong verandah with sleeping strangers only a yard away. There were half a dozen identical huts in our little hamlet, but I had no idea where it was after walking so far along the beach. I started to search in iridescent moonlight when the ground below me disappeared.

One of those absurd cartoon images flashed across my mind where a character steps off a cliff and hovers in mid-air until realising the mistake. Legs started pumping as I dropped a couple of feet into a steep-sided storm drain. A brutal concrete lip tore into my shins and one big toe took a severe stubbing. I stumbled off with the sarong around my neck to keep blood off, and my dignity dangling in the breeze. The only way I could identify the right hut was by the washing draped out to dry. Any observer watching a semi-naked man scrutinizing damp knickers in the half light would have been forgiven for jumping to the wrong conclusion.

By breakfast time, the wounds were beginning to hurt, so I reverted to my hobby of people-watching – one of the great sources of entertainment during independent travel. An insipid Englishman sat opposite his soppy girlfriend with a pronounced lisp in the restaurant. He ordered scrambled egg, a poached egg and four rounds of toast. She wanted omelette and chips. Everything was going fine until the order appeared with no poached egg and no chips. The bemused cook, who only spoke a few words of English, was summoned to be asked, "How can I eat all this toast with no poached egg, and where are the bloody chips?" The chips appeared immediately but limited cooking facilities meant not everything could be produced at the same time. The poached egg followed but the complainant was upset the toast had gone cold. The girl had a go at a waiter who took her exaggerated lisp as a quirk of the language, replying "yeth" to her question. "You people thould learn to thpeak Englith better," she demanded.

Imagine a Thai visiting a Bournmouth guest house and complaining the *padthai* (noodles) or *cowpat* (same with rice) did not have enough nuts and the waiter only had a nodding acquaintance with *their* language. I felt like telling them to fuck off back to Croydon and pay fifty pounds rather than

145

five for bed and breakfast – and without the idyllic surroundings.

To the Thais, the *felang* are verging on aliens, demanding weird food at strange times and assuming everyone speaks English. The British have a history of unforgiving arrogance from a time when we clocked up national conquests building an empire and have not really improved much since. The only travellers I have observed exceeding this uncompromising attitude, are young Israelis, who do their nation and religion no credit at all. One youth came close to punching a Thai cook for charging five *baht* (a little under ten pence) for two boiled eggs. Thereafter, he bought bread from a shop, demanded the restaurant toast it free and then he smothered it with ketchup and mustard standing on the table. Life is too short.

We were fortunate to find that sleepy little backwater where most multi-cultural Westerners take on the gentle pace of Thailand. The sea was warm, the living cheap, and the palm-fringed beach practically deserted. Apart from concrete storm drains, there was little to complain about. I was happy to sit and watch palms grow with only the lapping of the sea to remind me the world was still rotating. Koh Samui was to be a radical but planned change for New Year.

After Puket, Koh Samui was the most developed tourist island resort. The place was heaving with whites strutting about in posing pouches and newly acquired sarongs. Only one bungalow was available for our first night and Rena manfully offered to make herself scarce for half an hour if Marian and I fancied a shag. I told her, if she caught me having sex with *anyone*, to write it in her diary as it would be an event worth recording.

Although Samui was geared up to accommodate every need of sun and fun-seeking tourists, the authorities had not made the mistake of so many destinations of building multi-story concrete hotels to attract greater numbers. There were a few posh hotels, but not a high-rise anywhere to interrupt the natural horizon. Tourism is a fragile economy and Thailand showed great sensitivity getting the balance right. Pioneer backpackers will move on to Vietnam or Myanmar and the Khoa San Road phenomenon will possibly be gone from Bangkok in a decade, as the islands react to the demands of a better-heeled traveller.

Most things were a little more expensive than the rest of Thailand, but still excellent value. I bought two beautifully embroidered sarongs for Marian to take back as Christmas presents for my daughters. Unashamed crimson for Sasha and sexy purple for Chantie. The vendor attacked one with a cigarette lighter flame to prove it was pure silk. While negotiating the transaction, I became aware of heavy breathing in my ear. I turned to be greeted by an elephant's trunk slobbering over my last clean T-shirt. The enchanting creature, with a very sparse crew cut as bristly as a hair brush and engaging little piggy eyes, was only a baby at four years old and much too young for a deep throat snog with someone of my age.

We spent most evenings flopping about on dance floors at the Raggae Pub or Green Mango Club. On one evening as Rena went to buy drinks, Marian, above three million gigawatts of Beegees, managed to drop a revelation into the conversation. Without even changing the rhythm of the sentence, she matter-of-factly announced she was 'seeing' an old flame again back home. She did say something else, but I missed it as I was attempting to re-start my heart at the time. I left the club on my own to try to get my head round this celibacy thing.

Since leaving the UK I had been 'unfaithful' twice, but the demands of travel had taken most thoughts of chance sexual encounters from my mind. Also, as most days I was somewhere new, it is difficult to get to know someone well enough to end up in bed. Marian was still living in our Brighton home, but her life had changed, perhaps more subtlely, after the person she professed to love had pissed off for a year leaving a gaping hole.

At the time I did not feel emotionally equipped for an analysis of our future together. At the risk of losing the most important aspect of my life, I packed up to head north prematurely for some introspective thought on the road.

I awoke early to find Marian snoring soundly next to me. We had one of those tense conversations that can go horribly wrong – before the tears. She is not given to open displays of emotion or passion, so her tearful little face stopped me in my tracks. The thought of wilfully hurting her was beyond comprehension, so I melted instantly and unpacked.

She was of course right. Storming off feeling sorry for myself was no solution and from then on we applied ourselves to enjoying the holiday and each other, as our scheduled parting was not far away. On our last night together in Bangkok, I scribbled in my notebook trying to rationalise the contradictions.

'There is an underlying dark side to this journal that begs too many questions. Why do I love this woman so unreservedly? Why has she become singularly the most important factor in my pathetic existence? It makes me so angry. M lies next to me in gentle slumber. The rise and fall of her breast, blonde mop resplendent on the pillow, the smell of her skin, the sound of her breathing. If life terminated now, it would be a good moment, to know that someone has loved you with every fibre of their soul. Tomorrow is another day and another six months apart if all goes to plan. Excuse me? – I don't even have a map so a plan seems a bit grown up. Tomorrow I set off for Burma with no idea how far it is, or where it is for that matter, but that's tomorrow's problem. Funny old World - and still half of it to go.'

As the girlies surrendered baggage to Thai Airlines, I stood in an empty room fighting back tears, trying to be brave, but not being the hero type, my taste for the road had soured with confusion and emotional turmoil. My heart was no longer in the adventure although I knew I would feel differently after a couple of days on the road without her. Back to my solitary world on the chessboard of life where I could be king one day and pawn the next. Physically, I felt strong and rested – ready to take on anything the rest of the world could throw at me. All I had to do was get my head into gear and concentrate on the problems that lay ahead, not read too deeply between the lines of an evolving relationship. 'What happens, happens.'" It had all been said before and running back to England would not have made anything better.

19. Guns, Roses and the Road to Mandalay

A smallish article on about page five of the Bangkok Post read something like, '....and two Christian missionaries died at the hands of Burmese border guards on the bridge at Mae Sot, northern Thailand. A Thai policeman was also killed attempting to save the missionaries.'

From where I sat, astride a very hot Triumph, at the point where a magnificent new bridge rose out of the rough, potholed road, blood-spattered concrete was clearly visible. The incident had happened just two days before my arrival and the bridge had been barricaded with heavily-armed Burmese soldiers preventing any attempt to cross.

I made some inquiries at tumbledown little shacks fringing the muddy river. For US$50, a Thai boatman would be prepared to take me – at night. Imagine the scene. A feeble white tourist attempting to get nearly half a ton of bike and baggage across thirty yards of mud, quicksand and rocks to a fragile craft. Then, at the other side, being unceremoniously chucked off to negotiate the same on Myanmar soil, in the dark, with no maps or any idea where the nearest road was – and trigger-happy troops everywhere. It was hopeless.

I was taking one last look at the bridge, forming a graceful arabesque, on the Road to Mandalay. Close to tears with frustration, as Myanmar had been a real ambition and my only direct overland route to India. Laos, China and over the Himalayas were probably not possible because of both politics and conditions, so I sat on the bike wondering what the hell to do next. A staggeringly attractive young woman approached. "I am Burmese and cannot go to my country. Nor can you. You are brave but very stupid to try," she said in excellent English, putting a hand round my neck and pulling me down to her diminutive size. She kissed me full on the mouth saying "Ride south my friend. You will live longer," and then turned to walk away. Despite threadbare clothes and bare feet, she had great dignity. I wanted to give her something for endorsing what I already knew, but that may have trivialised her sentiments and her problems were far worse than mine.

The ride north to Mae Sot, the last crossing point, had been uneventful enough, except for those heart-stopping 'I miss Marian' moments mixing tears with sweat. Someone had told me of a guest house to stay in, but apparently it had been destroyed in a mortar bomb attack, so I found a place called Number Four Guest House. I was a little concerned for the other three.

In the seclusion of my mosquito net, I sat cross-legged on a mattress contemplating my options. There was only one. 'Ride south my friend – you will live longer.' The beautiful young woman had said it all. She had been denied her country by the vicious political regime. No hope for an old white man then. The pitiful state of those refugee camps full of displaced people brought home the cruelty of greed and ambition. I had no grounds for feeling sorry for myself, as all I had to do was ride about 2,000 miles out of my way and shell out a small fortune to get to India. Those poor humiliated people could not even go home for fear of persecution from their fellow countrymen.

Nevertheless, the anger was hard to contain. You know how annoying it is to miss a motorway junction and have to drive a dozen or so miles to get back to where you started. I anticipated having to ride a round trip of nearly 4,000 miles to get back to Singapore to find a boat to India. The road back to Bangkok was only too familiar and I decided to make enquiries at every coastal town in search of a solution.

Riding from port to port along the coast for the elusive passage to the sub-continent took me through breathtaking scenery, where the villages sound like descriptions of noises – Bang Tap, Klong Klap, Klung Klik – phonetic translations from a melodic language. My best hope was Puket Island but, after exhaustive research, I was told all sea traffic went via Singapore to Madras. I did not particularly enjoy Singapore the first time round but I could certainly ride the distance quicker than a boat, and so I was resigned to retracing my steps through Malaysia.

It was the fourth time the Trophy had faced the unpredictable road to Hat Yai, but the absence of a map meant I still got lost. The sea loomed on my left which meant I was on the east coast when I needed to be on the west of Thailand to cross into Malaysia.

After finding the border again, due to the magnificent roads and signs I could read, it was only a few hours before I was chatting to Aussie Bill again in the Hong Kong Bar, Penang. "Just couldn't keep away, could ya?" he said, wrinkling his face into a welcoming grin and he introduced me to a shipping agent who thought that Klang, the port for Kuala Lumpur and biggest in Malaysia, may be a solution.

Many ports are a little unsavoury, but Klang surpasses all bounds of undesirability. The place simply stinks and is not a typical reflection of that multi-cultural nation. I have only one favourable recollection of that unappealing town. After sleeping out on a beach next to a filthy fly-infested rubbish tip, I found a splendid little street restaurant that was not much more than a railway carriage with a few tables on the pavement. The slog in 98% humidity round all the shipping agents had been fruitless so, feeling very disappointed, I fell into the Muslim cafe for roti, a sort of egg pancake served with curry sauce and dhall, and to let my sweat-soaked T-shirt dry out. Although eating during the day was almost unheard of, I needed to sit and think. For some reason the restaurant was not cooking that day, but the owner had been out to buy roti for his family and put one on a plate for me. While tucking in, I noticed an old Indian tramp on a street bench, hiding behind a matted grey beard that joined wild unkempt hair, not unlike my own on that day. He was only a few feet away, between me and the bike and from my vantage point, I could see three plastic bags bulging with his worldly possessions under the bench. I glanced at the Trophy overloaded with just about everything I owned. The restaurant fed him and in turn he shared his bowl of rice with a rather mangy-looking dog. That guy was probably someone's dad but lived, like me, on the street. In the depths of my loneliness and failure to get to India – his country – I felt a curious bond. We were two solitary vagrants with no home and no particular place to go.

He did not beg, but the odd passer-by dropped a coin into his hand. He and the dog stopped eating their shared rice to nod thanks in a dignified fashion. The restaurant would not accept payment for my roti as it was a gift from the proprietor. I passed the old man's bench on my way back to the bike, and dropped the one ringget, about 50 pence and the price of breakfast, into his hand before patting the dog. He simply touched his forehead with both hands, then brought them together as if in prayer. The thought of his leathery smiling face kept my spirits up all the way back to Kuala Lumpur, where I found a saviour.

Kalvin Lee was Cantonese Chinese, about my age and ran an air freight company dedicated to flying fresh fish just about anywhere. Over the next two days, we became firm friends as he worked for no money trying to get me to India. Like most Chinese in Malaysia, he had to speak the national language (by law if you wish to work there), his own Chinese dialect, Mandarin (the common Chinese language) and near perfect English for international trade. He worked tirelessly through all the regulations regarding motorbikes and assured me that both the bike and I could travel together by Malaysian Airlines to Madras. After shedding another considerable wad of dollars to Singapore Airlines, he led me to the bike packers, then to the airport to sort the endless paperwork needed for Indian customs. India thrives on unnecessary mountains of paper.

He performed the task very efficiently while standing at a counter typing in triplicate on an ancient portable. Hours passed before he presented the bundle of documents to the customs official and then I heard a high-pitched voice ring out. Men with those squeaky voices are always trouble and this one was to be no exception. Squinting from behind tiny glasses that kept slipping off his nose, he quoted paragraph 48, section 122 of the AITA bible. It clearly stated that Indian air freight is unique in that they consider motorbikes, even drained of fuel and with a disconnected battery, 'dangerous cargo'.

The only way round this is to have a letter, not a fax, from the Director General of Indian Civil Aviation. "So, where do I obtain this document?" I asked naively. "New Delhi, of course," replied the squeaky voice. Weeks could have elapsed before getting confirmation from India and my flight was due to leave for Madras in a few hours. I could not afford to waste the ticket. Kalvin could see I was getting ready to punch squeaky's lights out and came up with a brain-wave. "What about Sri Lanka?" he said, studying a map on the wall. Suddenly everything changed.

I boarded the plane carrying only a camera bag, two tripods and a newly-acquired full-face crash helmet purchased for the princely sum of £25. Not up to the standard of my stolen Shoei, even with a bullet hole, but the open face helmet was too noisy and uncomfortable for long-distance riding. Some guy asked if I always flew with a crash helmet. I told him the Malaysian flight should be fine, but next I had to fly Indian Airways and anything could happen.

As I flew, Kalvin worked out the logistics and we communicated by fax from Madras Central Railway Station. He told me the Triumph would arrive at Colombo airport, Sri Lanka by Singapore Airlines in two days. His commission for all his efforts was 28 litres of fuel drained from all my petrol tanks. Was it fate or just luck that I had met some of the really good people in the world? So far on the trip, I had needed help from many people and had been very fortunate to find willing sympathisers to my cause. Sure, there had also been a few people I would rather not meet again, but I was delighted that good far outweighed the forces of evil. Had Kalvin not been there, I would no doubt have found someone else, but he was and I loved him for it.

Madras is probably farther from the Western idea of normality than anywhere in the world. There is so much going on that every inch of space is used around the clock for some practical use. Even when the pavements are full of traders and pedestrians, activities like welding rickshaws or slaughtering livestock spill into the streets. Torches crackle and spit blue fire next to hammer and anvil in the construction of complicated bits of metal with no obvious function while animals of every description dart about dodging sparks and opportunist restaurant workers looking for lunch.

The truth is that very little meat is consumed anywhere in India as I discovered attempting to take advantage of a legacy left by the vanishing Empire. I breezed into a little restaurant lusting after a genuine Madras curry. The waiter suffered a severe attack of rubber neck syndrome with his head wobbling from side to side in confusion. This seemed to be a common trait of most Indians and it could mean a multitude of things. In this case it meant 'What the hell are you talking about, you stupid white tourist?' There was no such thing as Madras curry locally. The cheap road cafes only served very tasty, if a little bland, vegetable Mossala. I asked for some extra chilli to spice it up a bit. 'No chilli here – this is Indian food.' I had ridden my bike over 20,000 miles to the heart of Indian cuisine just to find the nearest decent curry was in Brighton and, to make matters worse, it was a question of starve or get the hang of eating without the benefit of cutlery. Scooping thick vegetable sauce from a banana-leaf plate with a piece of chapati and tearing pieces of bread with your right hand only is one challenge, conveying the mixture to anywhere near your face is another matter, especially after making the mistake of ordering rice. I lacked the dexterity of locals in forming a ball of rice and mixed vegetables with delicate fingertips. The word must have got around amongst troops of cats and dogs that an Englishman was in town and they all benefited from the meal dripping off my elbow and beard. I needed to be hosed down, but made do with the sink provided. This is my theory as to why the limp rupee notes are so difficult to read - they are all stained greeny-brown from mossala-encrusted fingers.

Cats and dogs were not the only four-legged street inhabitants. Cows roamed freely, interrupting already congested traffic, grazing on market stalls. For what it is worth, I believe the cow is kept sacred to curb a population exceeding a billion, the largest democracy in the world as in the space of a minute I witnessed two unrelated incidents where cows were indirectly responsible for life-threatening situations. One was a motorcycle crash, as it skidded across the road and under a bus after hitting a particularly fresh cowpat. The other was an elderly man on a push bike. He fortunately managed to manoeuvre himself between the wheels of the following bullock cart, but his bike did not. He got up, wiped the cow shit from his eyes and hobbled off with a very bent bike over his shoulder.

Pigs, goats and the odd camel, with no apparent owners, add to the chaos as autos (Indian tuk-tuks), cars, buses and evil Tata trucks belching smokescreens of diesel fumes force their way down the road. People who are either dead or asleep fill in the gaps like pieces of a jigsaw obliterating any paved surface.

I picked my way between reclining bodies and broken bits of machinery to the nearest in my budget hotel. Checking-in is a time-consuming business with the proprietor laboriously copying every word from your passport into a vast dusty ledger, before stamping lots of receipts and taking a few rupees. Checking-out is similar. Forget throwing the keys on the reception desk. Sit down for twenty minutes and get the paperwork right over a glass of *chai* - tea. Sending a fax is far more complicated!

My flight to Colombo was confirmed and as there was only one seat available on the plane, I had to pay the extra four quid for a first class seat bringing the total to a bit less than £30. In reality the only difference between first and economy class is the passengers spit into the sick bags rather than over the hostess.

It is hard work achieving very little in such a labour-intensive society and by the end of the day I was in need of refreshment, but discovered to my dismay I was in the alcohol-free Moslem quarter. A lengthy walk eventually revealed a dingy basement bar in a Hindu hotel. The eyes take a while adjusting to near darkness after squinting into evening sunlight. I only knocked half a dozen tables over searching for the bar where a peculiar anti-corruption activity was in progress. Two inspectors carefully emptied in turn the contents of each open bottle into a measuring jug, recorded the findings against sales, then used a funnel to refill the bottles. Blue label Johnnie Walker to Smirnoff vodka were routinely checked – twice a day! The jug was not rinsed between bottles which must have had a bad effect on VSOP brandies being mixed with cheap gin. I assumed this had more to do with providing employment than preventing theft.

Feeling my way back to the hotel through prostrate bodies strewn on the pavement only a couple of feet from raging traffic, a cow trotted up from behind and firmly head-butted me across the shoulders. I landed neatly between two slumbering figures at the foot of the hotel steps and started to chuckle at the spectacle. A sleepy voice said, "Clean room early, we have much work." I had been impressed with the cleanliness of the building, especially when two small boys entered my room at 7.00am to scrub it and were polishing the stairs at 10.00pm. I deposited all my loose change into a grimy little hand stained and cracked with domestic chores and retreated apologising. My heart ached for the child as he in turn deposited the change into his sleeping friend's pocket and curled up behind him for a little comfort. I was grateful my children had had the advantage of a Western upbringing and had more than a concrete pavement for a pillow.

20. Tiger Tiger Burning Bright

The independent state of Sri Lanka greeted me with even more turmoil than the streets of Madras. Only hours before my arrival, a desperate suicide bomber had driven a truck packed with explosives into a central bank. The result was nearly 200 dead, people who had just popped out for a roll of toilet paper or to cash a cheque. I visited the site with a concealed camera and managed to film through rows of security staff. Not a building within a block had a window left in place. Plate glass and debris filled the streets as impotent soldiers crunched their way around searching everybody. Dark ominous blood stains sat in pools on a skating rink of glass sheets an inch deep. Most must have been caused by pedestrians wearing flip-flops lacerating their feet. At the centre of the carnage, twisted vehicles, even street lamps, showed the magnitude of the attack, with buildings so badly damaged demolition would be necessary to make them safe. Frankly, I felt blowing up Colombo was the best thing that could have happened to it, but that is no consolation for 200 bereaved families.

With the capital on security overload and a forthcoming public holiday, I decided to escape the city squalor for a small coastal village about fifteen miles north. The local buses may have been slow but, for a couple of rupees, passengers can ride in or cling to the outside and, on that occasion, I managed to get a seat next to a window. Well, it was more of a hole in the side of the vehicle than a window as recognised by most transport companies. A fat sweaty woman carrying a large box of squawking chickens decided there was plenty of room for her as well as the other three people sitting on a seat made for an intimate couple, pinning me against the hot bus side. In heavy traffic we lumbered over a railway line and the engine stalled while we were across the track. Attempting to get some air into crushed lungs, I stuck my head out of the widow and saw a goods train doing warp nine in our direction. All efforts to restart the bus on the starter motor failed as the train accelerated towards us. I started to fight my way past the mountain of flesh in a bid to escape via the window, for fear of joining the obituary column in Motoring & Leisure magazine. About 120 people nearest the doors jumped out and started pushing. The bus coughed into life and several hundred tons of rusting metal that had not had a hope of stopping missed us by a couple of feet, leaving most of the paying customers on the other side of a very long freight train. Sri Lanka was certainly not living up to its reputation as a desirable holiday destination, but Negombo was a vast improvement, where I found a cheap room facing a backwater of the Bay of Bengal.

Dave Barr had said 'Motorcycle travel is a daily catalogue of problems and catastrophes. Riding from one place to another is the easy bit.' His words were no comfort as I considered how I was going to transport the bike and me to the sub-continent practically visible over the pounding surf. A local fisherman offered to take me for a huge wad of rupees, but that would have made me an illegal immigrant in India and cause problems trying to gain access to Pakistan. Air Lanka said we could fly to Trivandrum (real name Thiruvananthapuram, but no one can say that) for a similar amount, so I embarked on the painful negotiations.

Much of the tiresome administration could at least be done back in the relaxed atmosphere of my guest house. My appointed accommodation was a tiny brick building separate from the rest of the guest house, just big enough for a bed and hosepipe shower.

The owner's pet monkey insisted on sitting on my head, but I soon got used to tiny fingers twisting ears and picking through my long unruly hair. Most of the day, she was tethered to a perch outside my room so she did not annoy guests by insisting on sharing their meals. In the evening she ran wild, jumping from mango tree to table top with astounding agility. Nimble fingers soon learned to remove a cigarette from the pack and tear off the filter before consuming. I had to stop this as it was getting expensive and I did not wish to turn her into a nicotine addict. Her nights were spent on top of, or under, my mosquito net in abandoned slumber purring only as a monkey can. I have woken occasionally during my life to some strange bed partners, but none as strange as that monkey with her wide amber blinking eyes and a startled 'who, me?' sort of expression. The best thing about animals is that, provided they are treated well, they do not discriminate, unlike humans and not for the first time I was suffering because of my colour. White tourists are an easy target in many countries, but in out-of-season Sri Lanka, when you are the only one, you attract more than your fair share of attention.

Walking the featureless beach, streaked black with volcanic sand, traders attempted to sell me brightly coloured plastic things or useless artifacts made from shells. They were rarely deterred by a firm 'no', and asked for cigarettes. Some asked to borrow money, claiming to be from my hotel and would repay that evening. I guess they thought they all looked the same to a pale face. Fortunately, I cottoned on to this one straight away and asked each of them for the name of the hotel without them realising I did not aspire to anything grander than a guest house. One persistent youth, angry at being found out, squeezed his nose between finger and thumb before departing. This I took as an abusive gesture and added it to a growing archive of different hand signals observed in other cultures.

In countries where one lacks any linguistic competence, there is an assumption that hand movements are a universal language. In parts of Greece an open hand is considered offensive, so friendly waving is done underarm, wiggling fingers from a half-open palm. In Central American countries, 'fill up with fuel' is indicated by an outstretched hand, palm down, moving from side to side. In Western society this would have been taken for 'enough' or 'stop'. In Thailand they tap the top of the tank with a clawed hand like a half-open fist. Two fingers spread in a V shape in Britain may mean 'we have won a war' or 'go away', but everywhere else it means 'two'. Traffic police in Tamil Nadu flap an open hand like a child waving to tell traffic to 'go' not 'stop' as I wrongly assumed. In many countries, showing your tongue is rude, but none more so than in Buddhist communities, but I challenge any westerner to eat noodle won ton soup with chop sticks and not lick their lips.

Cultural differences may seem like details, but when you are the foreigner, you should make an effort not to offend and mis-understanding a policeman's gestures in murderous traffic can be dangerous. Observing how others act in public can give you a clue, but how do you know if they are being polite or abusive? I am not aware of making any severe social blunders, but who knows and it can be hard to resist patting a child on the head occasionally, which is considered a put-down to Buddhists.

Two intensive days were spent trying to release the Triumph from one shipping agent and transporting it still crated to Air Lanka. No mention was made of the 'dangerous cargo' clause and I was not going to let them into the secret. Sri Lanka was turning out to be by far the most corrupt government-sponsored society so far, demanding fees that someone dreamt up that morning while shaving. Fortunately, it was all well-catalogued and receipted so I had evidence of payments when they attempted to charge me twice for the same service. The government, Tamil Tigers and bad-attitude locals with their short-sighted, 'grab it while you can' philosophy were effectively screwing their economy and decimating tourism, the country's most significant industry. In reality, it did not add up to as much as five minutes with a New York agriculture officer, but I found it most disheartening and, after running the gauntlet of five different and totally uncoordinated security checks in less than a hundred yards at the Air Lanka building, I vowed never to visit the place again. At each one the packaging was torn apart and the bike strip-searched, X-rayed and generally humiliated. My tool kit was unrolled several times and the contents scrutinised – fiddled with and then passed on to the next grim faced official for inspection. There was no humour in the proceedings making them all the more sinister. A tin of chain lube and piece of self-adhesive velcro caused heated conversation so I told the man to keep them before he lost control of his rubber neck and suffered a head injury. The packaging was in shreds, but I managed to repair most of it with a roll of tape and the self-adhesive Velcro. Just as we were starting to make progress, a smart-arse official with a shiny head and well-pressed uniform said the tyres had to be deflated. The back one was already soft because of the buckled wheel and I did not want them pushing the bike around at the other end on flat tyres. I told the slap-head all the other airlines liked them that way and letting tyres down would have loosened the straps so the Triumph would fall over on the pallet. I was climbing the wall with frustration when he conceded to leave the tyre valves in place and then warned me this could happen all over again in India with Celanese cargo.

All thirty one documents had to be examined, stamped and signed at each security check. At the last I was getting irritated and asked why they did not just speak to the other three police departments, but they all had their existences to justify. Their objective was to prevent the movement of firearms and the irony was that my revolver and fifty rounds of ammunition were stowed under the seat. The wretched thing had created more problems than it solved and I was beginning to regret ever buying it, especially when the bike was passed through an X-ray machine, but no one seemed to know what they were looking at. All that hard work just to transport me and the bike not much farther than from England to France. I could not wait to escape that money-grabbing, bureaucratic society, thriving on legalised corruption, for the beckoning sub-continent.

At most international airports, check-in is two hours before take off. In Sri Lanka four hours were necessary for security checks before a 45 minute flight. It started at 2.00am, and with the watery glow of dawn, the flight was being announced. To my horror, as the procession of passengers made its way across the tarmac, I saw the Triumph sitting on its pallet with about twenty uniforms surrounding it. "Mr. Marshall, is this your motor bike?" Shrewd guess as I was the only bugger carrying a crash helmet. The official, with a name like a remote Welsh village, said it was two inches too high for the hold. I started tearing at the packaging in search for tools. I yelled at them above the roar of jet engines that the windshield had to be removed. Twenty heads in assorted uniforms spontaneously went into a severe attack of rubber neck syndrome to a chorus of 'rhubarb rhubarb'. Waves of limp wrists, everyone shouting in Celanese – it was enough to turn a Muslim to drink. The pilot was waving at me to get on board and every passenger had their noses pressed against the windows. Sitting astride the Big Blue Babe, looking down an immaculate runway, for two rupees I would have cut the restraining straps, fired up the engine and done a wheelie to entertain them. The official promised to have the bike on the next flight as it was a bigger aircraft and it would have a horse for company and I was off back to India for another nail biting wait for the bike to follow.

Trivandrum was a pretty uninspiring town, but with everything so much cheaper (despite the devalued Sri Lanka rupee) and the relaxed attitude of locals, I was relieved to be off the island. Anyone visiting Sri Lanka should have a T-shirt printed saying 'I may be white but I'm not completely stupid'. After an easy but time-consuming customs release (with no mention of 'dangerous cargo') I had my first taste of riding on Indian roads.

India was refreshing in that it was one of the few countries to reject American and Japanese manufacture. I did not see one McDonald's in the whole continent. They do have Coke, but Thumbs Up, their own equally good version, is half the price.

Cars are mostly home-produced Ambassadors, loosely based on a Morris Cowley, and anything bigger, a Tata. Most motorcycles were magnificent single cylinder Enfields, identical to the war-time Royal Enfields produced in Britain before the factory closed due to Japanese enterprise. The choices were 350cc or 500cc petrol and amazingly enough, diesel engines, that sound like dumper trucks and are started with a rope round a fly-wheel. They were, however, far more appropriate than a water-cooled four cylinder Triumph on appalling roads with menacing traffic. Everything from camel carts to free-range cows have to give way to buses and trucks, which is the root of India's biggest problem as they do not give way to each other. The carnage on their roads must claim more lives each year than any global conflict. In an average day, I would see up to thirty recent crashes. They were so common no one stopped. I saw one bus on its side across the road with people inside and probably crushed hangers-on underneath. The tanker in front of me was determined to get past so drove off the road and tipped over next to the bus on a steep slope. I managed to squeeze between them as the tanker came to rest on its side. The warning, 'high explosives', was written all over it in several languages!

Across Texas, the Triumph had managed a little under 800 miles in a day as the roads were good and the scenery mind-numbingly boring. In India the best I achieved in ten hours' aggressive riding was 322 miles, such was the state of roads and traffic. India at that time possessed an arsenal of nuclear weapons, but not a decent stretch of tarmac to be found outside New Delhi. Just a tiny bit of the defence budget would have supplied some modern construction machinery, but they resorted to a more leisurely approach. Men broke boulders into rocks with big hammers. Women broke rocks into gravel with small hammers and children carried the tar. Little children struggling under the weight of heavy buckets, covered from head to toe in black goo was a pathetic sight. By contrast, women swinging pick-axes dressed in puce, saffron, or emerald saris with gold trim, sparkling under a fierce sun was a surreal spectacle.

India was an experience I wanted to savour, so I took my time through the state of Kerala. Filming had become a big part of my everyday life attempting to capture scenes that gave a true flavour of the world. I wanted to present a balanced view of geography, cultures, wild life and population. India had so much to offer in all those criteria that I was concerned the final presentation would not be a true reflection of a fascinating continent. I had, however, worked out how to put a microphone in my helmet to record spontaneous remarks and thoughts that would have drifted off on the wind long before being committed to paper and for the first time I was not talking to myself on long rides.

Basic beach resorts peppered the coast providing gentle entertainment for the scattering of pale faces on holiday. I will never know the name of one of them where a cool beer was consumed in welcome shade. The label read 'Marco Polo Beer. Only for resale in Tamil Nadu' (the next state). It claimed to be 8.7% proof and then went on to say 'Liquor ruins country, family and life'. The packet of Wills Navy Cut warned 'Smoking can be injurious to health'. Neither of these could compete with tap water, air pollution or bus rides as a health risk in most towns.

Most of the population of the small town were sculptors chipping away at marble blocks, making images of Hindu Gods or sturdy elephants for tourist consumption in Bombay or Goa. The rhythmic, tick tick of hammer on chisel filled the air giving the impression of frantic industry. Families of pigs roamed the beach in what appeared to be a fishing boat graveyard. The assumption was wrong as outboard motors and nets were evidence that the crude vessels were a working fleet. Logs, fifteen-foot long, were fashioned into square sections, slightly turned up at either end. Five of these lashed together floated just about long enough to cast nets.

India was proving to be a reward for me, but punishment for the Triumph on dreadful roads. The wheels had suffered so much that my first task each morning was to re-inflate tyres with an inefficient Chinese-made foot pump purchased in Bangkok. The light-weight construction was not man enough for the job as bits kept falling off. When a screw dropped out, I had to replace it with one pinched from the bike and twenty minutes careful and methodical pumping was needed each morning to get the tyres roughly the right shape. Air hoses in garages, or at least ones that worked, were a bit of a novelty, so I was pretty dependant, especially as sometimes I awoke in some rather remote areas.

Although accommodation was cheap, I slept out much of the time as it was difficult to find in rural areas. In such situations, I went out of my way to find a secluded spot, but was always woken by an assembled crowd of twenty or so, squatting in a circle round my pathetic camp, waiting for the day's entertainment. Often an English-speaking spokesman would nudge me and fire a barrage of questions as the sun peeped over a distant horizon.

The excitement would rise to fever pitch as I got vertical and dusty feet pushed forward trampling my sleeping bag into the dirt. They crowded in so tight that moving around the bike, cleaning teeth, packing up, pumping tyres was a hot sweaty business, even before 6.00am. I developed a sharp two steps backwards strategy with little regard for the first half dozen rows suffering the domino effect. Opening a pannier caused even more excitement as wobbling heads tried for a better look. During one intense inspection, I got so pissed off, each item was withdrawn from the pannier for all to see. Billy can for cooking – tripod for camera – ball of string for everything else.

All well-intentioned stuff, and they were being no more inquisitive than a curtain twitcher on a UK housing estate. I liked their openness, but after riding away over a few keen spectators I was exhausted before the main task of the day had begun. All the switches were flicked by inquisitive fingers at every stop. Kill switch, hazard lights, even the clock buttons prodded to satisfy a raging curiosity. Despite this, I never felt any of my possessions were at risk from theft.

Riding the N17 north, on a road not wide enough to merit a white line, my technique became progressively more aggressive in an attempt to stay upright for a whole day. Driving in India is a constant game of chicken, aiming your vehicle at on-coming traffic, blowing your horn and waiting to see whose nerve cracks first. If you hug the curb and you are at the mercy of everyone who wants your bit of road and there is absolutely no safety margin.

State borders frequently offer a dramatic change and none more so than leaving north west Karnataka.

21. Goa Way

The road terminated abruptly at a beach with two curious Venetian bridges spanning a rivulet looking for the Arabian Sea. My poor bike had been gasping all day, shuffling along in oppressive heat. It, rather than I, needed a rest in the shade of a broad-leafed banana tree. A wide beach, dotted with quite sophisticated bars offered shelter to more white people than I had seen since Koh Samui. A guy from the East End of London put me right on geography. We were in Cova Beach, Goa, which was something of a revelation as I was not aware that western India had such a flourishing tourist industry for Europeans in search of some winter sun. As tourist resorts go, in the grand scheme of things, Colva was small and low key, but far by the most developed I had seen India. Concrete hardstandings shaded by fabric awnings gave an impression of permanence to beach bars that even sold some familiar western products like Marlboro cigarettes and Coca Cola. I preferred the impromptu shacks seen further south, made from a few poles and palm thatch, with soft sand for a carpet. They generally sold only locally produced products for half the price of the western equivalent, which was one of the things I really admired about India. If they could not manufacture it locally, it was generally not available. Because of inadequate road links and the size of the country, 'local' generally meant within a couple of neighbouring states, giving a whole new sense of adventure to ordering a beer.

Watching other white folk sprinting from one patch of shade to another, across blistering sand, was not really the India I wanted to experience. Had Cova been a resort for the indigenous population, I would have found the scene more interesting although the formula of beach and booze is fairly universal. The bottom line is, regardless of race, colour, religion or financial status, we all appear to have the same expectations and desires, but one of the less attractive aspects of many Westerners at play is the total disregard for the sensibilities of local ettiquet. The sign saying 'no topless bathing' was perfectly adequate, even if you had considerably less than 20/20 vision, yet women insisted on grilling their breasts to a crisp with no attempt at seclusion.

Fortunately, Colva was not typical of Goa in the same way that Goa was not typical of India. Despite its size, many Goans were seeking independence from India's political administration. The Portuguese legacy lived on with nearly half the population fiercely clinging to a devout Catholic heritage, maintaining an air of old colonialism in architecture and attitude. Even their famous vindaloo was originally a Portuguese dish. The undeniable beauty and serenity of the tiny state had been rediscovered by European travellers some three decades before, but showed little sign of being seduced by pale-face dollars.

The state is a labyrinth of rivers and waterways feeding the population on a diet of fresh fish, so riding inland was often necessary to find a bridge. The uncluttered rural roads took me over devastatingly beautiful palm-clad mountains punctuated by vivid green almost luminescent paddy fields. Laughing school children in crisp uniforms waved at the strange sight of a biker wearing a crash helmet, which is rare anywhere in India. Lazy water buffalo with eye-brow horns wallowed in the glutinous mud, munching lush grass. Most of India's farming is free-range to the extreme, with well-fed cows, goats, pigs and chickens roaming roads and beaches scavenging. Even the multitude of dogs, like wild dingoes, looked healthy in short sandy coats. In the colourful villages, little bars spilled into the streets and markets buzzed with energy.

The ever-present problem of money drove me to the State capital Panaji. It is often referred to as Panjim, as the British conquerors were either too stupid or arrogant to learn many of the Indian names. A country where most towns have two names can be confusing to a mapless traveller.

Without exception, Panaji was my favourite Indian town so far, with broad streets skirting well-tended municipal gardens, watched over by the imposing Church of Immaculate Conception. Its gleaming white walls tempt many tourists to climb towards heaven up rather too many steps for the high humidity. From the shade of a bar, it was easy to imagine the intrepid, early Europeans in pith helmets sweating their way through tropical safari suits, as lazy ceiling fans disturbed reluctant air. Surprisingly, the traffic flowed without the constant use of horns, but there was still only one bank that accepted a Visa card for rupees. This is the chink in Goa's tourist trade. Allow the best part of a day to fill in the paperwork which has to be laboriously copied down in vast dusty ledgers. Not a pulsating computer screen in sight, as an unreliable power supply made them less reliable than the pen. Just as I thought I was making progress, an ancient Sikh security guard hung up his equally ancient Lee Enfield rifle and announced the bank was closed for lunch. Not a country of convenience.

One big problem was beginning to depress me after negotiating another bucket of rupees. The foot pump that I was so dependent on packed up. To you this may not sound like a big deal, but without a means of blowing up tyres on a daily basis, I was helpless. A little creative arc welding would have done the trick, so I selected one of the many workshops crackling in blue pinpoints of light. The young man grasped the job in one and proceeded to attack the pump with a fierce gas torch disregarding my protests. Within seconds it was reduced to a shapeless, molten blob, then burst into flames. He cooled the offending object with a bucket of water, then scraped it off the concrete floor with a shovel, before handing it over with a gentle smile. I could have throttled him on the spot, but resorted to shouting at him in a foreign language. So incensed was I, a trip to the police station was called for to complain and find out where the engineer could find me a replacement. Several officers turned the impromptu sculpture over in their hands with smirks on their faces. In unison they shrugged, wobbled their heads for a while and said I should not have gone to such an incompetent engineer. It was not *his* fault he was useless at his job, so I had to contain my anger and remember I was in their country with different rules.

The best part of the following day was spent trying to phone Marian and track down a new pump. The call to Marian was brief and expensive. I paid the equivalent of a week's rations up front for the two-minute call from a corner shop, keeping an eye on my watch counting down the seconds. There was just not time to cover the niceties, for fear of being cut off mid-sentence and the call had a purpose other than 'just keeping in touch', so an element of verbal economy was essential.

The foot pump, after exhaustive enquiries, was eventually discovered in the bowels of a bicycle shop and it was a monster. India thrives on low-tolerance engineering and low-tech everything else. This brute was massive with a totally unnecessary gauge of metal and an eighteen inch stroke – but it worked, sort of, even if I did have to hire a couple of sherpas to carry it back to my guest house.

India is a destination to hate or to love and curiously enough for the same contradictory reasons. The administration in banks could be frustrating, even challenging, but the satisfaction of scoring after pushing through crowds rather than queues was exhilarating. Public transport was notable for its lack of pace and counting votes after a national election took months. It is a continent running on its own rules and very much at its own time zone, which dictates the speed of everything, including overland travel. After racing the length of South East Asia trying to get to India, I was more than happy to trot along at their speed rather than gallop.

Food is another classic example in the love – hate relationship as I have never known anyone to be indifferent about it. Personally, I love the predominantly vegetable-based dishes that have to be fresh in a climate where nothing keeps for long and refrigerators are a luxury. The downside of that phenomena is the lack of cold beer as most things are served at room temperature, which can be pretty high. Many countries offer tourists nourishment they are used to, may even expect, but in India you would never be offered a 'full English breakfast' anywhere outside a posh international hotel.

It had been a trying day but I was elated with my purchase and began to enjoy the gentle pace of Panaji. My guest house room was a gem for a couple of quid, overlooking a mish-mash of tiled roofs casting interesting shadows on a sluggish green river. Before leaving early that morning to trawl the shops, I noticed a tabby cat just outside the window lying amongst fag ends and monkey nut shells on a rough red earthenware tiled roof. Marian and I had a tabby 'cat child' called Buttocks, so I took a little interest. Eight hours later, it had not moved, so I assumed it was recently dead and chucked a couple of dried-up chillies at it for a reaction. It stretched, looked at me with some disdain, as most cats do and slunk off to catch a rat. I do admire their independence.

My room was like a palace after spending a couple of nights on the road. No two walls were parallel and they were painted a dark crimson to shoulder height. The rest was once white, but had suffered the stains of age. The high ceiling was criss-crossed with wires to a disturbingly unbalanced ceiling fan and inevitable fluorescent light. Two big gothic-style windows peaked at soft triangles reminiscent of ecclesiastical architecture, making my space light and airy. Reflections from the river danced across every surface. A wash basin with no taps was cocked at a jaunty angle and two high steps led to a sit-down toilet. It was like sitting on a throne perched so high up with a fabulous view of the sleepy river.

In the evening I walked the active waterfront in search of a celebratory beer, so pleased was I about finding a foot pump. It never failed to amaze me how these apparently insignificant details, the sort of things that would be mundane in normal life, elated the soul more than achieving a major conquest. In Sri Lanka, I had felt similar joy acquiring a roll of toilet paper. After searching the shops in vain, I had gone to an expensive hotel for a drink and pinched two rolls from their 'guests only' cubical. Being white I was not challenged by the attendant but, getting out, dropping a limp rupee note into his tray with a bulge under my T-shirt was not so easy.

Sound rather than sight attracted me to a little bar pretending to be a British pub. From the outside there was nothing to it – a panelled door and 'olde worlde' bay window with small panes of glass covered in dense yellow cellophane to keep the sun out. Inside, there was even less of it. A tiny bar was backed by mirrors doubling the image of shelves crowded with bottles and optics. Four barstools were occupied by locals going all rubbernecked over the Western music and filled half the space. Two small round tables and half a dozen chairs competed for the remaining square inch. I ordered a beer and small Goan brandy through the half-light. Local brandy was very palatable and about 40 pence a bottle. The barman claimed to only have imported spirits so he could charge more, but I reckon bottles of Remy Martin and Johnnie Walker were refilled with equally good home-produced products. Wedged into a corner after passing the time of day with the other drinkers, I started catching up on notes, when two young white women entered, blinking as their eyes adjusted to the gloom. Only two seats were available and at my table, so the notebook was folded away to give them nearly enough room for their drinks.

Vanessa and Alison were two 'good time' girls who had left their nursing jobs in Lincoln and bought round the world tickets, starting in India.

They had had the brains to research before leaving and knew the good places to stay and visit. Neither had been on a motorcycle in their lives before, but had rented a couple of scooters to visit Panaji from their beach resort in Baga.

I confessed there was nothing pressing on my agenda for a day, so followed in their dust to a superb roomy guest house set in the shade of leafy palms and papayas. The village sprawled on unmade roads to an uncluttered beach where there were more cows than people taking advantage of a row of beach loungers. A gauntlet of make-shift palm-clad shacks offered devastating food and cool beer for a few pence before the welcoming waves of the Arabian Sea.

Dusk blushed the sky with a streak of crimson and the girls were determined to show me their favourite place to watch the sun set. Vanessa jumped on the back of my bike and Alison led for quite a distance along rough sandy tracks. A 49cc 'twist & go' scooter really comes into its own on such terrain. You can practically pick one off the ground with a single hand. A 1200cc Triumph with pillion is not so easy. The front tyre sank in a soft bit, hit a rock and Vanessa and I were pitched into the bushes. The only damage was to my ego, being the experienced rider on a performance machine. The aptly named Sunset Bar was worth the effort, cut off on one side by a tidal stream shallow enough to wade through. All our biking effort was to find a bridge inland when we were only a few hundred yards from where we were staying, as the crow flies.

With the aid of delicious Allo Gobi, Kingfisher beer and a few joints made with local grass, we sat self-satisfied watching a huge orange orb being extinguished by the sea. Those unexpected delights were few and far between, but made a year on the road worthwhile. Riding back in the dark, stoned and half-pissed was a doddle – I think.

Shadows of waving palm leaves animated my room at first light. The temptation to find my bearings in daylight prompted me to explore while the sun was still low in the sky. There was no block system to walk round to avoid getting lost, but the beach formed an arterial route to other villages, so all I had to do was find the sea again to get back. The villages of Candolim and the much busier Calangute crept imperceptibly into each other in a wide arabesque of coconutpalm-fringed beach contained by a headland at each end. Dilapidated Portuguese fortresses, some dating back to the 16th century, squatted stoutly on each rusty cliff projected seawards. Inland, the markets were in full swing for locals to shop for food. The tourist stalls waited for the white folk to emerge later in the heat of the day. *Mad Dogs and Englishmen* should have been written by an Indian. In clear early morning light, sounds and smells are pure, distinct, without being smudged by heat, disturbed dust or the bustle of traffic. Pungent spice stalls groaned under heaps of turmeric, saffron and fresh chilli. The best deals were to be made with those who just spread their wares on a sarong on the ground. For a few rupees I bought a huge bag of assorted red and green chillies. Their colour and texture were so perfect, they could have been moulded in plastic. I told the trader I only wanted a few as they dry up so quickly, but he insisted on filling the newspaper dunce's hat as he had no change for my lowest denomination coin.

Some hours later I returned to find the girls sunning themselves on the beach, sucking on slices of water melon. The green skin and pink flesh gave the appearance of a grotesque grin as juice dribbled off their chins. An over-affectionate calf joined Vanessa on her lounger licking her face for salt and moisture. Cows are opportunists that will eat money and passports as happily as meadow grass.

As I was only going to be there for one day, they were determined to show me the sights, so we boarded a fishing boat 'taxi' to Anjuna market for an extravaganza of colour and activity. The scene was a blaze of billowing fabric, carved hardwood and sparkling silver jewellery. Traders were a mixture of Tibetans, northern Indians and even some bad-attitude long-stay Europeans, taking advantage of the sub-continent's biggest concentration of tourists, which still did not add up to a great deal.

I had become irrationally attached to my two new friends and that evening set out in determined mood to enjoy the last one together. Maybe we were so comfortable together because of my experiences with Marian and Rena. Who knows? – but I was beginning to really lust after Vanessa. To keep the memory alive, I filmed them on the beach in the soft evening glow. They will never see the footage of two uninhibited, sparkling young women on their lifetime adventure.

I scored some cheap grass from a beach trader for us to smoke strolling the beach after dark splashing in warm lapping sea. The munchies hit us at the same time so we selected a shack to eat in at random. The mouth-watering gut-buster of Goan fish curry, vegetables and chapati, with two large Kingfishers, added up to the price of a pint of beer in a UK pub. The girls finished off with enormous ice creams served in half pint glasses. Alison suggested we sprinkle grass on our meal which had the most rewarding result of prolonging the effect. Walking the long beach back to Baga, I attempted, in fits of giggles, to demonstrate the luminous algae effect in the surf but the little sods refused to perform, leaving me with no good purpose for a skinny dip.

Only two hours after the fabulous meal we all felt a little peckish, so fell into another shack for a drink and a snack. Incredibly, we all consumed another huge meal and *they* finished with ice cream – *again!* Marijuana does a great deal for one's appreciation of food and lacking the sensation of hunger, it is the only time I really enjoy eating.

From the candle-lit sanctuary of our table we observed a small boy letting off rockets on the beach. Goans are big on home-produced fireworks despite their unpredictability. The rockets were about as controllable as a fart in a wind tunnel, exploding in all directions. Many of the rockets never made it off the launch pad as the small boy threw himself backwards into the flanks of a spectating cow, in an attempt to avoid the erupting pyrotechnics. One simply refused to perform and was kicked over in frustration just as the cordite ignited. The thing came snaking into our shack like a cruise missile a foot from the ground. Shrieking diners lifted their feet attempting not to impede its progress. Seconds later there was a loud bang and much cursing from the shack's tiny kitchen. It poses the question 'have their nuclear weapons the benefit of better guidance systems?'

After more local brandy, the girls retired to their room from mine in the early hours. I had hoped Vanessa would stay behind, as there was definitely a point of contact between us, but I did not want to be pushy in case it caused a rift. The girls were out of bed at a reasonable hour for my departure. I did not take addresses but gave them mine with the promise they would stay in touch. Six months later I received a postcard from the Great Barrier Reef,

Australia but, sadly, no more from two fun-loving nurses from Lincoln.

For me, the road north held no more pleasant surprises as the temperature dropped with latitude and altitude but with Delhi in my sights, a Tata truck was to change the course of my adventure.

22. Near Death Near Delhi

Motorbike travel is a little like playing chess, trying to work out a strategy several moves in advance, but with your opponent constantly changing the state of play, putting obstacles in your way. The ride from Goa was painfully slow and not without incident as I attempted to find a road going north to Delhi. I made the mistake of riding late into the night in tortuous traffic. Rounding one tight bend, I was presented by two trucks abreast hurtling towards me on a road wide enough for only one and a half of them. Each truck only had a single headlamp working, so I was a little confused at first as to how many vehicles were about to end my life. The overtaking truck teetered at a precarious angle with two wheels off the road, so he had slammed into the other to get a better foothold. The plan did not come up to the driver's expectation, as he bounced off leaving me nearly enough room to scrape between them. The truck bumper squarely caught a pannier bursting it open, spilling my possessions over the road, before smashing into another truck a few yards behind me. The impact and steep verge forced him off the road, holding up traffic long enough for me to pick up the important belongings strewn about in the halo of headlamps. Precious foot pump, sleeping bag, document file were stuffed back in and amazingly the lock still worked. The remains of Wayne's hat and emergency poncho, that had served so well from New Orleans, were left to fend for themselves. On a lighter bike I would probably have been thrust under the wheels of the competing truck. The incident was so unnerving, I needed to get off the road and find somewhere to camp. This was not easy, especially at night, as it was impossible to see what lay immediately off the road and there was generally only a couple of feet between me and the following truck bumper. One of those bumpers made the decision for me with a hefty thwack. The bike dropped six or eight inches into the darkness off the road not knowing if we were heading for a river, swamp or large concrete structure. With the wheels locked up, bumping over rocks, the Triumph did not need my help to fall on its side. Naturally, the truck did not stop, so the driver still does not know if he killed the only British bike and rider team in India.

Fortunately neither of us were badly hurt or we would probably have been recycled into 'Welcome to Bombay' ashtrays. Everything had to be removed for me to wrestle the bike upright, then I noticed in fading torch light, the trauma had flattened the back tyre. I had no choice but to struggle a few yards farther off the road and wait for morning. Removing and storing contact lenses in the dark is a difficult but essential practice and I vowed to clean my teeth twice in the morning. The noise of traffic just a few yards away was fantastic and occasionally pieces of gravel flew off churning tyres making a dull thud against my sleeping bag and a more musical note when they struck the Triumph.

Thoughts of 'what the hell am I going to do now' crowded my brain when a hand out of the darkness tugged at my sleeping bag. The accompanying voice said the land was private and much too dangerous to sleep on. I never discovered why, but three helpful strangers assisted me in getting the bike back over the bumps, across the road (nothing could have been more dangerous than that) and through some steel gates, all on a flat back tyre. Not easy.

The 'Bossman', who spoke a little English, showed me into a little room where several bodies lay in slumber. The shapeless mounds made it difficult to determine how many there were in the flickering of home-made oil lamps. They did have electric light, but that was their day for a power cut. A plate of cold Allo Gobi and chapati miraculously appeared. That was the first nourishment of the day and gratefully received. Bossman looked startled when he learned I was heading for Pakistan. "You Pakistani?" he asked, alarmed. "Do I look Pakistani?" I replied. "I don't know. I have never seen one."

I was escorted to a half-built structure, and invited to stay the night. It looked like someone had run out of money just after the concrete pouring stage, but there was a roof to keep the dew off. Bossman brought half a bucket of water and bid me good night at around 1.00am. The concrete floor was less forgiving than gravel and dawn, at about 6.00am, was a long time coming.

The bike was half-obscured by a plume of mist as I inspected the damage inflicted on the back wheel. Air was escaping from the Mexican dent and it would not reseat on the rim. Bossman came along with a glass of hot sweet and very welcome chai, but with the less welcome news that it was

Saturday and there would be no one around to help until Monday. I had noticed a small office block with names on the doors beginning with 'Doctor' or 'Professor', and ending in 'Chief plant psychologist' or some such grand title. I was in the grounds of The Research Institute for Indian Rubber. A good place to get a puncture, you would be forgiven for thinking. No such luck and with senior staff away for the weekend, I had to fix the problem or wait two days for a lift to the nearest repair man.

Dave Barr had given me some soft rubber patches that I forced into the dent with glue and then welded into place by setting fire to it with lighter fuel. It made a disgusting smell and lots of black smoke, but after endless pumping and reassembly, the bike was ready to face the road once more. Bossman received a Swiss Army knife for all his help. He could not believe his good fortune and proceeded to show everyone, with all the implements sticking out like a porcupine. Living in a dry state, the only gadget they could not fathom was the corkscrew. After a half-mimed, half-verbal explanation he was not convinced a metal pigtail was necessary for opening wine.

By Rajasthan, the roads had deteriorated considerably. It is a huge state that skirts the Pakistan border, but Theo, in Bangkok, had told me to head north west from Delhi, crossing at Lahore because of the impending conflict. By mistake I visited Jodhpur instead of Jaipur, but was glad to say I had been to where the trousers come from. I can not fathom how a garment adopted by the British ruling class got its name from a town where the only working animals were noble camels.

The bad roads were punishing tyres and in a couple of hours the bike suffered two punctures in the rear. The tubeless repair kit had got so wet in Guatamala, or somewhere, the instructions had been reduced to half a diagram of someone having sex with a tyre as flat as a Rajasthan chapati. Nevertheless, I calmly worked it out sitting in the dirt next to homicidal traffic and was gratified to find how easy and effective the rubber grommits were. Punctures and near misses, however, paled into insignificance some fifty miles from Delhi when a half-ton British-built missile took on a vomit green Tata.

India appeared to suffer from a national surplus of vile green paint, frequently used on home-produced Tatas that grind nose-to-tail across the sub-continent. One such monster, approaching from the other direction made a last-second decision to turn right across my path – with no warning and without slowing down.

Like so many trucks I had seen lying on their sides, this one was packed past its stability limit, and took the turn on two wheels. This was probably the reason for the driver's attention being directed away from a bright blue motorcycle, with headlight burning, speeding towards him. Fully loaded, with me in the saddle, the Triumph weighed 480kg and had I not struck the truck broadside, it would have toppled over and crushed me.

Three things flashed through my mind in the milli-second before realising disaster was inevitable and the world went dark. One, this was going to hurt (death did not occur as an option). Two, why do they paint trucks such a disgusting colour and, finally, this is the end of my attempt to ride a motorcycle around the world.

I do not remember getting to my feet, or removing my crash helmet to survey a very fucked Triumph lying in the road. It was not the closest *I* had been to terminal injury since leaving home, but it was the first devastating damage to the bike and without it the trip was over. 'Red mist' anger took over from shock, as I sprinted over to the stationary truck with murder in my eyes. There was no handle on the driver's door, so standing on the foot-plate, I leant in, grabbed the guy by the scruff of the neck and started dragging him out of the window. Curiously enough he did not resist, but clearly he was not going to fit through the hole – then I noticed blood trickling down his face and neck. The palm of one of my hands was bleeding profusely and so was the thumb on the other. I glanced back at the bike to see a crowd had accumulated and people were picking up bits strewn across the road. The terrified driver being assaulted by a mad long-haired white person was released, as I turned my attention to the theft of possessions. I had misjudged the situation and they were just moving everything to the side of the road to prevent traffic from running over it. The offending truck driver took the opportunity to drive away, doing nothing at all for my karma.

The crowd pushed in tighter until I had to stand on the tank of my battered friend. Not even splashing blood at them from gushing wounds deterred their interest. From my vantage point, I spotted India's version of a Willis Jeep approaching and got a warm feeling about the smart young man riding shotgun, with a neat moustache and red-rimmed glasses. The vehicle pulled up and I asked him if he spoke English. "Of course I do," came a friendly reply. I dropped to my knees with relief. The gravity of the incident was sinking in – and bits were beginning to hurt!

Naveen Vashistha, sales executive for Drawmet Wire Private Limited, or so his blood-stained card read, could not do enough to help. He found a man who owned a truck and had seen the whole incident. With Naveen acting as interpreter, the quiet stranger offered to transport me and the bike to Delhi for no reward just to prove 'not all Indians are bad'. I thanked him and said he did not have to prove anything. He gave me a dubious rag to quench the blood before shaking hands. It looked like it had been wedged up someone's bottom for a long time, so I dabbed around the wound.

For the first time in India, I found a use for the sodding crowd that accumulated everywhere I went. With ease they picked the bike up and placed it gently in the back of the open truck, along with a lot of broken plastic. I insisted on straddling the bike for the two-hour journey as it was rather unstable and likely to sustain more damage rattling around by itself.

Two hours to inspect the damage to the bike, the damage to my body and think about all that had happened and what may have been. We had traversed more countries than I had fingers and toes – not a bad effort in anyone's book but, as a team, the adventure was about to come to an abrupt end. I could not see anyway of making the bike roadworthy while in India. Just getting the necessary parts imported would have been logistic nightmare and where was I to find all the special tools needed for reconstruction? 'If only' is not an expression I dwell on because there is always a darker side to fate. If only the driver had seen me – if only the flipped coin had come up heads not tails when choosing a route. Granted, things could have been a damn sight rosier, but I had just survived another life-threatening encounter and escaped with a few cuts and bruises, which was more than could be said for my poor bike. I was saddened that it was probably not going to be economically viable to ship it home. After all we had been through together, I was going to have to leave a sick friend in a foreign land, but there was plenty to think about before then, like finding somewhere to stay that could accommodate a smashed up motorcycle.

Fortunately, Theo, in Bangkok, had told me of a place called the Tourist Camp in New Delhi where many overland travellers accumulate. A multinational task force was recruited to unload the bike and park it between rugged four-wheel drive vehicles. All standard rooms were occupied so I settled for a deluxe one. The only difference between them was the deluxe version had a sheet on a bed that filled the tiny room. My baggage covered every inch of floor space. The presence of so many other travellers, all willing to chat, sympathise and advise made it a good location to be. Battle-scarred Land Rovers and VW campers littered the place and again, I was surprised by the number of young children with shrill voices playing in a multitude of languages. Big sinks were occupied by women washing clothes Indian-style and a funny little open-air restaurant boasted a European menu of sorts. There must have been about thirty breeze-block 'cells' painted orange contrasting with the red earth and a semicircle of white stones marked a camping area big enough for half a dozen tents. It looked more like a refugee camp than a tourist camp, but I was glad to be amongst other travellers. We were all people searching for something within ourselves that went deeper than just chalking up destinations and I never heard anyone *boast* about their travel. There were no complaints about the lack of facilities or lack of spare parts for a VW camper van. We were all there through choice, not necessarily under the best circumstances, but no one forced us to spend our time and hard-earned money travelling.

In a sombre mood, I patched my wounds as well as possible with limited medical knowledge and even more limited medical kit. My thumb had been cut to the bone but thankfully it was the worst injury. Notes scribbled in my book for that day said it all:

'29th February - Tourist Camp, Delhi

Death came knocking again today. How many times can someone *nearly* die? My nine lives were used up long before taking on this task – and yet I walked away from a 30mph collision with a solid steel wall – and am depressed because my thumb will not stop bleeding. It is difficult to write with a bandaged hand and, yes, I am wallowing in self pity, but must move on, with or without my trusty friend.'

According to intelligence gained from locals and others experienced in Indian travel, getting the bike repaired anywhere on the sub-continent was a non-starter as import duty on 'luxury' items was prohibitive. I could have purchased a fleet of home-manufactured Enfields just for the price of shipping a Triumph front wheel, so my choices were to dump it or take it somewhere else. Gloomily, I studied the world wide Triumph dealer list reading aloud to myself making sure nothing was going to be missed. 'USA, Mexico, Australia, Singapore – I've already been there and some of them are farther away than England. South Africa, Dubai – Dubai – where the hell is Dubai? It must only be across the Indian Ocean somewhere – and surely it's a town not a country – so what does UAE stand for – and what ever did I do with the business card that lovely woman Sue gave me on a train in New Zealand?'

I did not exactly run about stark naked shouting 'eureka', but all of a sudden there was a spark of hope, just a small one, so not time to get too excited. Several knowledgeable Tourist Camp residents confirmed the only obstacle between me and the United Arab Emirates was the Indian Ocean. Just one obstacle – one big obstacle, but it was worth trawling every shipping company in Delhi before booking a one-way flight home.

New Delhi is a city that looks as if a town planner sat down one morning with a blank piece of paper and had the guts of a logical, well laid out design by lunch time. From Connaught Place in the centre, three wide circular roads of different circumferences are joined by wheel spokes radiating outwards. Well tended parks graced with sculptures and fountains were strategically placed between identical and uninspired office blocks identified alphabetically. This was where the logic fell apart. An aerial view may well have revealed what was in the planner's mind, but on the ground, chaos was firmly in control. My target was F22, which was next to M19 and no one on the ground had a clue. A whole frustrating day was spent searching for shipping agents. I visited five and the last one told me to go back to the one I started from. There is something about the Indian work ethic that says avoid it at all costs and it was obvious the task was going to take time, tenacity and vast wads of rupees.

Returning to the tourist camp, tired and angry, a small tent had been pitched a few yards from my deluxe chalet. An old but obviously well maintained 850cc Moto Guzzi was being attended to by a good-looking guy in his mid-thirties. Phil Holden was nationalistically confused, carrying an Australian and a British passport, but calling himself English despite an Aussie twang. He had ridden from Perth via Madras en route to London. We immediately recognised kindred spirits and I am glad to say we have remained in touch ever since. He reminded me of my ex-business partner and friend, Steve Rolls, with short-cropped dark hair and disarming grin. It prompted me to think about the company I had deserted for a very different lifestyle that was not going too well at the time. I hoped Steve was doing better than me on that day. They were both over a decade younger than me and shared an encouraging optimism coupled to a reassuring attitude.

He put my problems in perspective, confirming the Triumph was not terminal and, being a nurse, he advised me about preventing infection in my open wounds and said it was a miracle no bones were broken. I was lucky to avoid an Indian hospital. He laughed wobbling his head like a local saying ".... not available", the most used Delhi expression. Even in the teeth of adversity there is a bright side, and I passionately believe that from all bad, comes some good making the chance meeting with Phil almost worth the trauma, so much did he lift my spirits.

We found a dreadful dingy bar called Thugs for a couple of expensive beers, then walked the streets looking for something to eat. Little food stalls crowded the pavements selling delicious mossala in a multitude of guises and fresh chapati for a few pence. The banquet was handed over in plastic bags, so we walked back to base to eat it out of billy cans, washing it down with beer. Phil smoked disgusting local cigarettes called Beedies, which are not much more than a tobacco leaf rolled up and fastened by a piece of pink cotton. Labour must have been cheaper than glue and a pack of thirty, wrapped in newspaper, cost about eight pence. Courtesy of a Dutchman in a wreck of a camper van, the evening was concluded with a joint that rendered Phil incapable of straightforward activities like walking and talking.

At 8.00am there was a knock at my door. "Cup of tea mate?" Phil had made excellent chai and scrambled eggs on his minute cooker. He even had a pepper grinder and Tabasco sauce! What a traveller! The breakfast set me up in determined mood to make some positive progress, armed with a wad of rupees nearly three inches thick. All I had to do was pay at the air freight office where Mr. Singh politely asked me to sit and wait. Not ten feet away he sat at his desk to eat lunch and read the paper for an hour. As he wiped his desk top with the last piece of chapati, he glanced over and told me to come back tomorrow. This could only happen in India, where the rulebook is different to the rest of the world and it was not my place to criticise. The packers said they had a truck coming from the other side of town, so could I get the Triumph to them for when it arrived. When I asked them how, they said rent a truck of course. You would not believe how much slapping of foreheads and neck-wobbling went on before they agreed to divert their truck half a mile to the Tourist Camp rather than me having to go and find another one.

By the time all arrangements had been made to transport me and bike to the nearest Triumph dealer, in Dubai, I felt several years older. Phil headed off for Nepal with promises of staying in touch, leaving me a day with nothing to do before my final encounter with Indian administration and catching my flight. The Tourist Camp was on the cusp of new and old Delhi, so I wandered off to see the town's roots. As a child I had formed an impression of the capital and was pleasantly surprised to find it clean and almost devoid of the beggars that had lined the streets thirty years earlier. India had been part of the military round Asia tour and a place my parents had a special affection for. They met and married there just after World War Two and my sister was born there, as the country moved bloodlessly from British Raj to independence.

I came to the conclusion the British were largely responsible for creating begging as a viable means of income. Prior to British rule, India had its enormous rich poor divide as did most of the world, but with the rich being a tiny minority, beggars must have had a difficult time finding anyone with any spare cash. Then came Mr. Paleface by the boat load and, although British forces and civil servants were far from wealthy, they were well catered for and perceived by locals as being rich. The scope for beggars had increased enormously so their numbers naturally swelled, increasing competition. Mothers would blind or mutilate their babies to equip them better for the task, but if begging ceases to be commercially viable, beggars have to go and do something else – or starve. Giving money exacerbates the problem.

Mahatma Gandi, possibly the world's finest politician, changed the face of India peacefully, forcing the British out, filling hungry bellies and bringing employment.

More by chance than design, I found the impressive Red Fort with impenetrable rusty stone walls, towering into the sky from behind a broad moat choked with grass. Disappointingly, there was practically no information about its heritage and the museum was a relic of old colonialism with displays of very dusty First World War firearms. In raging noon-day heat, I could not be bothered to tag along with a melting crowd of pale faces having a tedious tour and, by chance, I discovered an impending Air India strike, was to bring my flight forward a day. I was off on a wing and a prayer to renew an acquaintance in the United Arab Emirates.

23. A Dish-Dash to Dubai

With very few preconceived ideas about Dubai, I struggled through the airport, weighed down by too much baggage. My best guess was it would be similar to Singapore, which was not far wrong, except not quite so sterile, but, compared to India, it was another world. Changing money was a breeze, customs took all of thirty seconds to check my passport and everyone spoke English. The Emirates are half a dozen wealthy states with no apparent barriers but, like the USA, each Emirate has its own local regulations.

From the air, I had seen unending desert, which gave way to opulent dwellings with a patchwork of green lawns, sparkling swimming pools and excellent straight roads disappearing into the shimmering heat haze. The impression on the ground was not dissimilar, with well-irrigated gardens adding greenery to a spartan desert landscape. Even central reservations on endless immaculate dual-carriageways are kept in bowling-green condition by miles of an intricate sprinkler system fed by regenerated sewage. Islamic architecture graces every horizon with mosaiced mosque spires, onion domes and minarets glinting under the ferocious sun.

The Emirates are obviously affluent and cosmopolitan, with only 20% of the population being indigenous Arabs. The bulk of the manual labour force are Indian, Pakistani, Celanese or Bangladeshi, with whites filling in many of the managerial roles. Arab men generally dress in traditional dish-dash, an ankle-length shirt available in a multitude of shades of white, topped off with matching or red check headdress. Local women perspire in black robes, frequently with the face completely obscured, except for the eyes, by flowing yashmaks making them resemble large black traffic cones. As both sexes dress in frocks, toilet door graphics show subtle differences in headdress.

Feeling a little desperate, I called Sue Al-Sobky, the woman who had in a weak moment given me her business card on a train in New Zealand. I had sent her cards warning of my arrival but, after such a brief meeting, I had no idea how a near stranger was going to react to a possibly unwelcome guest. We arranged to meet the following day for lunch, so I struggled off to a five-star youth hostel, far superior to any hotel I had stayed in so far.

With the bike still in transit, I walked the couple of miles to our designated Pizza Hut rendezvous to meet Sue. It had rained hard during the night and I was surprised to see so much surface water hanging around. You would have been forgiven for assuming every drop would immediately be absorbed by desert sand, but a high water table does not allow natural drainage. I still can not work out why this phenomena refuses to make the desert fertile. The Emirates' wealth became more apparent with the absence of buses and bicycles and, as people avoid walking in 40 degrees centigrade, most roads on my walk through Sharjah were edged by waterlogged sand rather than pavement.

Jumping between puddles, my mind focused on the telephone conversation with Sue. There had been a little apprehension in her voice and I did not wish to force myself on her hospitality. I can not bear the idea of being tolerated, but a desperate situation calls for drastic measures. With a smashed-up bike and very little money, I needed all the help on offer.

Sue was cool, smart and to the point. I was welcome to stay in her home, but she did not live in domestic bliss with her Egyptian husband, Hany. He had not worked for five years and seemed content to be kept by a wife who slept in a separate room and was actively seeking a divorce. This for any woman with a Muslim spouse, especially in an Islamic country, is difficult if the husband does not agree and Hany was not going to lie down and relinquish his meal ticket. Sue, with a demanding job and even more demanding eight-year-old son, was not having a particularly easy time but, typical of strong women, she threw herself into my problems with a reassuringly positive attitude. We reflected back to our first meeting under very different circumstances and she paid me the complement of my life. She said meeting me on a slow train to Christchurch had been the highlight of her holiday because 'it had given her hope, and the knowledge that it is never too late to change your life'.

Credit to Hany, the invitation to disrupt their lives was endorsed and Sue showed me to Omar's room as he manfully volunteered to share with his mother. The house was a rambling concrete bungalow she described as being old and falling apart despite it only being thirty years since the footings had been dug in soft sand. Few buildings saw that age as the concrete is made with sea water and erodes at a frightening pace. The regeneration of buildings after a decade or so is encouraged as land prices rocket and a more salubrious dwelling can be constructed to secure higher rent, but I liked it just the way it was with a lived-in feel, reflecting the character of the occupants. From the cool of the air-conditioned sitting room, I gazed out at a small lawn skirted by various outbuildings, including servants quarters and a sizeable but redundant swimming pool that must have passed its easy repair stage and was awaiting demolition with the rest of the property.

Omar's den was crammed to the ceiling with toys, books and expensive clothes, to pacify a hyperactive brain. Hany, in attitude at least, presented himself as more of a child than Omar. He was suffering from a chest infection that Sue said was a common occurrence for him. She had had to practically push him out of the door to go to a pharmacy for medication, which understandably she found exasperating. He was a big man, with great presence and still displayed signs of youthful good looks and an engaging sparkle. A round pudgy face and rotund body, with more than his fair share of thick, wavy black hair, eliminated any doubt that he was Omar's father.

Sue drove me to her offices at the Gulf Agency Company (Dubai) LLC, a Swedish organisation controlling freight flow. Her suave forty-something boss welcomed a scruffy biker with immaculate English. He could well have been a native of Bournmouth rather than Stockholm. One wonders whether such people are born with charisma, or is it something that develops with power and status. With a wave of his hand, lesser mortals were briefed to assist me through customs - and of course transport could be arranged to take my battered bike to the Triumph dealer. Sue was turning out to be the fairy godmother who could make everything better with a wave of her wand and I loved her for the dynamic energy that oozed from every pore.

Back at the house, I started work to resolve my immediate problems. I faxed Bruno Tagliaferri at Triumph pleading for parts, but he stoutly refused to budge from his previous offer of a back wheel replacement, which meant I had to find the money for a complete front end rebuild and arrange to have everything shipped out. In fairness to Bruno, he had other things to do than devote his working day to an irritating customer several thousand miles away. The only person who did offer to help in my dilemma was Tony Brown at Redhill Motors back in Brighton. Not only was he prepared to work his way through the logistical nightmare of sending me the appropriate parts, but also arranged a set of complementary tyres which I badly needed. He had been following my adventure with interest and erected a notice board in the showroom displaying cards sent from every destination. Marian repaid a loan, Triumph paid import duty and Tony went to work with a vengeance making arrangements. All I needed was the money to pay for the rebuild, even though I had volunteered to assist the mechanics at Gorica Trading, the only Triumph dealer for several thousand miles. All this sounds easy enough, but it took several weeks of dedicated work to achieve a result.

During those first few days in the Emirates, once the day's administration of faxing and letter writing was over there was not a hell of a lot to do accept acquaint myself with the local area and trying to keep out of Hany's way. I did not wish to cause Sue more grief so busied myself with repair work around the house and entertained Omar after school. We combed the beaches playing silly games with his pompous friend Rohan. He was the same age as Omar and not desperately likeable, but his mixed birth meant he was fluent in German, Hindi and English. Being a linguistic paraplegic, I admired his advantage. Other days we would sit and draw, which may have helped justify spending five years at art college, but the boys just found more and more complicated things for me to sketch in their school books, defeating the object of the exercise

I thought this would contribute to my keep and help Sue but, in reality, it just made Hany feel all the more inadequate. Unwittingly, I had rubbed salt into their domestic wound and it was left to Sue to tell me to leave. She was close to tears with anger and embarrassment explaining that Hany thought it was time for me to move on as 'having house guests is not the Eastern way'. I packed up, thanked Sue for her hospitality and apologised for exacerbating her domestic problems. Secretly I was livid with Hany for not having the balls to chuck me out himself and, from a logistical point of view, it did present a big problem.

By the time my wet washing had been crammed into a heavy rucksack it was after 10.00pm and raining hard. I walked the couple of miles into town stopping at the first affordable hotel. It was still outrageously expensive as Dubai was celebrating a shopping orgy attracting thousands to the state and

186

giving hoteliers an excuse to double their room rates. Panic nibbled at the corners of my confused brain. A tent in the desert would have suited me just fine, but mobility to embassies and the bike repair shop was essential in such a spread-out community. Predictably, my stressed-out fairy godmother came up with a solution and I moved into a colleague's spare room feeling even more like a fish out of water.

Sonja really did not have a clue what she had taken on by offering accommodation, rent free, to a passing stranger, but she displayed the bubbly confidence of a woman in control, so I thought she would not hesitate to tell me when it was time to leave and, thankfully, she had no qualms about putting me to work around her home, painting woodwork and repairing fly screens. This helped justify the roof over my head, but was not resolving the problem of paying for bike repair, international telephone calls and visas to countries that offered a logical route back to the UK. I set about the media in the hope of attracting a sponsor, but only managed a few articles in the Gulf News and one TV interview that lifted a flagging ego but did nothing for the bank balance.

One gratifying result of the media attention, however, was an invitation to a charity bikers' rally. Bikes are strictly weekend toys for wealthy people in the Emirates. About fifty Harley Davidsons gleamed in the sunshine posing for TV cameras, all trying to steal the show. The son of a sheik turned up on a gold plated Fat Boy which most riders thankfully found a little distasteful. A couple of inches off his front mud guard would have repaired my bike and got me home in style. Breakfast was followed by an hour's ride to lunch, where I was asked to speak about my travels to the assembled company. Unscripted and unrehearsed, I was a little apprehensive, but it went well with most people laughing in the right places. An English couple who ran a bar for US Mariners invited me to the opening of their new bikers' bar and asked me to speak again to raise a little cash for the cause. The crew of the USS George Washington were in fine spirits and, after I had thanked Harley riders the world over for their help, an amazing amount of crewmen pressed a dollar into my sweaty mitt with every handshake. I was grateful for every donation and the hospitality of some extraordinary people, but importing necessary parts for the Triumph was causing dreadful problems, and I still did not have the funds to pay for the rebuild.

Sue threw herself into the task of getting me mobile again with introductions to all her influential friends and, because of her considerable professional clout, took me to places well out of my league. The Hyatt Hotel was by far the poshest venue in town despite being an architectural monstrosity towering 25 floors above the elegant Islamic skyline. The top floor was a revolving restaurant where we enjoyed quite the most lavish lunch of my life and the evening was spent in the opulent bar with her friend Khizar Edroos, an unassuming self-made businessman who showed what could be achieved with hard work and considered my problems rather minor.

Days began to merge and I established a disciplined work routine balancing Sonja's home maintenance with the fruitless hunt for sponsors. On spec, I wandered down to the red marble palace of Emirates Petroleum to see their public relations manager. Oil alone is responsible for the country's astounding wealth where no one has to pay income tax and no expense had been spared on making an architectural statement that left no doubts about who was in control of the purse strings. Wearing my very best torn jeans and least travel-stained T-shirt, I sank into a crimson leather settee worth a good deal more than the sponsorship money I needed to move on. The lofty reception towered six floors to a glass dome with cool marble stairs meandering between carved office doors. Twenty-foot palms sprang from a jungle of tropical plants in stark contrast to sparkling steel, tinted glass and polished granite. After an hour of watching empty scenic lifts glide silently between burbling waterfalls, I again interrupted the receptionist's phone call to her friend. "The PR Manager's secretary will be available," she hissed between giggles. I never did find out when she would be available or what for, so sunk back into the sumptuous settee to wait another hour. We judge the business practices of others by our own experiences and this one was in a different time frame to mine, so I had another stab at a dialogue with motormouth as she paused between social calls. Before I had a chance to speak, she stood up and walked away saying she had to go and pray. Did the well-oiled wheels of commerce grind to a halt until she returned? A smart young man in Western dress eventually put me out of my misery by saying the PR Manager was out for lunch. "Shall I wait? Will he be long?" "Only two days. Maybe you should come back when he is not so busy." Well, it was worth a try.

Most evenings I would stroll the couple of miles into the busy part of town refusing the twenty or more cab drivers who stopped and insisted it was unseemly for white people, even scruffy ones, to walk. After working out the bus system (they ran every other Thursday) I enjoyed the company of Asian workers while trying to figure out where we were.

The streets of Diera in central Dubai were always lively and second only to Las Vegas in the flickering lights department, with animated neon stabbing the star-spangled sky. Shops stayed open late, but failed miserably to attract customers, unlike most of the restaurants. Dubai had an obsession with American burger and pizza establishments, but I much preferred the Indian and Pakistani cafes with authentic cheap menus and the traditional style of eating. The clashing and clinking of steel water cups and plates under an unnecessary amount of flourescent strip lighting added to the energy. Despite the Muslim culture, alcohol was tolerated in discrete bars always within the confines of hotels. The best I found was a reasonable attempt at a British pub called the George and Dragon, deep in the bowels of the Ambassador Hotel. Timber panelling, dark green paint, even a dart board made ex-pats feel at home while sipping one of half a dozen draught beers. They even had Guinness on tap which flowed like Arabian oil on St. Patrick's night. Several people recognised me from the newspaper and TV coverage, so frequently I had my beer bought for me. It did not help me get the bike fixed, but did take care of the evening's entertainment on many occasions. One evening I fell into conversation with a Scottish ship fitter by the name of George Smith who quizzed me about my travels and then asked "Why?" This was not something I had ever really stopped to think about, yet I was prepared to spend a year of my life and more money than I possessed fulfilling an ambition without much apparent, or at least obvious foundation. Not everything stands up to logical critisism. I can never understand the desire to walk to the North Pole or climb Everest, but those explorers chose their quest for discovery and I had chosen mine. Despite mounting problems, the enforced stay in one place had taught me that travelling had become a vocation. A way of life that suited me very well and seemed to have been mapped out by destiny. Reflecting back over my 46 years there had of course been times of joy, challenge, hardship and achievement, but I could not recall a time when life took on greater personal purpose. The trip should have been a prologue to the real thing and I hoped that, while there was strength in my body, the road should be my home, if only I could get back on it.

24. Assault on Mount Susan

All my faxing and phoning had been in vain as only one item turned up, so as the invoice was for all the parts, it was sent back and a new one had to be prepared. When the crate eventually did appear, the tyres, windshield, fairing panel and front wheel were still missing. I could ride with half a fairing, no windshield and even make the tyres last, but the front wheel was pretty fundamental piece of kit, unless I was going to be the first person around the world on a motorised unicycle. The good news was the British Embassy supplied a new passport within a couple of days so I went back to the Iranian Consulate to attempt to secure a visa. While sitting in an endless queue, I noticed the guy next to me in traditional dress with his passport renewal forms. The photo of him was just fine, but the picture of his wife had her in a yashmak with just one eye visible. It would take a clever customs official to differentiate her from his own dog. The women must feel a sense of security walking around in masquerade and what a good way of avoiding people in the street you did not want to meet. An English woman I met, who ran a lingerie shop, told me they wore the most outrageous clothes underneath their black robes and smutty underwear was always in demand.

My Iranian visa was going to take weeks and I had to be out of the Emirates in two, or suffer financial penalties. Saudi Arabia was an option, but I had been informed they may confiscate cameras and I could not take that risk. Oman was an option but the Yemen stood in the way of Africa and I had been warned that overland travel would not be permitted as renewed hostilities made it too dangerous. To cap it all, a very good friend of mine called Simon Jones had had the courtesy to telephone me for an update on progress. He had been following my exploits in Motoring & Leisure magazine and was largely responsible for securing the commission. In his usual dulcet tones he asked if I knew the Le Mans Race, my start and finish point, had been brought forward a week leaving only thirteen not fourteen weeks to get back to France. Under any other circumstances 51 weeks rather than 52 would not have made a great deal of difference, but on that occasion the news was profoundly depressing. Nevertheless, we arranged to meet at 1.00pm in the bar, just before the start of the race.

Tenacity won over bureaucracy and bike rebuilding changed up a gear. Meanwhile my social life was improving and I was getting fat from too much Guinness with new-found friends and burgers with Sue and Omar. Khizar Edroos, a very private man for whom I have enormous respect, was becoming a friend. He took a crowd of us to watch horse racing on the night of the Gold Cup – the world's richest sprint across a desert. The prize money was four million US dollars and it went to the favourite, Cigar, an American racing phenomenon who had won fifteen races on the trot (or should I say gallop?). The sin of it all is that these fantastically lucrative prizes go to the people who need them least. Personally I found the camel racing more entertaining with child jockeys bouncing around on noble beasts with permanently nonplussed expressions.

Another social event came as the result of embarrassingly bad journalism in the Gulf News. Ken Hassall ran a small advertising agency and was planning to ride a BMW back to England. We met over a couple of beers and immediately found a point of contact, but not just because of our professional background. He was of similar age, shape and height to me and expressed surprise that someone so skinny could ride such a heavy bike across rough terrain. I told him it was a bigger surprise to me – and there was worse to come. Despite being useless at ball games he invited me to join their boules team and we spent several balmy nights playing delightful multi-national games.

Then one phone call was all it took to change the gentle pace of an emerging routine – it was Floyd at Gorica Trading to say the bike was ready. The press were informed to cover the handover and keep the cost down, but I still did not have the money. Edroos had raised a little from his wealthy friends, but *he* came up with the majority in cash – fantastic generosity. Most of the Triumph panels were different colours as the wrong ones had been ordered and the standard of workmanship left a good deal to be desired, but it was running sweeter than ever.

I was still grinning after being reunited with my travel companion when the phone rang again. It was Sue to say she had made the break and found a new home away from Hany, but it was 'in need of work, so you can't leave now!' I could not have left anyway as politics were interfering with progress and escaping without a route was impossible. In truth, I was delighted to attempt, in a small way, to repay her for all the effort she had so selflessly squandered on me.

Her major concern was the garden, which was a walled piece of desert and she wanted a lawn. "What you need, Boss, are a couple of tons of top soil," I said trying to sound knowledgeable. "You're not in England now. Here we do things differently." The very next morning I went round to find a heap of sand, a good deal taller than me, blocking the drive. There were fifteen tons of the stuff, and to my untrained eye it looked identical to that already in her garden. The helpful Indian guy who delivered it thrust his hand deep into the wet grit and pulled out an anaemic little root about an inch long. "Look – good stuff for growing – very special." The expression 'I may be white, but I'm not completely stupid', came to mind again, but Sue just shrugged and said, "Told you so." All I had to do was transport 'Mount Susan' in an inadequate wheelbarrow to the back garden and level it off – in 43 degrees centigrade. The heat was not a problem as it gives me energy, but I must have looked a sight stripped down to brightly coloured shorts and dripping with sweat. The hard physical work was welcome to get my muscles and flabby burger belly back into shape for the road ahead and gave me an excuse for well-earned Guinness at the George and Dragon. Two Indian guys working on another house, who spent most of the day sitting under shady trees drinking water, came over to inquire if I was doing manual labour for the exercise. "No," I said, "I'm English." The explanation seemed to satisfy their curiosity.

A new newspaper, imaginatively called 'Gulf Today' was being launched and I was keen to try and get Edroos, my benefactor, a little publicity. We arranged to meet a journalist and photographer at their offices for a shoot and interview. It did not matter much but Edroos was pleased to see his photograph plastered over the first issue sitting on the back of the Triumph, all branded up in his company livery. He suggested I had my hair cut for the occasion, but I had to decline as it amused me to see it getting longer and longer during my video filming. Also the sun had bleached it a delicate shade of beige which surprised me as it had been grey when I left the UK. Sue, being such a high-profile person in a small community, was sent an invitation to the Gulf Today launch dinner. She did not want to go, so gave me her ticket. The last line stated 'Dress: formal or traditional'. The traditional bit was for the Arabs who understandably preferred a dish-dash to dinner jacket. I had neither, but was determined to bluff my way in. The best I could come up with were a pair of dark green cotton trousers I had bought for a pound in India and which were starting to look a bit threadbare. These were partly covered by a long shirt with toggle buttons bought in Thailand and I tied it at the waist with a sarong to cover the worst stains. The fashion statement was topped off with another sarong wrapped around my head in an elaborate turban. I was impressed the head-dress did not fall off as I rode through the night to the glitzy Holiday Inn, but the bouncer was a little suspicious of the curiously dressed guest who turned up on a motorcycle.

He was British, well over seven-foot tall with heavy bone growth on his forehead, cheek bones and chin giving him a skeletal look. Once inside, I felt a tap on my shoulder. "May I see your invitation please and are you aware of the dress code?" I turned to see the poor man bent double so our faces were more or less on the same level. The next bit took some thinking about and it was important not to crack up laughing. "The invitation says traditional dress," I said. "This is traditional Kashmiri dress." "Are you Kashmiri?" said the skull head who could have consumed me in one bite. "I am half Kashmiri, and that half is in traditional dress," I said hoping the sun tan was holding up in the glitter of crystal chandeliers. "If you have a problem with my country, I will pass it on to my Father, the Prince." The skull went very red and begged forgiveness. Two Indian waiters standing right behind him were wetting themselves with laughter and then the English photographer who had taken the shots of Edroos and me came over to join in. "Excuse me, Odd Job," he said waving the bouncer to one side, "I must get a shot of the only royal guest." Unfortunately, I never got to see the photographs, but would have liked to have had a copy to take on the next bizarre stage of my journey.

Once again my tireless fairy godmother came up with a solution to my problems and set up a devious escape plan. Using her considerable influence, she approached a Japanese sister company who had a ro-ro vessel about to sail for Mombassa. I had overstayed my time in the Emirates, but

Sue assured me the 900 Dirham fine would be paid by Gulf Agency. I could not understand this and hoped it was not her way of getting me off the hook. Her home, if not complete, was habitable and looked a lot more inviting than it had before I got hold of it. The last couple of days were a whirl of 'thank-yous' and 'good-byes'.

It blows my mind how apparently insignificant incidents can completely change the direction of a life, and the sequence of events that lead up to that sultry evening, as I packed up my rucksack with sweat running into my eyes, was no exception. How far back do you take it? A day's delay in Peru for repairs had meant I had had to wait weeks for the Triumph to be shipped from South America to Australia. As a result, I had seized the chance to see New Zealand and ended up on a train opposite Sue. The war in Myanmar had forced me to chang my route across India where I was nearly annihilated by a truck – and Dubai just happened to be the nearest and only accessible repair shop. Obviously, if those events had not happened, equally strange ones may have done, but it does make you wonder if there is someone pulling the strings. Without Sue there would have been no Sonja to shelter a tortoise without its shell and no Edroos, without who's help continuation would not have been possible. With a team of that calibre behind me, I was feeling optimistic about the way ahead.

The good ship Nada Five (what ever happened to the other four?) was to sail at dawn, so plenty of time for a farewell pizza with Sue, Sonja and Omar. I gave him the most complicated Swiss Army knife in Dubai (a proper one), as he had been fascinated by mine, but told him he had to give it to his mother until she decided he was old enough not to do himself an injury. He immediately opened a blade and cut his finger which made the point. The last meeting on Emirates soil was with Edroos quite late in the evening. We chatted for a while and he said there would always be a job for me if I needed it, inviting me to return. "But Edroos," I exclaimed "you don't know what I'm capable of." "Yes I do," he replied. "You are riding a motorcycle around the world, which is not easy and you are the sort of person who gets things done. Sue trusts you. I trust her judgement." Such accolades from the mouth of success itself. He then stuffed five US$100 notes into my hand and wished me good luck. Was there no end to this man's generosity?

At around midnight I sat on a packed up Triumph watching the Nada V manoeuvre sedately into Sharjah dock. The ramp was dropped for me to ride on board a vessel whose lower decks were crammed with second hand cars bound for Africa. I had thirteen decks to choose from and one of the Filipino crew members took pleasure in securing the Triumph smack bang in the middle of the empty top deck. The five-foot tall Captain Ishimaru greeted me with limited English, a big grin and gaping fly zip. All seven officers were Japanese and the crew of about thirty Filipino. I was shown the luxury of the pilot's huge cabin, with comfortable bunk, writing desk, settee and shared bathroom with the first mate. Sue really had pushed the boat out with the VIP treatment. As the vessel was not permitted to carry passengers, I was listed as crew and, as I sipped from a bottle of Johnnie Walker donated by Sue, I speculated what tasks would be given to me during the week-long voyage. Not even the whisky could induce sleep as pastel shades of dawn silhouetted iron skeletons of floating oilrigs and the Nada V inched its way into the Indian Ocean. A flock of seagulls had taken over from the butterflies in my stomach as we picked up speed and headed for the mysteries of Africa and a new continent of discovery.

25. Sea Sore

As the crew and the officers didn't speak each other's language they communicated in a strange pigin, making the simplest instructions complicated and time-consuming. I hoped they at least knew how to say 'abandon ship'. Resting in my cabin after a sleepless night, I gazed through the large porthole at the unbroken horizon of the Indian Ocean. I had seen rougher bath water and the endless blue sky exaggerated the enormity of the scene. I strolled onto the top deck for a better look. Look at what? The sky and the ocean, without any reference points, were quite the biggest things I had ever seen. Standing on the highest point above the bridge I rotated my view 360 degrees again and again until totally disorientated. Without knowing the time of day, it would have been impossible to find any point on the compass.

The crew member who had secured my bike came on deck with a pot of paint and a brush. The metal bulkhead must have been red hot so strokes had to be short and in a random direction. With my newly gained domestic maintenance skills I offered to help. No such luck. The crew hardly had enough to keep themselves occupied so there was little chance of me joining in. Fortunately, most of the Filipinos spoke better English than the officers, so conversation at some level was possible. Within an hour, I had seen all the decks, read every notice taped to the walls and committed to memory a chart of every flag in the world. I was gratified to see the Marshall Islands had a colourful and interesting design. One notice that caught my attention was on the connecting door of the shared shower room. It stated there were only three hours in every twenty four when the first mate could use it, so I was careful not to disrupt his 'Toilet Schedule'. How can people legislate about when to use a toilet?

A hand-written note appeared in my cabin with meal times. Breakfast: 0730, lunch: 1200 and dinner: 1700. The evenings were going to be long, but three meals a day would punctuate the boredom. I was instructed to eat with the Japanese officers, which was a shame as judging by the noise from the crew's quarters, they were having much more fun. On my way down to the dining cabin, I had said hello to the cook who was Filipino and I wondered if I would have the choice of food from two nations. They were both enticing and the officers were served with an interesting spread, but to my dismay, they had attempted Western food for me, which amounted to a piece of dead animal with the looks and texture of the heel of a Wellington boot with a dubious mix of vegetables crouching threateningly on the side. As my lunch companions Captain Ishimaro, First Officer Chang, a surly-looking Chief Engineer and two others, tucked into scrummy Japanese food slurping soup and clashing chopsticks. I asked the Captain if in future I could eat the same as them. Chang, who was a little less stand-offish than the rest of the officers and spoke better English, conveniently translated where necessary. "Being a traveller, I prefer to eat local food and the Nada V is as close to Japan as this trip takes me." The message was passed to the Filipino cook who was being taught how to prepare Japanese food by the Captain.

Dinner was not just a vast improvement, but a whole new adventure. Watery vegetable soup, drunk straight from the bowl (it took all week to perfect the slurping noises) two tiny, dry and very bony fish, then a meaty casserole thing served with a powerful but delicious mustard sauce. There was always a vast bowl of glutinous rice and continuous flow of refreshing Chinese tea. Before we finished, two cans of Budweiser were placed before me and, as Chang was going on watch, my ration doubled. Things were looking up. In the evening the crew invited me into their mess for 'Karaoke', which struck me as a culture swap. What a difference their side of the deck was. Lots of laughter, beer and friendly inquisitive people.

With precious little to do during the day, I was granted permission to film the bridge and engine room. According to a naval friend, there are definitely two types of mariner. Those who work above the waterline and those below and I had seen the 'aboves' so time to have a look at the 'belows.' A Filipino engineer took me in a lift that descended seemingly to the bottom of the ocean. We picked our way along clattering steel catwalks, up and down ladders avoiding pipework and vibrating bits of machinery. Within seconds, I was sweating buckets in the oppressive still air heavy with the smell of diesel and hot oil. The noise was fantastic and the answers to my questions were all lost in the mind-numbing din. After a couple of hours filming a cathedral of throbbing engines, with pistons pumping and tappets tapping, we arrived at the single prop shaft. All that energy and activity to rotate one solid steel rod about eighteen inches in diameter. The prop itself must have been massive to shift 13,000 tons of floating muti-story car park through dense seawater at about twelve knots.

I could not wait to escape back onto the upper deck where the air moved and the sun shone. There is still, however, an undeniable feeling of captivity on a ship. Once you have walked from the pointed end to the blunt end, the only place to go is back again. One piece of ocean to a novice seaman looks very like another. The only excitement is seeing the odd ship steaming the other way, or a hint of land in the shimmering distance. We passed an apparently uninhabited island. A barren rock devoid of vegetation but, as it was dinner time, I resisted the temptation dive overboard and explore. Regrettably, there was no beer as it was only permitted on Saturday night and the officers alone ran the ship on Sundays. The rule was only broken on special occasions like birthdays. I spent the evening in my cabin wondering how I could convince the Captain it was my birthday, or Karl Marx's, Shakespeare's, anyone's to liven up the evening.

My notebook took the brunt of my boredom.

'26th April, Nada V, Indian Ocean.

The tedium is getting to me. This morning I dutifully arrived at breakfast at 0730 only to find the clocks had gone back half an hour and it was only seven. Returning to my cabin I noticed the clock above my bunk had miraculously changed during the night. Breakfast, when it came, was a fried egg on a bed of rice with another bony little fish. Good stuff, but it was tricky consuming a slippery fried egg with short pointed chopsticks. As ever, I sat back for a moment to observe how the others coped before making a total prat of myself.

Each meal, I ask Chang to teach me a couple of Japanese words, but am finding the pronunciation very difficult and write everything down phonetically. He also taught me to write my name in Japanese. I asked him what Karaoke meant, as Japan was its birthplace. I assumed it meant something like 'sing-along' but he just said, "it mean Karaoke, of course." He didn't actually say, "You stupid English person," but his expression did.

Last night I finished Sue's whisky, so the highlight of today was writing a note saying $100 reward for contacting this address. I put a single dollar bill in also for some incentive and chucked it overboard. It will go to India, Africa, or the bottom of the ocean. This occupied me for a whole hour. After that there was little else to do except contemplate the curvature of the Earth which is easily visible. I tried counting all the rivets on the foredeck but even that got dull after two million.

This is a vast ocean that must be teeming with life, but the only natives I have seen are shoals of tiny flying fish that look suspiciously like the ones served up at every meal. As many as fifty at a time dance above the ever-flexing and relaxing muscles of the sea – silver bodies as reflective as mirrors fly as far as a hundred yards, then duck back into the blue en masse, hitting the water like automatic gunfire.

There was a message over the tannoy. Something was going to happen at eight this evening. Hoping for some entertainment I inquired at the radio room, but Sparks said it was only the clocks going back another half hour making the long evening even longer. Once again, I read *Zen and the Art of Motorcycle Maintenance* even though I had not enjoyed it much the first time. Strange that the book had been given to me on another ship - but that was a lifetime ago.

To many people, a week on a ship in glorious sunshine with nothing much to do would be bliss. After having my wings clipped in the Emirates for so long, I can't wait to see the open road again and, thanks to Sue, I am going to see Africa after all.

27th April, Nada V (again), Indian Ocean (still)

According to Sparks we have just crossed the equator – my third time since leaving home. One of the chirpy crew invited me into their games room. I didn't know there was one. The bookshelf is crammed with publications in Japanese (badly targeted reading for the Filipinos) and a guitar with no strings hangs from the ceiling. In the centre is the sailor's version of pool. It is played on a four-foot square table that revolves so players do not have to move to take a shot. Instead of balls, flat plastic discs are struck with a very short cue and skid about on a chalked wooden top. I played several games before a splendid dinner of sukiyaki, prepared by Captain Ishimaru.

Before sitting down to eat, we shout 'Hi' at each other in a rather aggressive way, but I still am not doing it with the enthusiasm of the others.

Getting the slurpy noises right eating noodles without stuff dripping off my beard is more difficult than with the soup. Maybe this is why the Japanese do not grow much facial hair. I noticed that the Captain had a rather tatty bandage around the middle finger on his left hand. The finger is definitely a little shorter than it should be and I did not like to ask how he inflicted the injury. Nothing sinister about this, except he cooked the sukiyaki and I can't think of any other times a captain would be around sharp knives unless he had been practicing with his Samurai sword.

Chang is a bit of a smoothy with vignette-tinted glasses and dapper hair style framing a narrow head on even narrower shoulders. His protruding nether lip makes him look as if he is speaking French. I am generally only spoken to if I ask a question and I always direct them at the Captain, but am generally answered by Chang.

30th April, Stuck in a car park somewhere on the Indian Ocean

Bollocks! Breakdown in communication. I thought we were docking today so spent last night packing up. We should, however, be in Mombassa tomorrow morning. A storm blew up in the evening making it impossible to play pool. The discs slid away before I had a chance to aim the cue at them. Blue sea turned gun-metal grey with white surf rolling down steep exploding waves. It was the first time I had experienced an angry ocean and found it all rather exciting. What was startling was the speed at which the robust sea grew from a mill pond calm reinforcing the notion it should always be respected.

I braved the elements to look through the ship's binoculars for my first sight of Africa as Somalia was only thirty miles away, but no luck – the stormy horizon gave no indication where the sea ended and the sky began.

Tomorrow we dock in Mombassa where I will be chucked off into a strange town, in a new country with absolutely no knowledge of which way to go – no concept of what it will be like, and of course, I have no idea what the rules are. If you do not learn them quickly, I could be in deep shit just for doing things we think of as ordinary. Terrifying but exciting!'

From the beginning, I had lusted after Africa but never knew if I was going to make it there. I anticipated it was going to be difficult and was glad to have had experience of travelling in other challenging places. Everybody I knew (and there were quite a few of them) who had ever ridden a bike almost anywhere in Africa had said 'Forget the travel rule book and rely on the survival book', but there are over fifty independent countries within that vast continent and each must be different. Bad roads (if you can find one at all), lack of fuel, bureaucracy, local conflicts, bandits, wild animals – the list was endless and all negative, but I refused to believe it was going to be all bad. The place was just so big there must be a multitude of unique delights and the thought of being able to explore some of them made my spine tingle. My biggest worry was the Triumph as it was so inadequately equipped for such an arduous journey and if anything breaks, it will have to be repaired not replaced. I have never met anyone who has attempted to ride the length of the East Coast on anything and several seriously experienced off-road riders laughed when I told them I was going to attempt it on a heavy road machine. Despite all that, I was full of confidence. The Triumph and I had already experienced half a dozen deserts, non-existent roads, fuel shortages, bandits – you name it, and resourcefulness had always won through. After such an easy time in the Emirates, I was feeling strong, fat, determined and ready to take on the next chapter of life on a motorcycle. One more night and I was going to find out for myself.

During our last dinner aboard the Nada V, I scored my only brownie point with the assembled officers. For a week, I had sat with those men and not heard the sound of laughter. I am too ignorant to say if this is typical of Japanese mealtime etiquette, but it is my limited experience. The Chief Engineer, who spent his day in the clatter of the engine room, was a man of few words and possibly deaf from working in such an inhospitable environment. He was a heavy-set man for a Japanese and commented to the Captain he needed to lose weight. Chang translated for me and I said tell him to eat with only one chopstick. There was a moment's silence and I thought I must have offended until they spontaneously roared with laughter. Captain Ishimaru was so delighted with the remark, he wrote it down in Japanese on a large piece of paper with a thick felt-tip pen and pinned it to the wall. I was glad to leave my hosts on a high note and there was a fair amount of hand shaking and shouting 'hi' before retiring to my cabin for the last time.

A blustery dawn greeted the good ship Nada V and, with it, my first glimpse of Kenya. By the time we gracefully slid through the gaping jaws of Mombassa harbour a mixture of excitement and terror gripped every sinew. Africa was more than another vast land mass, but a whole new adventure.

26. It's May, so this must be Africa

After a week of unbroken sunshine, I was disappointed to see heavy overcast skies. My timing throughout the trip had been appalling, catching the rainy season just about everywhere. My bike was released from its moorings and everything packed up in preparation for a wet introduction to African roads. Oh foolish fellow! Was I really so naive to think a white man on a big motorcycle could just ride off a ship and exit the port with nothing more than a stamp on his carnet?

On board, the immigration had been a doddle. Four officials sat around smoking and chatting armed with a suitcase full of rubber stamps. The most senior was anxious to move on to the next stage. "Now the formalities are over, it is time for gifts." I do not recall ever hearing a man in uniform so blatantly asking for bribes. Captain Ishimara looked confused. Maybe he did not understand the guy's English, or perhaps the Japanese culture did not comprehend the concept of bribes. "Gifts – gifts, what gifts?" The Captain turned the word over in his mouth like an unaccustomed taste that he was unsure if he liked. "Whisky, cigarettes, pens, shirts, anything you have for us," replied the big official who looked surprised a sea captain did not know what a gift was. Sparks, who seemed to run the ship, jumped into the breech stuffing a few US dollars into an official's gaping top pocket. "No whisky, but we have cigarettes, pens and smart shirts with our company name on." They know how the world goes round in the Philippines. While eager hands were being filled, I took the opportunity of saying goodbye to all the officers and crew, thanking them for their hospitality and an enjoyable trip. The ramp was lowered for the very first new generation Triumph to experience Kenya. My senses were immediately bombarded with unfamiliar sights, smells and sound. Mombasa Port was a vast labyrinth of tumbledown offices and warehouses in sad need of repair , covering about three miles of coast. Two giant cranes sat expectantly, their claws waiting to be fed. A third had fallen over through the roof of a huge shed, crushing and trapping cargo under its stout, twisted, steel legs. Judging by the rust and debris, this had happened quite some time before, but no attempt had been made to clear the wreckage or release someone's shipment.

With some difficulty, I found the port exit and produced my carnet, but was sent back to the Transport department for documentation. The friendly but firm security guard drew me a hopeless map, but at least it pointed me more or less in the right direction. He said I would have to hurry as they closed in a couple of hours. Two hours for one stamp should have not posed too much of a challenge for such an intrepid traveller who had experienced Central American and Asian bureaucracy. When I eventually found the right brick-built hut with half a corrugated iron roof, the Transport Manager was cleaning his stamp. It was like a piece of an old newspaper letter-press with each character etched on the end of a metal shaft and held together in a wooden block. There must have been a hundred bits of shiny metal soaking in a rusty tobacco tin full of paraffin. Each one was laboriously pulled out, examined, rotated and replaced. This had to be done with some care as the last piece, when tapped into place, held the entire thing together like a key-stone to a bridge. I asked if he had another stamp, or could he just sign the document as time was short. No reply, just a slow shake of the head and a tut tutting noise as big fingers, not given to delicate tasks, grappled – prodded each piece into place. About two thirds of the way through getting the intricate jigsaw back together, it all fell apart. Quite calmly he replaced them in the tin and walked away. He shouted to a colleague who produced his own stamp, which was spat on to make a smudged mark in the appropriate place. "Now go there. See Boss," he said pointing up the road. "Where?" I said as there was nothing visible in the direction of the stubby finger. "Automobile Department." On my way to the automobile department, I passed the exit gate again and had another stab at bluffing my way out, but no joy, so eventually, found the Boss sipping tea in an open air canteen. He was very jolly and immediately mounted the bike grinning at his friends. Very few people appreciate how heavy it is and I only just caught it as he went off balance. His office was already closed and no amount of "Is there a fee I can pay?" would produce a signature as he said all goods have to be inspected first. "Where is the Inspector," I asked looking at my watch. "I am the inspector," he replied, "but my office is closed. We have procedures." An expression that was to be engraved on my brain over the next day or so. "Come, we store your bike and you return for permit." He took me to a lock-up riding pillion. We went the scenic route so he could wave at his mates all over the dock. My success with Kenyan officialdom took another down turn when he said, "Tomorrow is a holiday, come back next day." With the bike locked and alarmed, I asked for a cheap hotel, which he obligingly drove me to in the back of his truck. The Polana Hotel seemed quite cheap but, without local intelligence, I had no comparison. The standard, however, was better than anticipated and, to my joy, was located smack in the middle of a boisterous part of town.

One of my Sunday lunchtime drinking friends back in Sussex had a charismatic companion called Richard Woodall, whom I had met on a couple of occasions and, as luck would have it, he lived and worked in the outskirts of Mombasa. He had received a card or two just in case I did get to Kenya, so my phone call was not a complete surprise. He was however snowed under with work attempting to secure a big contract, but said I was welcome to stay and suggested getting a taxi to his house in the morning.

Feeling pleased at making contact with Richard, I set about exploring the city. As dusk fell, several rooftop bars illuminated with coloured lights were visible from my third-floor room. The smartly dressed doorman advised, if I had to go out, to be very careful as walking the streets at night was hazardous enough for blacks and white people were a real novelty on that side of town. He nodded approvingly when I showed him the shiny steel of a cheap flick knife purchased in Bangkok. If it came to the crunch, I would never have had the balls to use it, but the loud click it made on opening was extremely threatening and all the bluff needed to make an escape.

I attracted a little more attention than I was comfortable with wandering round dimly lit streets, and the doorman's warning was echoed by several friendly passers-by. The English are not very good at reacting to complete strangers crossing the street for a handshake or friendly clap on the back, but a few strong beers from the plethora on offer did a lot for the inhibitions. Danger is relative and I felt much safer on the wrong side of town in Mombassa than I did in New York. The bars were a delight. The air was heavy with the scent of sex as young men and women in brightly coloured clothes postured and posed to the sound of booming reggae. Any white person dressed in such clashing colours would have looked ridiculous, but this was African chic and they carried it with grace and style. After a couple of hours in the bars that proliferated in the area, I discovered why Africans move like they do. It is the beer. Cheap, strong, tasty and does something weird to the pelvic bones. By midnight I could be seen slinking about with no idea where my hotel was or what it was called. I had forgotten all my golden rules of getting a card with the name and address on, then walking in a block system to avoid getting lost.

The next morning, I casually sauntered up and down a taxi rank outside the hotel negotiating a price to Diani Beach. Richard had said it was quite a distance, but I was still a bit upset that the best price on offer was 1500 shillings, about £20.00. In India that would have been food and lodging for a week, but staying with Richard was going to save on accommodation for a couple of days. The taxi was an ancient black cab that three of us push-started. The two drivers who helped got in with me. They had probably just come for the ride, but at least there would be willing help if more pushing was necessary.

To get to north Mombasa we had to take a ferry across the gaping estuary mouth. While boarding the rickety car ferry, the Nada V slipped gracefully past as only a floating car park can. Captain Ishimaru was clearly visible on the bridge and my Filipino friend was still painting the same piece of bulkhead and Sparks with a watering can tending the plants that softened the ugly angular vessel. That ship was their world until they could see family and friends again, mine had got much bigger since setting foot on African soil and I idly speculated about who would get home first.

The only thing Kenya and the Emirates have in common is the lack of proper addresses. Everything is done by PO Box numbers and, although Richard had given me landmarks to look out for, he remained elusive until I stopped to ask a Diani Beach resident. Richard's name only produced bemused looks, but a detailed description did the trick. "Oh, you mean Truly. Two driveways down." Several explanations were offered as to why the likeable man was known as Truly Wonderful, but none were particularly convincing.

His drive was contained by dense vegetation and blocked by two large baboons sunning themselves which Richard practically ignored as he welcomed me with 'jambo', the traditional Swahili greeting. The taxi driver must have been impressed he spoke the language as they shared a little joke together, Richard laughed on cue as the taxi coughed into life after a little push. "What was so funny?" I asked when the dust had settled. Richard laughed again, "No idea whatsoever. He probably said your friend looks like an orangutan, but I never got passed learning jambo."

Being an architect, he had designed his own home.It oozed style and elegance without ostentation. The span of a palatial sitting room was supported by two massive tree trunks and the roof by smaller twisted timbers still in the round. There was no obvious demarcation between the house and the lush tropical greens of a substantial garden. The rampant plant life attracted iridescent dragon-flies, butterflies and massive millipedes with legions of legs moving in waves. Much of the organised jungle was shaded by a canopy of trees where agile monkeys played hide and seek in an impressive display of aerial acrobatics. A path of some fifty yards led to the bottom of the garden and terminated at one of the most idyllic beaches I have ever seen. In bright sunlight the bleached sand was blinding and the sea, blue, warm and, inviting.

Richard showed me a spacious spare room and introduced me to Christopher, his house boy who immediately grabbed all my travel-stained clothes and started washing.

Left to my own devices, I strolled the beach. Ali Baba's Beach Bar appeared like a mirage with a warm welcome and cold beer. Fupi, the ebullient manageress, introduced me to Kenyan Guinness that demands some respect at 7.5% proof. Remarkable though it may seem, Guinness is very popular in many African countries, although the local brews are quite different in texture, taste and strength. Back in my advertising days, I had held the Guinness Brewing WorldWide account and I had been surprised to discover Nigeria was third only to the UK and USA for consumption. Because it is so strong, it is marketed as a blatant aphrodisiac and I recall designing a half page advertisement for a Lagos newspaper, with the other half page given up to a serious article about cures for impotency. I am not qualified to comment on the validity of this claim, but I can vouch for its aftermath.

I could have done without a raging hangover the next morning as Richard drove me to the port authorities to claim my bike. "It will take about a week and a big wad," was his not very encouraging parting statement.

Getting the bike released from customs was without question the most frustrating day of my life. For anyone contemplating inter-continental travel with *any* vehicle from a bicycle to a bus, this next bit is important. Accessing a new country overland can be tiresome, time consuming, even expensive, but is easily achievable if you stick at it. At very worst, if they do not let you in, you can turn round, retrace your steps in the hope of finding another border crossing, or even access your goal via another country. However, if you have to release your vehicle to air or sea port authorities, everything changes. They have got you by the short and curlies. You cannot officially enter the country without the right authorisation (and they can make this up as they go along if they do not like the colour of your eyes) and there is no easy way back, as they can charge what they like, or even prevent your vehicle being loaded on to the next vessel out. Sjaak, the Dutch biker I had met in Bangkok, for example, had had his bike flown to Thailand by Honda from Japan. Thai customs refused to release his bike because the paperwork was "not in order" but did not tell him in what way. I do not know if the Thais were being obstructive or opportunist, but it took over a week and an intervention by the Dutch government to get his property released. This had been one of my fears in the administrative turmoil that is India and one of the reasons why I was so passionate about an overland route. Sri Lanka had been tortuous enough, what was Kenya going to be like? Fortunately, I had the Triumph to race about on from one department to another as they were frequently a mile or so apart. The port authorities, unlike immigration, had undergone an anti-corruption crackdown and discreet offers of bribes did not speed the procedures. Having 'procedures', one can live with, but regrettably no one knew what they were, which caused tremendous confusion. A very helpful young man called Simon with appalling halitosis clung to a stack of paperwork on the back of the bike directing me from one department to another. I will never know what they all were and with corrupt senior staff behind bars, everyone was hell bent on doing things by the book. Unfortunately there was nothing in the book about motorcycle import for travelling overland. The ridiculous thing about all the procedures was, as soon as I got past the gates, no one would care. The ordeal started at eight in the morning and by five that evening I had not made much progress and had to report back to E block where I originally started. It was closed, but I saw the senior officer getting into his car. I had evidence that the bike belonged to a crew member of the Nada V. I could prove that the bike was mine, therefore *I must have been that crew member*, was the gist of my plea through an open car window. As I had ridden the bike off the ship instead of having it unloaded it was classified as personal belongings just like the rest of my luggage. The kind, lovely man took the stack of documents from sherpa Simon, threw them in a bin and told me to follow him to the gates where I was released. After nine hours' hard bargaining, all that was needed was one throw-away gesture from the right person – a rule that seems to apply everywhere. Richard was so impressed I had managed to retrieve the bike in a single day with no money changing hands that we celebrated in Ali Baba's magnificent subterranean restaurant. Millions of years ago it was a submerged hollow coral reef, but the sea had given up Nature's amphitheatre to leave the most sensational labyrinth of lofty caverns. It was the most inspired restaurant I had ever seen, with food to match. Kenya was revealing some remarkable surprises and I looked forward to experiencing more.

Another surprise was ending up in bed with Fupi, so maybe its true about the aphrodisiac qualities of Guinness. Whatever the reasons for it, there was no guilt felt on my part, I was happy to snuggle up to a soft warm body, and it was something Marian and I would talk about one day. It really can not be analysed, but the feeling probably lay somewhere between desire and a craving for affection. She always said, "*When* it happens, make it meaningful, memorable and do not just do it for carnal gratification. Every event in every life has some influence, some purpose and they form the building blocks that make us the people we are." There were still several weeks and more adventure before our reunion. I fell asleep with her philosophical words ringing in my head. Maybe it was those thoughts that inspired a remarkably vivid dream of my return to Le Mans. We were sitting with a mutual friend called Simon Jones and he asked me what it was like to travel in Africa. I was struggling to give him an answer. "You've been there," he insisted, "what was it like?" "I don't know, I can't remember, difficult I think" was not a satisfactory answer, but showed my apprehension about, about what was to be the most demanding part of the journey.

27. 'Follow the Stones'

I would have quite happily stayed on in the comfort of Richard's home for several years, but time was running out and I anticipated the next stage was going to be very different. There was nothing I could really put my finger on, as no one could give me any qualified intelligence on what happens north of Nairobi. Richard waved an encouraging finger across an atlas. "I'm sure you will find a coast road – or something – that should take you all the way to Egypt." The silly old bastard had not got a clue. He only went to places where he could be sure of finding a good pub. His own round-world adventure would be the perfect way to catch up with old friends and his target was eighty bars in eighty days.

Thanks to Fupi, I had somewhere to stay in Nairobi, so had to get a move on to make sure I arrived before dark. Too many warnings about travelling at night had come my way to ignore them. This was real 'Boys' Own Annual' stuff. Man and machine against the elements of Africa. With possibly the exception of Antarctica, Africa is the least explored, known about, charted, continent in the world and, all on my lonesome I was going to take on the forces of nature and all it could throw at me. The clock was ticking, no one could even guess my chances of success, or even if the task was feasible, but my pioneering spirit was at its peak and I was thirsting for something new.

If, and it was a very big if, everything worked out just dandy, there were only about three thousand miles to go before making the leap back to southern Europe. Three thousand miles of mountains, deserts and war zones. I needed the best part of a week to ride the length of Europe back to Le Mans leaving me an absolute maximum of four to negotiate a distance that was *only* the width of the USA. It had taken nearly a month to traverse North America with a few detours, but it had been easy on Interstate Highways with food, fuel, flushing toilets, friendly people, Triumph dealers…… Same amount of time, same distance, except now I was approaching some of most hostile and inaccessible places on Earth.

The ride to Nairobi was a very enjoyable easy start, on reasonable black top most of the time. Being a National Geographic addict, I had salivated over photography of Kilamanjaro – what a name to conjure with – and there it was, just over the border with Tanzania, half lost in angry skies warning of a premature rainy season. I had to get moving quickly before the rains prevented cross country travel in the north, but not before soaking up the stuff dreams are made of. Seeing African wildlife on film can be pretty stimulating, but actually being there, watching ostriches sprinting along, troops of baboons sunning themselves by waterholes was really exciting - riding next to a herd of galloping zebra was exhilarating – all this before reaching my first African capital city.

Fupi's friend, Judy, lived in a rambling wooden bungalow with her Italian husband, Marzio, and their very small child. An army of cleaners, gardeners, guards, nannies and cooks slumped around in the evening sun. My hosts' neighbour came round for drinks. Darsi Jan Ruysenaar, was straight off the pages of the adventure books I had coveted as a child, complete with proper safari wear. Like Owen in Australia, he was in his late fifties with a remarkably fair complexion and glinting ice blue eyes. He spoke the native language and lived off his country's natural bounty. Where Owen sold kangaroo tails, Darsi ran sightseer safari trips all over east and south Africa. I couldn't be in better hands and in a soft BBC voice he offered to help.

He drove me into town in his very serviceable 24 year old Land Rover in search of an Ethiopian visa and a map, which he said was essential for desert travel. Anywhere else in the world his chosen transport would have been called a wreck, but it ran well and Darsi knew how to fix it. "Everything has to be pushed a little harder and a little longer out here," he explained. "When something does break, you have to improvise and Africans are the best at improvisation. If you have been short of a regular supply of just about everything for a couple of generations you get pretty good at it." In the Aero Club that evening, his pale penetrating eyes scanned the map for the best route, but his words were not too encouraging. "Corrugations are going to be your problem," he said rather gravely. "On your bike with hardly any ground clearance I seriously doubt your chances and the north is bandit country." It was not all doom and gloom and I was grateful for accurate and honest information from a gentleman adventurer who really knew what he was talking about.

Every journey has milestones, punctuation marks in geography or events and I was approaching one such memorable occasion. At approximately 26,000 miles long, the Equator is the longest line of latitude. An invisible line where night and day are equally divided all year round and the sun is directly overhead at noon. Because it is the shortest route from the sun to the Earth, it is generally hot, but there I was, crossing it for the fourth time with fingers numb from the cold. The crossing was not quite as miserable as Ecuador, but billowing dark skies made Mount Kenya look like an erupting volcano and was a further reminder that I needed to get out of the mountains before the rains. At least I had a proper leather jacket to keep the chill out but, before descending into the arid northern desert we were caught in a Bromdignag hail storm. Stones the size of marbles bruised my hands and soaked the second hand jeans I had purchased in a Nairobi market for less than two pounds. There was a satisfying poetic justice in a pair of jeans, probably given to a charity shop in Bognor, being sold on by a poor Kenyan to a poor white traveller.

The change in scenery was as staggering as the rise in temperature, descending from the lush green mountains to parched scrub. Water holes were drying up, driving the proud Masai tribesmen north with herds of cattle and goats. Tall, with Arab like bone structure, they were far from the archetypal indigenous African. Their vivid red robes could be seen flapping in the breeze miles into the shimmering heat haze. Naked children waved and cheered as I picked my way through dust and pot holes. They showed nothing but uninhibited glee for their first encounter with a white man wearing a space helmet on a huge two-wheeled machine.

Isiolo is a small but quite pleasant little town where the last of the green bit of Kenya gives way to the vast expanse of desert and all roads as we know them stop. For a couple of quid I secured a room and the last of anything recognisable as food for a few days. The customary crowd of people gathered round the bike but, unlike India, no one touched or fiddled with anything. The owner offered to remove the furniture from the restaurant for me to get the bike off the road for the night, but his furniture would have been under more threat from theft than the Trophy. Locals were very friendly and a few spoke enough English for a chat. One Ethiopian youth advised me to

213

face the rough road to Eritrea as there was a twice weekly ferry up the Red Sea to Port Said. According to him, Sudan would be impossible to cross as civil war was raging. Djibouti was the only other option and that was going to be expensive. Another déjà vu scenario reared its head as the conflict in Myanmar had stopped my progress and resulted in a massive detour. Sudan is the biggest country in Africa – nearly a million square miles and over ten times bigger in area than the UK, so finding a route round it was going to take months not weeks. Because it is so vast and mostly desert, I speculated that not all of it could be a war zone and people must have been getting on with their lives with some normality. Guatemala had been suffering a protracted civil war but I saw no evidence of it. In Sri Lanka, I had witnessed the aftermath of a terrorist attack, but was never in any personal danger. I had to take a big chance and my best estimate was a week's hard graft to drag the bike across the deserts and mountain ranges of North Kenya and Ethiopia to any Sudanese border. Curiously enough, the war was of little concern to me, provided it did not prevent entry to the country, but the terrain, finding fuel and even water could become serious problems. It was make your mind up time and I was painfully aware that the next decision was a crucial one if I was to stand any chance of getting back on time. West to Uganda and Zaire, or north across the wilderness to Ethiopia. It was no time to start flipping coins, there was too much at stake. I have absolutely no belief in astrology, but do know I am never really comfortable being far from the sea and some people may say that being born under the sign of the crab, a water sign, influenced my choice. North it had to be as the Red Sea beckoned.

Before dawn, I was parked up at the last military checkpoint waiting for a convoy. Intensive bandit activity meant all vehicles had to travel in convoy and carry armed guards. As the sun peeped over distant mountains, the heat hit me like a brick and the enormity of the task ahead became evident. There were only about 340 miles of nothing to cross before Ethiopia, on a 'road' that was a heap of sharp boulders partly obscured by loose sand. On a dangerously overloaded bike with bald tyres and a few inches ground clearance, I began to hear Darsi's words of warning.

Looking at the bike and then the 'road,' I did not know whether to laugh or cry, but would the route going west have been any better? The biggest obstacle, as I saw it, was every time the bike fell over, an absolute inevitability, I would have to strip it to get it upright again. Maybe, just maybe, if I could shift all unnecessary weight, the task would be possible – just wait for a convoy.

Two bulging trucks appeared in a magenta dust cloud. The least overloaded took all my luggage except camera and spare fuel for about a fiver. The details of every vehicle were recorded by the military and checked off in Marsabit in case of breakdown or bandit attack. As the officer took my details I realised two things. The first was that I had left the map in my room. I came to the conclusion fate had not meant me to have a map and what use was it anyway when the "road," or at least direction of travel was hardly visible? Secondly, and much more seriously, I was attempting to cross one of the most hostile places on Earth, on the most ridiculous form of transport and I had forgotten to obtain any water. A stunningly beautiful Ethiopian woman sitting in the shade of the military hut partly solved the problem by selling me some green oranges. She could have been Miss World, but instead she covered her poverty with threadbare robes and sold oranges to truck passengers. I wanted to marry her, settle down and have lots of babies but, before there was time to propose – we were off, with my heart pounding.

I quickly came to the conclusion that riding in front of the trucks was the safest plan so if I fell off, (an absolute inevitability) they would see me and help, and I would not be blinded by flying grit. In reality they could well have left me to the bandits and taken my possessions to the market. The trucks crawled along at five or six miles per hour and at that speed the Triumph radiator was boiling in minutes. I had no choice but to push harder, stopping periodically to let the engine cool down and let the convoy catch up. The threat of marauders was very real, so the .38 was cocked and kept ready for action. I had already seen the guards on the trucks check their automatic weapons.

The protruding rocks and soft sand would have been punishment enough without the threat of ambush, but then our first experience of corrugations. Darsi knew what he was talking about and his concern for the bike was justifiable. Imagine a rippled river bed or sheets of corrugated iron set at ninety degrees to your line of attack – and magnify it by a factor of between two and five – and you have The Great North Road of Kenya. Small ones, even at a walking pace made riding feel like the bike had square wheels. The big ones that sometimes went on for half a mile or so had to be attacked at an oblique angle to avoid grounding and the back wheel spinning in soft sand unable to gain traction. Remarkably, I only fell off nine times in the first day's riding.

By mid-afternoon the convoy's dust had long since disappeared from my vibrating wing mirrors as I followed what I thought was evidence left by other road vehicles. A little village of a dozen sun-baked huts appeared out of a mirage. All my concentration was so targeted on the ground two feet in front of the front wheel that, I was next to a gaudily painted shack of a bar before realising people lived there. A good enough place to wait for my luggage, check if arms were still in sockets and wheels still round and hang up a sweat soaked jacket to dry in the sun.

The only drink on offer was very warm beer which I consumed in the partial shade of an acacia tree, but real relief from the devastating thirst came from tart oranges cut into quarters and sucked making my saliva glands burst painfully into a dust-coated throat.

A group of about twenty – the entire adult population – left the shade of their homes to investigate with children running between them giggling. Some stood within arms reach with mouths gaping, studying my every move. Suddenly, like the Red Sea parting for Moses, the crowd fell away as a Masai, wiry as a thorn twig and well over six feet tall flanked by two warriors carrying machetes and bows with arrows in the firing position approached. My hand closed on the .38 concealed by a sodden T-shirt and my matted hair stood on end. They had the advantage with the sun behind them and all I could see, squinting into the furnace, were skinny black things and I was an illuminated target.

"English?" demanded the stately leader. I nodded not knowing if the gesture meant yes or no. His next question floored me completely, and not just because he spoke my mother tongue so well. "Do you think John Major will still be premier after the next election?" After recovering my composure, all I could do was laugh hysterically.

That elegant man dressed in traditional vivid scarlet loin cloth and shawl over one shoulder, sat and talked of Westminster, the Commonwealth, the Royal Family and British agriculture. He was chief of his tribe and had learned to speak English from listening to the BBC World Service on the radio. At the risk of sounding patronising, I was surprised and elated to meet anyone in those barren wastelands who spoke English. To be able to discuss the affairs of state in Britain with 'a savage out of the desert' was startling. In another society he could have been living the White House, but was probably better off in the wilderness where the air is pure, the view uncluttered and getting run over would be a real challenge. His uninhibited laughter at some of my tales is still fresh in my mind. Ear lobes extended by heavy copper rings flashed and jingled in the sun as he rocked back and forth with genuine amusement. We shared the last of my oranges engrossed in debate.

With my guard down, a tug at my unruly beard from an invisible assailant was quite a surprise, but, still managed to be on my feet, gun in hand, in one movement. An enchanting, naked child burst into tears waiting to be rebuked. "You must forgive my son," said the chief, "he has never seen a white man with yellow hair before." His statement worried me. The child must have been at least four years old. "You have not seen a white man in how many years?" I asked. "Never here," he replied. "Sometimes they come near but stay on the path to Marsabit." "So this is not the road to Marsabit?" I asked. "There is no road, but trucks come near and although I have never been there, they talk of Marsabit." "Bollocks," I shouted out loud, "I'm fucking lost." The infant started to cry again at my harsh words so I sat him on my knee and gave him a beaded bracelet bought under pressure from a woman in Nairobi. He was not desperately impressed but the sparkling stones made him smile.

By that time shadows had lengthened, my luggage was miles north and I had not a clue which way to go next. My illustrious friend put my mind at rest - nearly. "You must not travel now as the dark will kill you." I never understood what he meant, but his grave face was very convincing. "Tomorrow, follow the sun and you will find the truck path." "How will I find it?" I asked feeling desperate. I thought I was on it. Like some medieval magician he blew into the sand for what seemed a long time. A shiny rust red rock appeared surrounded by crests of sand. "When you see this turn this

217

way," long expressive fingers indicated left, "and follow the stones." He was beginning to sound like, Merlin but, without the benefit of a tourist board rep, it was the best information on offer. "If bad people come, tell them their chief says they must help." I could not imagine any self-respecting bandit being put off his murderous task with that information. "Now I must go and tend my goats and wives." He really did say that before rising gracefully, thanking me for the oranges and departing with silent guards and small child in tow.

From the bar, I managed to purchase beer, oranges and a very old bottle of sickly Fanta orange juice, not so much because they were needed, but they were the only things on offer. No sign of food of any description, but I was more tired than hungry, so parked the bike up on the eastern edge of the village to settle down for the night. Unfortunately there was absolutely nothing to make a fire out of and no features to camp near. The man from the bar had said I could sleep on his floor as it was dangerous out at night. I declined as the sand was softer and if a bandit could find me in the dark, I would probably have a fifty fifty chance of winning.

Night falls like a brick in open desert and I was pleased it was not as cold as I had experienced in some other deserts. As the sun faded in the west, the sky became electric in the east with more stars than you could point a telescope at in a lifetime. It was a staggering sight with more space given to pin points of flickering light than inky blackness. Picking out star formations in England, when you can see any, is relatively easy as there are so few visible on the brightest of nights. In that sky, finding one prominent enough to navigate by was near impossible. Periodically a shooting star would join the dots, then I was privileged to see God's own firework display. I had witnessed night skies camping out all over the world, but that meteor storm, animating the sky with brush strokes of bright light, was by far the most astounding. A humbling experience that made me feel very small in a desert wilderness.

At first light, to reduce weight even more on the back of the bike, I emptied all the spare fuel into the tank and with some difficulty, stowed the empties as best I could on the rapidly disintegrating pannier racks. As instructed by the Masai chief, I set out across the rocky desert in pursuit of the rising sun and noting the compass direction. I had the bottle of Fanta and two small green oranges and there was absolutely nothing to head for giving no impression of distance. We are used to moving from one land mark to another which gives a feeling of progress. The Masai had said it was about three hours and I assumed that meant on foot. My speed was not much more, but improved after the first two as I began to recognise and avoid the areas of soft sand that prevented all forward motion.

The wheels would sink, spin and the bike would go over again and again as my foot rarely had anything solid to keep balance. With no assistance, the only way to get vertical again was to put a packing strap around one wheel at a time and drag the bike to firmer ground. The effort was draining what little strength I had left and constant sweating was alarmingly dehydrating. Every time shiny stones appeared I stopped to look for evidence of vehicles and by the time three acacia trees were visible on the horizon, panic had started to set in, increasing my already profuse perspiration.

For no particular reason other than it was something to head for, I set off for the trees in a vain hope there may be water, or at least a little shade to die in. It must have taken nearly another hour to reach them and to my delight, there was a clearly perceptible dark line of sand polished rocks snaking into an energetic heat haze. The waves of sand created by the chief blowing on the ground were crests of loosely packed rubble on the verges. It was just as he had demonstrated but on a much grander scale. Moments like that are heart stopping and the revelation was as startling as finding humanoids on Mars.

Nothing moved in the parched landscape – no breeze to move the sparse shade – no wild life, not even insects or ants disturbed the ear shattering silence. I guess the sensation was like being profoundly deaf. The Fanta was disgustingly sweet and made me even more thirsty. I was contemplating draining some coolant but decided the bike was in greater need than me, when a twisting, pulsating shape became visible some distance down the road. It turned out to be a youth carrying a plastic bottle with no lid. He showed no surprise at seeing me and handed over the bottle of smelly hot water, but it was water and the *only* water. I gave him the remains of the Fanta which he swallowed in one with a big grin. Not one word passed between us as he sat down next to me expectantly. Only a few minutes passed before he pointed at a distant whirlwind that had sprung up in the heat of the day. It was not a twister but the dust from a vehicle.

The UN jeep full of armed soldiers slid to a halt and the white driver told me to move on to the next settlement only a couple of miles away. He was an Italian doctor working for the Ethiopian relief project and said there had been bandit activity during the night. His parting remark was, ".... and take the kid with you." My silent friend needed no encouragement to hop on the back and I was careful to put his bare feet on the foot pegs to prevent them being burned on red hot exhausts. It was only two miles but it took us over an hour to reach the village, bigger, but not dissimilar to the previous one. We only fell off twice, but the kid was so weak another pair of hands did not make a lot of difference. He did, however, learn the art of desert pillion riding very quickly, rising out of the saddle over big rocks and stood full height holding my collar to wave at friends through the village like a victorious gladiator.

I asked about trucks in the hope of seeing my luggage again, but a newly arrived driver said one had been attacked in the night and there were none behind him. Marsabit, the half way stage to the Ethiopian border, was seven hours drive – there were about six hours of daylight left. I had to take a chance and follow in the hope of retrieving my luggage. The ride proved to be the most demanding of my life bouncing over boulders and sliding about in soft gravel. Without me noticing, the desert changed to black volcanic rock with smooth boulders, sharp stones and deep tracks moulded by truck tyres.

Riding the crests of the tracks was hopeless as the bike skidded in loose stones and slid to the bottom often three feet deep. On one such peak the bike disappeared leaving me standing a yard above it straddling the narrow sided rut. The bike was firmly wedged in place. It took a good half hour stabbing at concrete hard mud with my knife to release it and I had to ride it out standing on the seat. As the sun set, the road improved slightly, so I continued for the last half hour to the welcome lights of Marsabit. It had taken a little over seven hours non-stop riding to cover forty-two miles.

The military post said my truck had not arrived and hoped it was not the one attacked by bandits. I found a room in a shack of a hotel and told the check point guards where I was if it did arrive, leaving a small cash incentive.

The hotel had no water, so I dragged my filthy, aching body to a bar for a quiet beer. There was no food being served, but I had discovered the very fortifying nourishment that could be gained from local brews. As I was enjoying the cool night air, my truck turned up. The driver had broken down and spent a day on repairs, so I went to bed feeling content that my possessions did not end up in the market, but worried about what was to come on the road north.

28. Addis? Addis? Where the fuck is Addis?

Daybreak revealed the devastation suffered by the Triumph. Nuts and bolts had been shaken loose or were missing and some serious reconstruction was necessary around the back end if the panniers were ever going to fit again. As an enthusiastic young man set about the bike with a welding torch, I tightened all the remaining bolts. Some had stripped threads so had to be held in place with a blob of welding rod. Bracing the pannier racks apart so they did not foul exhausts was essential, but no convenient bits of metal were available. Living in a desolate town, where everything has to be transported by truck for a couple of days meant Peru-style recycling. If it can not be fixed, it can be turned into something else of use, so nothing is wasted. The welding engineer asked me to help drag oxyacetylene tanks over to the outside of someone's house, where he cut off a six-foot length of shower pipe and made a very satisfactory repair job on the bike. After that, I noticed many pipes had suffered the same fate. All buildings were equipped with bathroom fittings, but the town had never had running water. What a waste of money and resources bringing them there in the first place. The other peculiar revelation was the lack of oil as the dip-stick was dry. Maybe it had not been properly topped up in Dubai. It could not have evaporated despite overheating, so I assumed it had leaked out of the loose drain plug.

The engineer disappeared for what seemed like a long time, returning with a metal jug full of oil the consistency of treacle. It was so thick, the last bit needed scraping out with a spoon. The dipstick was still dry so off he went again, this time I followed. In a deep gully, a truck lay on its side. It looked as if it had been there for some years. The engineer removed the gear box drain plug and refilled the jug. Well, it may get me to the next supply, I thought, and beggars can't be choosers. The best part of a day's work cost me a set of Gorica Trading overalls given to me by Floyd in the Emirates. He did not ask for money once he clapped eyes on the immaculately pressed garment still in its plastic bag.

I have never been unfortunate enough to suffer real starvation, but my experience of going a few days without eating is that my already pathetic appetite completely disappears. Yet again beer was the only nourishment to fortify my emaciated body. Back at the hotel while attempting to obtain enough water to clean my teeth, a BMW Boxer pulled up outside. A young Swiss guy practically fell off the bike with exhaustion. He had just ridden from the Ethiopian border, on route to Diani Beach to meet his mother on holiday.

I told him about the road south. "It cannot be as bad as going north," he said. His bike was a properly equipped off-road machine, much lighter than mine, with knobbly tyres. He was several inches taller, several stone heavier and much stronger than me. "You haven't a hope on your bike," he said over a beer. I had serious doubts about the Triumph or me surviving much more punishment, so I set about finding a truck to transport us to Moyali where Ethiopia, and roads began.

A price was negotiated and I followed the truck to a dry river bed where it was reversed up to a bank the same height as the truck floor. Riding a flat tailgate into the canvas-clad interior was easy. I checked out of the hotel and slept on the canvas roof wedged between steel supporting hoops. The only incident during the sleepless night was nearly breaking my leg jumping into darkness going for a piss. I had forgotten how high the truck roof was and misjudged it by about six feet when launching myself into the dark.

In reality, the route north was a vast improvement on the one south. My Swiss friend must have had a rude awakening. Corrugations miraculously vanished making the road much easier to negotiate. Huge termite mounds, much bigger than those in Australia, became the dominant feature, many of them humanoid in shape and well-formed enough for Henry Moore to put his name to. For me it was a new experience sitting for ten hours on the truck roof with a bunch of locals and armed military and it gave me an opportunity to film. A strong wind soon covered everyone with a thick crust of red dust and my travel companions were amused to see we were all the same colour.

We stopped for lunch in a village of not much more than a few mud huts where my first meal for days was a bowl of rice with chopped up hens' feet in it. What a feast! The truck convoys were the only lifeline to those desolate villages. Donkey trains trekked up to fifty miles to obtain water.

For the last couple of hours the gradient increased, air cooled as the truck's grinding engine took on a note of urgency. The desert petered out to sparse vegetation at first, then fertile land fit for agriculture.

Moyale, my gateway to Ethiopia, looked like so many small towns as the truck was yet again reversed up to an escarpment, but a precarious ramp was needed to span the distance. Locals were all asking for money to help unload, but I told them if they came to *my* country no one would expect money for a little help. Okay, so we were in *their* country, with their rules, but it worked and with a good deal of pushing and shoving the bike was on terra firma once more – perched about eight feet in the air on a very steep mound. The assembled crowd were nearly as impressed as me as I slid the bike down to road level with both wheels locked up and not falling off.

Customs was closed so I found a mosquito-infested room for the night. When asking for water, I was rewarded with a bucket and directed down the road to the communal tap – next to the communal toilet, which was a bottomless pit surrounded by a corrugated iron wigwam. The bucket leaked spilling my hard-earned spoils over the dirt road. My hair had turned to dreadlocks and it was impossible to guess what colour my T-shirt used to be.

Ethiopia greeted the Triumph with what used to be a tarmac road and me with courteous officials. No one asked for bribes, but one pleasant guy asked if I had any books written in English as he enjoyed reading the language. I did not think he would be too impressed with *Zen and the Art of Motorcycle Maintenance* so said 'no'. He then asked if he could sign something 'official' for me. The carnet was produced along with one of the cheap Bic biros purchased for such an occasion. After finishing his flourish, I produced a red one asking for another signature in a different place, leaving both pens with him. "Welcome to Ethiopia," he said satisfied with the transaction. Ball point pens are currency in many African countries. Despite a disturbingly high rate of illiteracy, everyone from politicians to school children are prepared to sell their soul for them, so they are a wise investment should you ever visit.

The first twenty miles of Ethiopia were on badly pitted black-top but, with no traffic, the Triumph was at liberty to wander about on the best bits. I had neglected to ask the friendly customs man which side of the road to ride on and, as there were no signs, I assumed it was the left like in Kenya. I stopped to examine two parked vehicles and noticed the steering wheel on the other side, so moved more or less to the right.

Ethiopia was a revelation. I had expected parched barren desert and hungry people. Climbing north through devastatingly beautiful mountains with food growing on every tree, the rain came down in buckets. Once the wet bit creeping up your arms reaches the stuff trickling down your neck, it becomes damn cold. Torrents falling off the mountains left heaps of slippery magenta mud to slide around in. Descending into Isla was one of the better moments of the day's ride as the rise in temperature penetrated my stiff, frozen fingers.

Isla was not an impressive spectacle, especially as the road had been washed away and neither of the two fuel stops had petrol. "Benzene all gone, try next." This was getting a bit worrying as everything ran on diesel. Supply was so short even locals were rationed. One came to my rescue saying his van ran on diesel so I was allowed his ten litre ration of precious "Benzene," which was carefully measured into the Triumph by a boy with a tin jug.

Local food was an equal disappointment with a limp, nut-brown chapati-like thing called incherra hanging over the sides of an enormous plate. The discus of rubbery dough was cold and not made from a crop of my acquaintance and sitting in the middle was a little steel bowl full of bits of gristle. It was one of those meals that would not go away no matter how hard you worked at it and without a convenient dog to be seen, I was a bit stuck.

The best thing about travelling in remote underdeveloped countries is that there are very few roads, meaning getting lost is a little more difficult although definitely possible as I had proved in Kenya. Decisions have to be made at every fork in the road and without much intelligence on where Addis Ababa was, the compass could not advise. Few people move around the country, so not even locals know, but will lie or speculate about a direction rather than confess ignorance. This was of no great concern as I was so delighted to be on a road that allowed me to get out of second gear.

In Dubai, there was a very popular record released that escaped the strict obscenity censorship. It was a remake of an old hit, ending up as 'Alice? Alice? Who the fuck is Alice?' Frequently I would wake up with a tune in my head and regardless of how tough the day had been, it would still be there at night. Sometimes the lyrics got distorted to suit my mood, and the Dubai hit became 'Addis? Addis? Where the Fuck is Addis?' as I slid around gracefully in glutinous red slurry dumped all over the road by escaping rain water.

The two things that really stood out in rural Ethiopia were white people and vehicles young enough to still have paint on. I overtook a shiny four-wheel drive – and in it were three pale faces – one even looked familiar. I pulled over at a bar leaving the bike in a prominent position hoping they would stop. The Italian doctor, from the road in Kenya, was accompanied by two Germans and an Ethiopian guide. He was delighted and impressed to see me over the border even though I did confess to cheating for a day. He paid for my beer and put me straight about direction. Luck rather than brain cells had me only about a hundred miles from Addis. He confirmed Eritrea was probably my best option, although he told me to expect similar travel conditions as northern Kenya before getting there.

Once hitting the tatty outskirts of Addis Ababa, I steered towards the centre looking for a hotel. One that looked very posh and way out of my budget appeared but, with several days filth held in place by red mud, a proper shower was called for. But joy of joys, my fabulous room had a bath. I filled it to the top with *hot* water, but after only a minute had to start again as the water had changed colour. The next morning I discovered prices were quoted in US dollars not Birr so checked out and found a very acceptable place for a tenth of the amount.

The Green Falls Hotel (the walls were green with mould and it was falling down) was clean enough, but it was back to the bucket method for water. The most notable feature was found in a drawer next to the bed where one may expect to find a Gideon Bible. Instead there were six condoms. This said a lot for the country's AIDS awareness and the sexual prowess of Ethiopian men.

Addis was not as bad as I had expected and all the facilities I needed were in easy walking distance. As capital cities go it was refreshingly low-rise and few people could afford cars so the well-surfaced roads were uncluttered by traffic. There were a disturbing number of monopedal beggars who had suffered a legacy of anti-personnel mines scattered like confetti during the recent conflict. Most advertising hoardings proclaimed the dangers of AIDS in English. A worthy effort, but those at greatest risk did not speak English and were illiterate in any language.

The only piece of reading matter I left home with was a little book containing riveting facts about every country in the world and the revelations about Ethiopia were disturbing. During the last century over ninety per cent of forests in the highlands were destroyed. Life expectancy for both men and women at the time of publication was only thirty eight, the lowest in the world, with an optimistic literacy rate of 35%. GNP was US$ 4.8 billion, US$ 104 per head. The UK for the same period was US$758 billion, US$ 13,129 per head even though our population was much higher. A chequered history of perpetual conflict and natural disasters unfolded from the sins of Haile Selassie to a two billion dollar arms budget to fight numerous wars when people were dying in the street from starvation. The price of a bullet would have fed a child all day – but they still bought bullets. The penalty for human greed is obscene. Why will we never learn? Perhaps there is less profit in peace.

Redundant, limbless, ex-military personnel resorted to begging and those still whole to menial labouring occupations. The one observation I made of most poor people was a greenish cud in the corners of their mouths. Gwat is a prolific wild plant turned into a cash crop for those who can not pick their own. The tough unyielding leaves have to be chewed with some determination to achieve a lift. With my usual enthusiasm to try all things local, I purchased some and likened it to consuming a privet hedge. After masticating dry, unpalatable leaves for what seemed a very long time my gums tingled, but alas no euphoria. There are some things that do not beg persistence and my aching jaws, after a humungus chewing marathon, told me gwat was one of them.

By contrast, marijuana grows as weeds do, just like in Colombia and a delightful young man in a bar offered to sell me a little. To keep in step with the rest of the world politically, it is in theory illegal, so discretion was essential. I put a price limit of five American dollars on the transaction as he was not impressed with the offer of birr. We met later that evening down a dark alley and he handed over a female head, the most desirable part. I smelt it and fondled it pretending to be a discerning buyer who knew his stuff. "Very good," I said. "How much?" "We agreed five dollar – okay?" I have no idea what it would have cost back home but was sure it would be at least ten times more, even though I was obviously paying tourist price. I agreed and handed over the dosh. In the darkness I had not noticed the huge black bin liner propped against his leg. He dropped the specimen plant head into the sack and handed over the lot. I was at a bit of a loss to know what to do next, but as the vendor had walked away happy, I made tracks back to the hotel looking like Father Christmas with a huge sack over my shoulder. In the privacy of my room, I discovered there were two whole plants that must have been four or five feet tall before being scrunched up into the bag. A fair amount of patience was demanded to reduce the best of it to a lump the size of a house brick, discarding the rest on a rubbish tip. With no proper information about the emerging new country of Eritrea, it was all disposed of well before the border.

The last challenge I faced before departing in search of a new country was obtaining money. There was not a banking institution in the entire capital that would accept a Visa card, so I phoned Marian for help. I had forgotten she was about to go on holiday, so the task was delegated to my loyal and hard-working bookkeeper Mary. If anyone could be trusted to get the complicated system right, it was her. She had to take a cheque, made out in pounds sterling, to a Western Union office in a Brighton supermarket. It was converted into US dollars and wired to Addis where it was converted into birr. This meant losing out twice on exchange rates. The only way to obtain American currency again (birr is useless outside the country and should not be taken out) was to lose more to an illegal dealer in the city.

After more expensive faxes and telephone calls, the deal was done and I was pleased not to have to scale the stairs to the Central Bank of Ethiopia again. The first time this task was attempted, I had been concerned about my condition as a breather half way up was necessary. Gasping for breath a guy asked how I found the air in Addis. It was clean, clear and unpolluted but, at 9000 feet, it was just the quantity that caused the problem. "The air is fine," I wheezed to the inquisitive stranger, "but we white folk need a bit more of it."

Road reports for the next four hundred miles or so were fair to crap depending on the time of year. During the height of the rainy season, the route was impassable through the mountains. Threatening skies and distant thunder was nature's way of telling me to get a move on.

29. Dancing in the Streets

Memories of South America flooded back riding dreadful roads on steeper and steeper gradients into the mountains. Fog, so dense I could not see the potholes, cold penetrating rain and succulent vegetation was not what I had expected for equatorial Ethiopia. With the possible exception of Colombia, the landscape was the most beautiful I had experienced so far – when the fog lifted long enough to see it. The Rift Valley, although inaccessible, was a devastating sight stretching half the way across the continent and the Grand Canyon came a poor second in nature's evolving art gallery.

Rivers of red mud became the enemy, hiding cavernous holes and denying any grip to the back wheel. Every time I put my foot down for stability, my boots were replenished with a fresh supply of sludge. After climbing out of one particularly unforgiving mud-filled crater there was a loud crash, as everything supported by the botched up pannier racks hit the ground followed by me. One of the exhausts had sheered from its mounting, luggage bounced about on bungie straps and I suffered a crippling pain that shot through my groin and abdomen bringing me to my knees. I must have looked a pathetic sight grovelling around in the mud collecting belongings dragging a leg through puddles. "Only a few thousand miles more," I kept repeating to myself through clenched teeth. A few thousand miles to where and to what were not at the forefront of my mind and, if that bit of road was all I could call home, I wished someone would put a roof on it.

The pain felt like someone had pushed a blunt instrument through my pelvis bringing tears to my eyes. I had to carefully lift my right leg on to the foot peg, where it stayed, leaving just one leg to keep the bike upright.

By Dessie, several more feet of shower hose and portions of dead truck were creatively welded to the rear end sculpture to keep the Triumph together. Less than 300 miles from Mitsiwa and news that a major bridge had been washed away did not seem fair. A ten-mile detour inland should not have been a problem, except it had to be accomplished through truck tracks and there was no way of assessing how deep they were in sticky mud. With one leg out of action, I had to be brave, accelerating into quagmires hoping to have enough momentum to get out the other side. I only got stuck once and was impressed that locals leapt into the muddy breech to assist.

The most common feature pressing north was the increasing number of deserted tanks and armoured vehicles abandoned after the recent conflict. Many of them looked in working order and I shuddered watching children play with live ammunition. Many men could be seen carrying automatic weapons. It would have only taken one opportunist to bring down a helpless biker struggling through the quagmire at a walking pace, but fortunately they recognised I was not the enemy and they proved to be very friendly and helpful. Obtaining fuel got progressively more difficult and I was rationed to a couple of litres at a time. I only ran out once and could do nothing except wait for assistance. I sat under a tree sticking out of the steep valley side attempting to keep the worst of the rain off until it got dark. Not the first long lonely night, but that one had some nasty surprises in store and the pain in my groin throbbed mercilessly. Shortly before dawn, water higher up the mountain found a new escape route. Flash floods are instant and devastating as tons of water seek the lines of least resistance and can build into torrents in seconds. Before I knew it, I was up to my waist in it, clinging to a tree feeling very cold, miserable and scared. All traffic stops during the rainy season as the road is really a dry river bed. I just had to arrive as it was undergoing the transition from a road back into a river. Fortunately, clear sunlight came with the dawn for me to asses the predicament. The bike had received a thorough wash, the crippling pain had miraculously disappeared and a gangly adolescent was fighting his way up the steep track with two plastic containers strapped to his back. He quickly grasped my message that a drop of benzene would go down rather well and both cylindrical containers were released from their moorings. One contained water – and the other, smelt about right for petrol. I could not believe what was happening, but took the precaution of pouring a little of the urine-coloured fluid into my Zippo lighter to test its flammability. The flame gave off thick black smoke, but it was worth a try. He only had about a litre, but it all worked remarkably well and he would only accept a few Birr as a reward for saving my life. If I had been stuck there for another night, a second flash flood caused by torrential rain higher up the mountain would probably have drowned me, and the bike would have been lost forever under mud slides. After stuffing the money in his pocket, the youth loaded himself up again and walked off in the direction he had just come from. I will never understand how he knew where I was or what was required to keep the Triumph team moving, but the bush telegraph is mighty efficient in Ethiopia.

It took another two days to cover the feeble mileage to Adigrat, in striking distance of Eritrea. I had been told there were only *two* mountains to cross, but I think he must have said a *few* after grinding up and down hour after hour. There is the danger of getting complacent, even in those atrocious conditions that elevated themselves above North Kenya in the undesirability stakes. Mudslides in places completely obliterated the road and water plummeting on to the gravel surface carved new dangers for the uninitiated. Rounding yet another hairpin, the front wheel got caught in a little rivulet only a few inches deep, but there was no way out of it. Fortunately, we were only doing about fifteen miles an hour as the bike veered out of control towards the brink where water plummeted to the valley below. I had less than two yards to make some rapid and serious decisions. It took all of my limited strength and even more limited courage to throw the bike on its side. The Triumph came to rest with the front wheel over the edge of an uninterrupted five hundred foot drop. I clung to rocks by my teeth and fingernails with nothing but fresh air under my feet. Damage to me was minimal, with just a few more bruises and abrasions to add to the collection. The bike looked okay, but any attempt to right it would have sent it over the edge. I desperately wanted to photograph it, but dared not fiddle with luggage as the weight on the back was the only thing keeping it in its precarious position. A pick-up full of road clearance workers came to the rescue. A rope was tied round the back wheel, and we dragged the bike away from the precipice and back on to the road. Remarkably, very little damage was inflicted during the ordeal and minutes later, I was riding the piece of twisty, descending road that had very nearly become a fatal short cut from that ridge several hundred feet up the mountain. That incident was probably the closest I got to death during the whole year. Shootings, crashes and flash floods paled into insignificance looking up with a shudder at the incident site.

Petrol was begged and bought from anyone who had a spare litre. A ragged man with a donkey cart offered me a banana . I gave him one birr (about two pence) and he handed over a complete hand of the dumpy green fruit, so that was breakfast, lunch and dinner sorted. He had been a commander in the Liberation Army, suffered drought and famine for his cause, followed by the humiliation of being demoted from important military person to poor Ethiopian again. Stories of political power struggles while the population suffered fell from his lips. He asked for a cigarette, but received a packet when he told me the road ahead was as smooth as a baby's skin. He was right. The last fifty miles to Adigrat were a joy, weaving along well-cambered black-top constructed to transport troops to the Eritrean war zone. The only mishaps were a cow's head smashing open a pannier and a badly bruised ankle from kicking a goat about to throw itself under the Triumph. There was even time to admire the changing scenery in warm evening sunshine. Forested flat-top mountains gave way to the arid northern plains that sustain very little vegetation of any kind, resembling the media coverage that I had assumed typical of Ethiopia.

Over the border into Eritrea and the scene became progressively more barren, riding sweeping bends through a dramatic lunar landscape. The well-surfaced road snaked its way thorough mountain passes before plummeting several thousand feet in a few miles through colourful villages of stone-built houses. One village, still under construction, was a rehabilitation centre for disabled war victims with stoutly constructed square buildings strewn with flags in preparation for their fifth independence celebration.

A large Coca Cola sign announced 'Welcome to Mitsiwa', where the mountains end and the Red Sea begins. A premature Independence Day parade was in full swing and a policeman stuck an Eritrean flag on the back of the bike and asked me to join in, much to the amusement of the cheering crowd lining the street. The town was a blaze of colour and awash with rejoicing locals.

I stopped at the first hotel, which was well out of my budget, but not the Italian doctor's. He was surprised and relieved to see I had made it, as he had to fly in after being told the Ethiopian mountain road was impassable. His job as a United Nations medical officer was to treat the sick in some very remote areas of Ethiopia, especially those that had been affected by the war. Lack of supplies and qualified assistance meant many victims of gun-shot wounds or mortar attacks died from infection, often long after the wound had been inflicted. In his opinion children treading on anti-personnel mines were the worst as, even if they did survive the resultant infection, a child without legs cannot work, so becomes a burden to a family with very limited resources.

He had come to Eritrea for some R&R and according to him, all sea traffic from Mitsiwa, the only port, went via Jeddah, which meant I would have to ride to the capital for a Saudi visa which would take more time and money than I had. Cruising the neat little port, I found one ship about to sail and there was not another for two weeks. The Sudan High Commission had told me in no uncertain terms that I would not be permitted to travel through southern Sudan because of the war and actually laughed when I said my plan was to follow the coast to Egypt. "How do you think you are going to do that? There is nothing there – just men with guns – go another way home." With only a couple of weeks before my planned return to Le Mans, north and west were bared by Sudanese, passage up the Red Sea was out of the question and the weather barred any route south. I was effectively a prisoner in a very small emerging country about to go into party overload. The thought of witnessing, even taking part in the festivities was tantalizing, but getting anything done would be difficult during a holiday.

I found an excellent hotel run by a very jolly, fat lady who spoke good English. The neat little bar and restaurant boasted more fans than Elvis Presley ever had and everything had to be bolted to the floor to prevent it being blown away in the manufactured force nine gale. My room was big and airy with shuttered windows at either end keeping out the fierce sun. The furniture was old and interestingly battered. Nothing matched, but was mainly in a utility style except for a splendid drop-leaf bureau that would have gone for a fortune in a Brighton antique shop. The view over harbour and town was quite a revelation. Mitsiwa had been the last strategic stronghold of the Eritrean Revolutionary Army during the long conflict. Without it, Ethiopia was landlocked, so the town was bombarded night and day for a month. Just about every building older than the ceasefire showed evidence from machine-gun pockmarks to half a mosque reduced to rubble. Ghosts of tanks and armoured personnel carriers rusted quietly in military graveyards.

By 6.30 the following morning I was packed and ready for the ride to Asmara the capital for more information on an escape plan. The heat was staggering even at that time of day and I drank a litre of water before even mounting the bike. Mitsiwa must be the hottest place in the world. After only a few miles, progress was interrupted by road works and I had to return. The nice man stopping traffic just said, "No road today. Come back tomorrow and we will have a new one." My jovial landlady was glad to see me back and laughed when I told her I could not bear the idea of never spending another night in her hotel.

I was effectively trapped in a town of a few thousand souls, in a country half the size of Wales. So, with no particular place to go, I cruised the streets until hearing an English voice shout "It's a Triumph!" Now you have to know something about bikes to recognise British engineering when most branding has been scratched off or is covered by a tank bag. Martin and Miranda ran an overland travel company and also did rather well importing trucks to Africa. He was exceptionally well-travelled and a good source of information as he knew the country well. They were also off to Asmara when the road reopened so we arranged to meet again on their arrival. "I need to buy a washing machine," said Martin, "It should fit on the roof of the Land Rover okay." It seemed a bit weird to me that these explorer types were giving up so much valuable space on their Land Rover roof for a washing machine, but he obviously knew what he was talking about.

Believe it or not, the following day there really was a new road. The happy chap who had turned me back the previous day said I was the first person to use it and hoped it was to my satisfaction. It certainly was, meandering up into the cool ochre mountains. It rose nearly eight thousand feet in sixty miles through scenery that belonged on another planet.

After a couple of hours' easy riding I stopped in a tiny mountain hamlet for a Coke and bum rest. The solitary shop only sold beer so I sat on the roadside at 8.00am sipping the warm brew from the bottle. Small stone-built houses clung to the mountain side or nestled under the arches of an impressive bridge. Blocks were so accurately hewn that no mortar was required in the construction. A constant procession of women and children walked to and fro collecting water from somewhere out of sight in a variety of plastic containers. The containers varied from bottles for the children to five-gallon drums for women, which they carried on their backs, supported by a thong around their foreheads. Many of the older women had necks like sumo wrestlers, so developed were their muscles. Many of the young children were dressed in nothing but a vest, most of which looked as though they had served several generations. They all stopped to gaze at me with extraordinarily big inquiring eyes. No one asked for anything and the bike was much admired but not touched. The distribution of a few ball point pens went down well although some of the enchanting kids had no idea what they had been given. Expressions of joy took over from confusion at the meagre gifts as they ran off with shrieks of joy, spilling much of their precious water. Without little children, the world as we know it will cease to exist and I was staring into the face of Africa's future. Bright eyes, big toothy grin and a vest that was more holes than vest. The distribution of wealth in the world is so unjust. My children did not have to collect water, naked save for a holey vest. I donated a travel-stained T-shirt and another to his friend, both had been given to me by the UAE Harley Davidson Club in Dubai and they very nearly reached the ankles of two poor Eritrean children. Being an observer, or sharing in the lives of others, is the best part of travel and sitting there watching life go by was my very reason for being there.

Asmara itself was another unexpected pleasant surprise. A clean orderly capital, small enough to walk round in a day. Women constantly swept the streets with palm fronds amongst constant reminders of Eritrea's Italian heritage. Authentic pizza and spaghetti houses punctuated orderly streets between cafe bars hissing and gurgling with ancient Gaggia espresso coffee machines. Strangers stopped for no more than a handshake and chat, all wishing to know if I was enjoying their country. Eritrea is undoubtedly a destination with vast potential for tourists in search of an 'alternative' holiday so long as natural assets are used and not abused

Martin and Miranda showed me round the markets as they searched for an 'overlander's' washing machine. The last one had apparently fallen off the roof of their Land Rover full of clothes. Martin was pleased with his acquisition of a sturdy plastic tub with tight-fitting lid. This was firmly lashed to the roofrack, water and washing powder added to dirty laundry and after a day driving over bumpy roads the result was very impressive. When the washing machine (dustbin to you and me) was not washing, it was carrying water, or it was a table and the lid was a frisby.

We strolled down to the museum in the grounds of one of Haile Selassie's palaces. Why the man is still revered by some Rastafarians in the world is a mystery. No dreadlocks were to be seen in the country where his brutal regime was responsible for a genocide of fellow countrymen on a par with Pol Pot or Idi Amin. In the great European-driven carve-up of Africa, Eritrea became an Italian colony and one Mussolini cherished as his foothold for Catholics surrounded by Islam. The British liberated the country after the Second World War, but then left them to fight for their independence against the might of Ethiopia. The museum was mostly a testament to those courageous men and women protecting their unique identity and culture during the conflict. Make-shift rocket launchers crudely mounted on the back of dilapidated trucks faced armoured tanks. Martin pointed out a Russian-made nine millimeter automatic rifle. In Uganda he had been on the receiving end of one as an over-ambitious young soldier tried to take control of his truck. After stopping a bullet in his left arm and another in the chest, he punched his assailant in the face knocking him off the footplate and drove himself to the nearest place that could be described as a hospital in war-torn Uganda. Only ten days later, he was back on the road minus a lung and had still not regained full use of his arm. Bit of a hero really, especially as the incident did not deter him from driving trucks through troubled parts of Africa and he still claimed Uganda was his favourite country.

That evening, the Independence Day celebrations got into full swing. Live bands played from open trucks. *Everybody*, including Miranda and me, were dragged into the street to dance. Policemen handed their weapons to children so they could join in the festivities. Being white, we were a novelty and kids to armed soldiers demanded we dance with them. It is not uncommon to see men walking the streets holding hands as they do in India. This has nothing to do with their sexuality, but it can be a comical sight to see uniformed officers clasped to each other gyrating to the buzz of *real* African music. The people are a startlingly attractive, not African or Arab in looks but uniquely Eritrean with fine features, nut-brown skins and wide grins that are remarkably disarming. That night on the streets of Asmara was one of the most memorable – and I desperately wanted to share it with Marian. When trying to resolve an issue, the silent pages of my note book was a battle ground of conflicting ideas and emotions. When there is no one to talk to, a scribbled monologue was as close to a debate as I could manage.

'29th May – Red Sea Guest House, Asmara, Eritrea

Although it is still far from over, this has been a journey of contradictions – life is a journey of contradictions, regardless of our chosen path. My chosen path has taken me around nine tenths of the world, yet I have seen so little of it. Travelling alone was the right decision, but how I would love to share these experiences with Marian. Writing them down, even filming them, will never reveal the pain and joy of actually being there. This evening, dancing in the streets, amongst so many warm and welcoming people was one of the most memorable in a year's travel, but I felt lonely in the crowd and wanted to share a unique moment. It will never happen again quite like this – the sixth celebration of independence will be different, and then there is the biggest contradiction of all. Provided a route out of Eritrea can be secured, I will soon be back in Europe, the Le Mans, then home. I crave the company of friends, I have not seen my children in a whole year – and then there is Marian to enjoy all over again. Our lives – our futures together – but never in my life have I felt so 'comfortable', so at home, as I do right now, so if we do have a future together, how can the adventure continue? Before then however, there is another tiny little problem – how do we get out of *here!*'

30. The First Day of The Rest of My life

Two days of investigation and hard bargaining resulted in an escape plan from Eritrea. Ethiopian Airlines eventually agreed a sensible price to fly me and the Triumph to Athens, meaning I would be taking one leap out of Africa into the relative comfort of Europe. I felt cheated because I was having to cheat. My intention had always been to ride overland wherever possible but, not for the first time, war had prevented progress. I was not there to try and prove anything and was delighted to secure a way out to anywhere as time marched on. Weight was reduced to a minimum by throwing or giving away anything I would not need in Europe. Old sprockets and two sad chains kept for emergencies, cans of lubricant and surplus tools were donated to a rather tumbledown workshop where a complete wall of the two-storey building and the staircase had been demolished during the war. They accessed the top floor via a ladder but found it difficult to get heavy objects up to the machinery, which was too heavy to bring down. He said he was going to use my redundant sprockets and chain to make a hoist as 'the gear ratios are very acceptable'. My water purifier, camping stove and a sack full of junk collected in a year on the road was offered to the guest house owner, but he was not desperately impressed. "In Eritrea the water is pure, it's the quantity that's the problem and not much can be made from the rest of this, but the little stove is *very* good."

Despite all my efforts to shed weight, the total was still beyond my budget. Airlines have a strange formula of volume and weight and charge you for whichever is the more expensive. I visited a senior director of Ethiopian Airlines with some of the articles printed by Motoring & Leisure Magazine to prove I was a travel journalist – of sorts. I said I wanted to write good things about their country, but this would be impossible if I could not continue my journey. I genuinely thought Eritrea had a future in tourism and I hoped it showed. He was very sympathetic and agreed to charge for the dimensions of the crated bike rather than weight. My flight was duly booked for the following day, leaving one more night in Eritrea.

A German biker with a severe stomach problem told me of a very good pizza restaurant called 'Have-a-shit'. I was unconvinced that a restaurant with such a name was a good recommendation from someone suffering from advanced food poisoning, but thought it worth trying. Something must have been lost in the translation as it was really called Hawasheit, serving authentic pizza and spaghetti. The depth of Italian culture in that small African country was extraordinary – a weird combination of the familiar and the unfamiliar – tagliatelli being served by an exquisite young lady in tribal robes and excellent local wine poured from something that looked like a cross between a pig's bladder and a hot water bottle.

On my way back to the hotel, I popped into a shop to buy some cigarettes. I had run out of money, and told the shop keeper I needed to go and get more from the hotel. He said, "No problem. Take the cigarettes and pay me tomorrow." Where else in the world can a complete stranger walk into a shop in the capital city and be told to drop the money in the following day? He did not know me from a bar of soap yet trusted a white stranger. We can learn a lot from those people. On my travels, stories of white backpackers doing 'runners' from camp sites or hotels were commonplace and frequently bragged about by the perpetrators. It is not clever and not funny. We white, middle-class travellers – pioneers – have a responsibility to the tourists of the future and it is a sad testament to the selfish backpacker to tar us all with the same brush. As Westerners forged deeper into uncharted territory, the first victims were animals and flightless birds who did not recognise them as enemies. Easy pickings for a man with a musket. We then progressed to plundering and enslaving. Now a new breed of traveller is robbing them. Will we never learn?

My last night was spent in a cheap hotel, with no water, shivering. It can get cold anywhere at nearly 8,000 feet, but my days of mountain climbing, on that trip at least, were over.

'30th May Red Sea Guest House, Asmara, Eritrea

Tomorrow is my last day in Africa after only a month. I'm sad, very sad, I can't ride the Nile Valley through Egypt, but thanks to a Tata truck in India and Sue in Dubai, I have at least experienced three countries on the continent. Without that chain of events, I would not be sitting here. The cynic may say I could have been somewhere better, but I doubt that.

Africa has certainly been very tough and nearly beat us with its extremes of desert and flood. It is not the fault of Africa that I have to fly with my tail between my legs, but human conflict in a struggle for power over a population who mostly do not care. I met a group of Christian refugees from the south of Sudan escaping Sunni muslim troops and, although the war is political rather than religious, any minority group is an easy target and they felt safer living with a common faith. All they wanted in their homeland was a fresh water supply and the freedom to farm in peace. They knew very little about the causes of the war but, after twice having their village torched by apparently two different armies, it was obvious they were being persecuted by both warring factions. A no win situation for them – and I am moaning because I can't cross their country. In the grand scheme of things, my grief and problems don't add up to a hill of desert sand and this time tomorrow I will be on my way back to Europe. Now, there is a bizarre concept. In New York a guy asked me where I was going and I said England, the long way round, so I was on my way home from the moment Marian kissed me goodbye. Then in Bangkok, the half way stage home and back to Marian was the objective, but it wasn't until this moment, a last night in Africa, that I feel any closer.'

At dawn the following morning I was at the airport with a dozen-strong crew to build the bike crate with a sizable amount of protected rain forest. "It's big," said the official inspecting my bike. "It must have grown with all the rain in the night," I replied making everyone laugh. Humour is a great leveller. One guy started cutting a piece of 3x4 across his knee with a blunt saw. We had only five hours before the plane was due to leave, so I set up a work bench from breeze blocks presumably delivered to construct an airport building – when they got round to it. A couple of hours later, we admired our work as the empty crate, weighing over eighty kilos, was manhandled on to a platform ready to be loaded into the hold. All I had to do was ride the bike up a six inch wide, 45 degree ramp into a box with slightly less than an inch clearance each side. The man with the nails and the man with the hammer knocked off while the man with the string set about securing the bike in the crate, while I went in search of another rubber stamp. When I returned, the lid was about to be nailed in place so I thought it a good idea to peep in to check all was well. Two pieces of limp string tied to the handlebars were the only support, so I insisted on more, climbing into the box myself. My experience of bike packing was limited, but more than theirs. I showed them how to tension rope twisting a block of wood (learned in India) and tie non-slip knots (Malaysia) before nailing down the lid. After, I thought they should be paying me rather than the other way round.

Once the bike was stowed safely in the cargo hold of the remarkably small aircraft, I could relax and say good-bye to the packing crew and officials who had attempted, at least, to help. The only thing worrying me was we had to change planes in Addis Ababa, the one hurdle that could prevent me getting back to Europe. Once in Europe I knew things would be relatively easy as it is a familiar continent and most of the journey back to France could be easily achieved overland.

My window seat at low altitude offered fine views of the little country I had developed such an irrational affection for. Across the north Ethiopian desert and then the lush mountains, the road that very nearly beat us had turned from a heap of unforgiving boulders to a raging torrent fed by swollen streams. I could not identify the precise spot where I could have drowned in a flash flood or where I came close to plummeting several hundred feet to my death – it all seemed small from the safety of an aircraft, but I knew its real scale and unforgiving power. In less than an hour we were landing in Addis, a trip that had taken a week's hard riding. This may reveal the idiot side of my nature as all the hardship could have been avoided if I had flown in the first place, but that is the difference between observing and experiencing.

Predictably, Addis Ababa administration caused more problems. Our connecting flight was ready for take off and there was not time to transfer the bike, but I was promised it would be on the next one and had no choice but to trust them. Leaving my most treasured possession behind in a poor developing East African country was worrying, but at least I would be in a country where I understood the culture to sort out the mess.

The vast expanse of Saudi Arabia, with sand-strewn mountains and immaculate roads criss-crossing an unbroken desert horizon, made me want to ride it one day. The Red Sea looked inviting, the Mediterranean welcoming

– Athens, my first taste of Europe in a year and the reverse culture shock, stimulating. After experiencing so many countries that 'have not', the buzz of a thriving cosmopolitan country took my breath away. Tall, fat, well-dressed people – old people – women in short skirts driving new cars and living in houses with no evidence of war. My emaciated body was down to eight and a half stone and it took several long hot baths to wash away the last grains of African dirt. This posed another contradiction. My objective of Le Mans at 1.00pm on race day was becoming a reality, but I watched the last evidence of Africa swirl down the plug hole with some regret. The political map of Africa is constantly evolving, but by my best reckoning there are 49 countries and if the privilege of a year's travel ever presented itself to me again, I would probably use it to explore that vast land mass in more depth.

There were precisely two weeks left until the start of the 24 hour race in Le Mans. This gave me ample time to ride the distance, but with the bike still in transit and Ethiopian cargo closed for three days because of the weekend and a public holiday, I was beginning to panic, but was totally impotent as there was no one to shout at. Nothing to do except sit on a gritty beach and watch the world go by.

The sand was strewn with plump, well-oiled, blonde, women in bikinis a size too small. An ancient, immaculately dressed man in three-piece suit sat with his fat wife and gold Rolex of a son. I came to the conclusion that the old man was dead as his son chatted incessantly on a mobile phone and Mum rested a newspaper on her ample bosom. A beach trader sat in the translucent light of a cloud of helium balloons doing good business with kids wearing Chicago Bulls T-shirts and I wondered why the spectacle seemed so alien. Every few minutes a jet would scream overhead almost close enough to touch. My eyes searched the sky for an Ethiopian flag.

For once the Gods were with me and the bike arrived in time for a complicated voyage through Greek authorities. My only concern was that my carnet had run out in Kenya, so I falsified an extension with bogus signatures and as many rubber stamps as I could find. Nairobi hotels and a post office had been more than happy to aid my conspiracy. Fortunately, nothing was questioned and I immediately headed west looking for Italy and hoping for a ferry to the heel of that long-legged country. The feeling of liberation was inebriating, riding the jagged coast with the sea sparkling left and right. When I ran out of land at the Ionian Sea, I visited the first building offering boats to Italy and purchased a foot passenger ticket as the bike travelled free. On board I met a truck driver called Mick who clocked up a hundred thousand miles a year in his own truck all over Europe. He was refreshingly down to earth about a job that sounds a good deal more glamourous than the reality. We drank a few beers in the bar before he disappeared to his cabin and I found a piece of deck space out of the cool breeze.

I awoke to hazy sunshine and a wet foot. A large puddle had accumulated from somewhere filling my boot. The ferry was docking much to my surprise as the ticket office had said it would arrive in Italy at 4.00pm and it was 5.30am. Mick appeared looking a little ruffled. "This is Corfu," he said, "I think we are on the wrong boat." It is so reassuring when a more experienced traveller expresses the same doubts and we were both relieved to find out the ferry stopped at several islands before landing on Italian soil.

Italian roads are the best engineered and frequently the most spectacular in the world. They have been doing it for a couple of thousand years longer than everyone else, so have had a lot of practice. An easy 450 miles across the width of Italy and half-way up the West coast through breath-taking scenery. I was the sole visitor to a manicured and orderly campsite. Not having a tent, they are generally bad value, but as the season had not really started, I stayed for free. A regiment of expectant caravans were lined up under a canopy of trees awaiting the tourist invasion. Scrubbed toilets, showers and launderette sat in silence, awaiting the assault.

Trying to remember Mick's advice, I skipped the boring expensive autostrada for the coast road that represents a marvel in civil engineering and passes through some interesting places. Red-roofed hamlets clung to sheer cliffs suspended over the deep blue Ligurian Sea. A switchback road of tunnels and spectacular bridges to Carrara where Michelangelo quarried chunks of marble to grace just about every art museum in the world. A far cry from the quarries of northern India where small boys and camels heave and sweat over gleaming blocks rather than mechanised gantries. Picturesque towns where trams whisper by, sucking power through overhead wires. Every wall was a cascade of magenta bourganvillia on pink and ochre houses, green shutters slammed closed against the sun.

Into Monaco and France on a coast road so familiar it seemed like home. Nationalistic differences became immediately apparent with roads in need of maintenance and a more rustic landscape. Every view was a Van Gogh painting with dark foliage contrasting with rust-coloured earth. There was nowhere open to access money with a Visa card, so I changed my last few dollars for francs to buy bread and cheese. Fortunately my pack revealed a tin of Ethiopian sardines and a bottle of excellent Asmaran brandy (30 pence per litre). Watching the setting sun, munching on the first meal of the day, I became consumed with apprehension about the next chapter of life.

Returning to England, old, poor and jobless was a frightening prospect. The travel would be over and with it a purpose to each day. I doubted very much if the past self-indulgent year would be the source of an income and I would need to find something quick as there was no one to lean on financially, even though Marian would be there for some emotional support. There hangs the hidden commercial truth behind such an endeavour. Travel is costly, and, in my experience, it is generally the unforeseen that drains resources so dramatically. Spend a year doing it and it can be very costly, but the biggest kick in the groin is no income is being generated during that time making a double negative. Earning a crust is one thing, accumulating funds to travel again is quite a different matter, but there *has* to be a way! The thought of having my wings clipped for the rest of my life was too painful to contemplate.

On the wealthiest stretch of coastline in the world, I spent the night sleeping next to an intimate friend with no money and not enough fuel to get me to get me to a bank in St. Raphael. I had more immediate problems demanding answers before debating the meaning of life.

The fuel did last so I fell into a beachside cafe for a carafe of local vin rouge to celebrate and to watch the French at play. The wine was cool, pale with a refreshing sour fruit taste and not the deep ruby colour, with the warm mellow taste of hot red earth that I was expecting. With a day in hand before the big reunion, there was time to make some observations about neighbouring countries. Italy is home to good taste and design. I had been under the impression every Italian woman became obese the day after her marriage, yet as a nation they were slim, good-looking – chic. They dressed appropriately for their age, size and shape, dapper and oozing class. The French seem less self-conscious and have a sexy lived-in appeal. Women to make love to rather than admire from afar. Sitting in the warm sun sipping 'precocious but good-humoured' wine – watching sex on a stick, between the ages of sixteen and sixty, parade by, sapped my motivation to get off my arse and face reality.

The gentle pace of rural France unfolded for me to enjoy, but I was already missing the urgency of travel and daily challenges that had become such a part of life. Most of us work better with a little stress and pressure and receive satisfaction for a task well done, especially under difficult circumstances. For me, on that last stretch to my goal, the desire for achievement had been replaced by shear enjoyment, as I followed the compass north for the last time, but with a fork in the road, the dichotomy of travel would not let go. On average this had been a decision I had been forced to take about ten times a day, so what was the problem with this one? On every road or dirt track, in countless cities, towns and villages, more countries than I was ever likely to see in the rest of my life – and this one – my last one hit me in the gut like a brick. I was well enough acquainted with the roads a few miles north not to get lost and Le Mans was well sign posted. An old wooden post pointed weather beaten fingers at two villages I had never heard of and it would be dark in an hour. I needed food, wine and cognac to celebrate my last day on the road and somewhere to sleep, even if it was to be under the stars. An empty Asmara brandy bottle spinning in the road made the decision for me. That was after it spun into a ditch a couple of times and then pointed steadfastly in the direction I had come from. I was beginning to suspect African 'spirits' were trying make me return to Eritrea, until it decisively pointed left. France is full of wonderful surprises.

'15th June – Somewhere in Central France.

At the spin of a bottle, I fell upon this delightful little town locked between undulating hills thick with elm and oak. As with many French villages, the dominant feature is a square given to playing boules by street lighting. Most spectators are pretty ancient with craggy faces, hats askew and a large glass of cognac. Across the square, the war memorial partly obscures my view of a couple of toothless old grannies on the corner of Rue de

Somnambulist (or some such name). Both dressed in black, one with a matching head scarf, the other with a white frilly bonnet, they nod 'bon soir' to passers by. The washing hanging from balconies above their heads writhes in the gentle breeze heavy with the scent of blossom.

So spinning a bottle got me here, I wonder what a flip of a coin would have turned up. Too late to find out now because tomorrow is D-Day and I'll be amongst faces I recognise, in a place I know – for the first time in 51 weeks – spooky thought!'

I checked out of the charming little hotel early, with a couple of hours in hand to arrive at the '*Aux Portes du Circuit*' bar, for my 1.00pm rendezvous. Some ten miles out of the village, I though I was getting the hang of the bumpy little country roads, often so narrow they could not justify a white line – and then I was heading for a huge, yawning, cavernous ditch brimming with muddy water. Wheels locked up across the grass verge, the front wheel made contact with something hard and large veering it off to a little muddy slope – planting me – back on the road. My knees were shaking by the time the bike slid to a halt and why was I having trouble stabilising the bike on the side stand? I dismounted, took one look and I kissed goodbye to any thoughts of a grand entrance and one o'clock drinkies. The back tyre was very hot and very flat. This tyre had been donated by a long-suffering Tony Brown at his dealership in Brighton, who had had it flown to the Middle East only to have it tortured across Africa. Four times it had suffered punctures and four times my emergency repair kit had got me moving again.

Those tyres were really not made for that kind of punishment and, judging by the heat, it must have been going down for some time and then I knew why I was having so much trouble on the road camber. If I had not had a crash helmet on I would have punched myself. How many times have I been on that bike when the back tyre went down, slowly or quickly – and still I did not immediately spot the symptoms, blaming something else for the difficult handling.

This was serious, not life threatening as Ecuador, India, Kenya or Ethiopia, but serious enough to start my heart racing again, just after it had recovered from nearly ending up in a terminal ditch. I was in the middle of rural France, so far as I knew about ten miles from the nearest village, or do you gamble and walk the other way? First I had to see what I could do and on closer inspection it seemed clear one of the self-repair grommets had been forced out , so set about replacing it. One only starred gloomily at me from the tin and the adhesive had gone solid. It may get me to the next village and after a mammoth pumping exercise on my Indian foot pump we were on our way again.

I did not stop at the next village or the one after, just kept riding and soon picked up signs for Le Mans. I had lost about an hour during the puncture episode, so still should be okay, if it held up but I was putting it under pressure as a renewed sense of urgency sped me forward. 'Read the road – double white lines – no problem for the Big Blue babe, scorch past the traffic – oh shit, what's that.' Your mind goes into a sort of shorthand riding fast. What I had spotted was policemen flagging down cars.

I was riding the solid white line next to a car trying to be inconspicuous on the blindside of the cop. It worked, or at least it did until the cop on the other side of the road attending to traffic coming the other way saw me. There was no escape as I could see more police up the road. I knew police targeted roads north of Le Mans to catch the Brits racing to the circuit, but had not thought they would do the same going south. In Franglaise on both sides, my offence had been to stray over the solid white line and they wanted 600FF – right now, and demanded my passport. What could I do, outnumbered by armed police officers and this was France not El Salvador. I counted up my money, only 448FF. "Vous acceptez la card s'il vous plait?" I asked flashing my visa card. No such luck. I had to ride about 15 miles to the next town, go to the bank and return with the sodding money. 45 minutes to an hour was the insistent copper's best reckoning.

The bank was closed. Can you believe that? In a civilized country with cheap fags, fab wine and a thriving economy – and the damn bank was closed! An old gentleman with a long gray beard and walking stick saw my efforts trying to force the bank door open. "Enface, monsieur." There it was, bless it, another one on the other side of the road.

A race back to the scene, money paid, passport retrieved and I was an hour away with an hour to go. As I leapt on the bike, the police officer was folding my money into his pocket telling me to slow down, or I would have another ticket. I could not afford the money or time , so took it steady.

Rather than attempting a dramatic entrance, I cruised past the bar and into the garden where a few familiar tents were zipped up against the sun, but devoid of people. I recognised several faces and voices through open windows in the bar, but I was not quite ready to face them. I sat astride the hot bike trying to contain my excitement. Who was there? Had Marian arrived? I just needed a bit of time to focus my thoughts.

This was it, I was back to where I started in the same time it took for the Earth to rotate around the Sun and nothing had changed. It was just like it was when I left. Time seemed to have stood still and the past 51 weeks was like a dream. I glanced at the dials on the bike and made a mental note of 36,792 miles since parking the Triumph in exactly the same space, even using the same piece of paving slab under the side stand to stop it sinking on the grass. When jockeys win a race, rather than saying *they* did it, they say 'I rode a winner'. That was exactly what I was feeling at the time, riding a real outsider and sure it fell at a few fences, but was there at the end of a one horse race around the world. An enormous bubble of pride, compassion and respect rose from somewhere inside me.

I laid a hand on the tank, wiped a tear from my eye and headed for the bar. Simon Jones, the man who had phoned me in Dubai to give me the race date strode forward with an outstretched hand. Then there was a shout. "He's here! The old bastard made it after all." Marian gave me a hug and long-awaited kiss. Someone put a beer in my hand and the celebrations began – rejoicing was the order of the day.

A note book fell from my pocket and someone picked it off the floor and handed it to me. It was the very first one I had scribbled thoughts in at the beginning of my adventure. The cover had been ripped off a million miles ago revealing the very first words recorded on my departure, 'This is definitely the very first day of the rest of my life'. It was as true then as it is now and is true for every mortal soul. We only get one stab at life, so we have an obligation to enjoy it and make it as rewarding and as fulfilling as we possibly can. Say it to yourself *every* morning and however you spend that day – make it really count.

Epilogue

"Don't come in here brandishing it about." The police officer was just being firm, although there may have been a hint of hysteria in his voice, it was difficult to detect over the phone. Understandably, Marian would not have the gun in the house and as luck would have it there was a firearms amnesty. The only condition was that it had not been used in a violent crime. You would think firearms used in violent crime would be the very ones they wanted. For all I knew, it was the most wanted gun in America and, although it had not been involved in any crime since I had taken possession of it, which was in itself a crime it had spent the best part of a year illegally secreted under the seat of my bike. I was beginning to regret not dumping it in the Indian Ocean, as it had caused more grief then it had resolved. It had been a gross error of judgement to buy it in the first place.

The gun and ammunition was put into a carrier bag and I handed it over to a woman police constable at the station. She gave me a big 'toothpaste ad' kind of smile as if I had handed her a bag of sweeties. "May I have your name and address, for the receipt" she chirped. "That's okay," I said making a hasty exit, "I won't be needing a receipt."

Shedding the other trappings of travel was easy enough as there were so few of them. Grimy clothes, dog-eared note books and miles of video tape. The note books revealed spontaneous thoughts, emotions and fears that made my palms sweat on re-reading, they were so evocative. Pages punctuated by the odd business card taken from a stranger, newspaper cuttings kept for no apparent reason, scraps of paper with names on that I could not put faces to, a betting slip for the Melbourne Gold Cup and pressed flowers from just about everywhere.

Forty hours of video tape were reduced down to just one to make a potted history of a year on the road. The most active, eventful year of my life reduced to sixty minutes of film, but it was at least the first solo round world account committed to celluloid. For the sake of continuity during filming, my hair had been left to its own devices, starting cropped and grey, but finishing long, unkempt and the colour of straw, bleached by desert sun.

The Triumph had been through more stages of metamorphosis, but fortunately, as it was my only source of income, it did not object to abuse and had more to come. Courier riding had to supplement earnings as a journalist as I had lost the taste for advertising design. After such an arduous trip the riding should have been easy, but it was not, as there was always someone telling me where to be and when. Finding the next country, next continent had been replaced by finding a particular address in Slough and I had forgotten how persistent the drizzle was in England, under perpetually grey sky. At the end of one such day after three Brighton to London trips in ten hours, we suffered the wickedest irony.

I recall thinking deserted seafronts on chilly wet nights can be spooky places. Street lighting created starbursts as rain drops splashed against my visor. I was looking forward to shedding wet leathers and falling into a hot bath and there was less than half a mile to go. You have to ride more carefully on a wet road and be even more vigilant about other traffic at night as motorists are often blind to a single headlamp. Second on the left and I would be home, just past the white van trying to access the main road at the first. It was inching out trying to see past parked vehicles, then it put on a spurt across my path. Brake hard, but not too hard, I did not want the wheels to lock up on the wet road. There was no room to pass behind him so I had to have a go round the front. It never amazes me how much information the brain is capable of absorbing and how many decisions can be made in less than a second. Mine was fixed on damage limitation as the van moved forward again and I became airborne, then unconscious.

There was someone near my head, my naked head, so where was my crash helmet? Rain fell into my eyes from the inky blackness above. A face appeared across my line of vision. "You bastard, you fucking bastard, you could have killed me," I screamed and may well have got up and punched him – if only my legs had worked. The poor man I was shouting at was only the witness who had come to help. The perpetrator of the accident stayed in his van in a state of shock because he thought I was dead. The ambulance men were a bit more positive strapping up my legs and neck while attempting to stop the fountain of blood squirting from my head. The next twelve hours or so in Accident and Emergency were a bit of a blur.

" One day, Robbie Marshall, one day you will be carried from an incident in a box, so just behave, act your age and not your shoe size." Big Jon had arrived to take me home. Marian was away on a week's holiday to 'think things through', and his was the only telephone number I could remember. The only available bed in the hospital was in the female geriatric ward so I was determined to discharge myself fast. "What's the damage, Jon have you spoken to the doctor?" "You'll live – this time. You have a crushed lumber vertebrae, but your legs work again; you received forty two stitches in your head and your left ear was ripped off – but don't be alarmed 'cause they sewed it on again the right way up – oh, and you may be deaf in your right ear." "What did you say Jon." "I'll rephrase that – you *are* deaf in your right ear." "…but my helmet, what happened to my helmet?" "It's fine," said Jon holding it up for me to see, "still with the chin strap tightly fastened." "And my bike, is it bad?" "Unlike you, Robbie, your bike's travels are over."

Marian returned from her holiday and left again with more than just a suitcase. There were no raised voices, no thoughts of retribution, just two confused people who knew their relationship had run out of steam, but did not know why. I tried to take a positive attitude and be thankful for the six good years we had spent together but now it was time to start a new chapter. There was little point in speculating if my year away was responsible for the demise of what we used to call love, and if I had remained at home, what would have happened to my yearning for travel? Would it just have vanished like Marian, leaving no visible scars to remind me of what may have been?

All I was certain of was a year on the road – a year of self-discovery had made a profound change to my perspective on life, which caused a dilemma. The sensible thing would be to say the adventure is at an end and now it is time to get on with life. Alternatively, it could be viewed as a beginning and become a way of life. That elegant and eloquent Masai philosopher had said it all as he sucked on tart oranges with a lost, white motorcyclist in a Kenyan desert – and I only asked him 'How far?' "The road is as long as you want to make it, my friend, every distance has a different length to different people, it just depends on how much you see on the way.' Oh, and in case you were wondering, the bike, the same bike, is ready to go.

Never Let anyone tell you the world is small – it is huge and out there for the taking.

TravellersEye Club Membership

Each month we receive hundreds of enquiries from people who've read our books or entered our competitions. All of these people have one thing in common: an aching to achieve something extraordinary, outside the bounds of our everyday lives. Not everyone can undertake the more extreme challenges, but we all value learning about other people's experiences.

Membership is free because we want to unite people of similar interests. Via our website, members will be able to liase with each other about everything from the kit they've taken, to the places they've been to and the things they've done. Our authors will also be available to answer any of your questions if you're planning a trip or if you simply have a question about their books.

As well as regularly up-dating members with news about our forthcoming titles, we will also offer you the following benefits:

Free entry to author talks / signings
Direct author correspondence
Discounts off new and past titles
Free entry to TravellersEye events
Discounts on a variety of travel products and services

To register your membership, simply write or email us telling us your name and address (postal and email). See address at the front of this book.

About TravellersEye

I believe the more you put into life, the more you get out of it. However, at times I have been disillusioned and felt like giving up on a goal because I have been made to feel that an ordinary person like me could never achieve my dreams.

The world is absolutely huge and out there for the taking. There has never been more opportunity for people like you and me to have dreams and fulfil them.

I have met many people who have achieved extraordinary things and these people have helped inspire and motivate me to try and live my life to the fullest.

TravellersEye publishes books about people who have done just this and we hope that their stories will encourage other people to live their dream.

When setting up TravellersEye I was given two pieces of advice. The first was that there are only two things I ever need to know: You are never going to know everything and neither is anyone else. The second was that there are only two things I ever need to do in life: Never give up and don't forget rule one.

Nelson Mandela said in his presidential acceptance speech: "Our deepest fear is not that we are inadequate. Our deepest fear is that we are powerful beyond our measure... as we let our own light shine, we unconsciously give other people permission to do the same."

We want people to shine their light and share it with others in the hope that it may encourage them to do the same.

Dan Hiscocks
Managing Director of TravellersEye

New For 2001

Jungle Janes   **Peter Burden**
12 middle aged women take on the Borneo Jungle: Seen on Channel 4
ISBN: 1903070058   Price: £7.99 $14.95

Travels with my Daughter   **Niema Ash**
Forget convention, follow your instincts.
ISBN: 190307004X   Price: £7.99 $14.95

Grey Paes And Bacon   **Bob Bibby**
A hillarious romp through the bowels and vowels of the Black Country.
ISBN: 1903070066   Price: £7.99 $14.95

What For Chop Today?   **Gail Haddock**
Experiences of VSO in Sierra Leone.
ISBN: 1903070074   Price: £7.99 $14.95

Riding With Ghosts: South Of The Border   **Gwen Maka**
Second part of Gwen's epic cycle trip accross the Americas.
ISBN: 1903070090   Price: £7.99 $14.95

Jasmine And Arnica   **Nicola Naylor**
An Indian Experience by the world's first blind travel writer.
ISBN: 1903070104   Price: £16.99

Travellers Tales From Heaven And Hell...Part 3
Winners of this year's competition
ISBN: 190307112   Price: £6.99 $14.95

Cry From The Highest Mountain   **Tess Burrows**
A tale of the struggle to free Tibet.
ISBN: 1903070120   Price: £7.99 $14.95

Already Available

Desert Governess   Phyllis Ellis
An inside view of the Soudi Royal Family
ISBN: 1903070015   Price: £7.99 $14,95

Fever Trees Of Borneo   Mark Eveleigh
A daring expedition through uncharted jungle
ISBN: 0953057569   Price: £7.99 $14,95

Discovery Road   Tim Garrett & Andy Brown
Their mission was to mountain bike around the world.
ISBN: 0953057534   Price: £7.99 $14.95

Frigid Women   Sue & Victoria Riches
The first all female expeditin to The North Pole
ISBN: 0953057526   Price: £7.99 $14.95

The Jungle Beat   Roy Follows
Fighting Terrorists in Malaya
ISBN: 1953057577   Price: £7.99 $14.95

Slow Winter   Alex Hickman
A personal quest against the back drop of the war torn Balkans
ISBN: 0953057585   Price: £7.99 $14.95

Riding With Ghosts   Gwen Maka
One woman's solo cycle ride from Seattle to Mexico
ISBN: 1903070007   Price: £7.99 $14.95

Tea For Two   Polly Benge
She cycled around India to test her love.
ISBN: 0953057593   Price: £7.99 $14.95

Touching Tibet   Niema Ash
One of the first westerners to enter Tibet
ISBN: 0953057550   Price: £7.99 $14.95

Travellers Tales From Heaven and Hell
More Travellers Tales From Heaven and Hell
Past winners of our competition
ISBN: 0953057518/1903070023   Price: £6.99 $14.95

A Trail Of Visions: Route 1: India Sri Lanka, Thailand, Sumatra
A Trail Of Visions: Route 2: Peru, Bolivia, Columbia, Ecuador
Vicki Couchman